Death in modern theatre

Manchester University Press

series editors
MARIA M. DELGADO
MAGGIE B. GALE
PETER LICHTENFELS

advisory board
Michael Billington, Sandra Hebron, Mark Ravenhill, Janelle Reinelt, Peter Sellars, Joanne Tompkins

This series will offer a space for those people who practise theatre to have a dialogue with those who think and write about it.

The series has a flexible format that refocuses the analysis and documentation of performance. It provides, presents and represents material which is written by those who make or create performance history, and offers access to theatre documents, different methodologies and approaches to the art of making theatre.

The books in the series are aimed at students, scholars, practitioners and theatre-visiting readers. They encourage reassessments of periods, companies and figures in twentieth-century and twenty-first-century theatre history, and provoke and take up discussions of cultural strategies and legacies that recognise the heterogeneity of performance studies.

also available

Directing scenes and senses: The thinking of Regie
PETER M. BOENISCH

The Paris Jigsaw: Internationalism and the city's stages
DAVID BRADBY AND MARIA M. DELGADO (EDS)

Theatre in crisis? Performance manifestos for a new century
MARIA M. DELGADO AND CARIDAD SVICH (EDS)

World stages, local audiences: Essays on performance, place, and politics
PETER DICKINSON

Performing presence: Between the live and the simulated
GABRIELLA GIANNACHI AND NICK KAYE

Queer exceptions: Solo performance in neoliberal times
STEPHEN GREER

Performance in a time of terror: Critical mimesis and the age of uncertainty
JENNY HUGHES

South African performance and the archive of memory
YVETTE HUTCHISON

Jean Genet and the politics of theatre: Spaces of revolution
CARL LAVERY

After '89: Polish theatre and the political
BRYCE LEASE

Not magic but work: An ethnographic account of a rehearsal process
GAY MCAULEY

'Love me or kill me': Sarah Kane and the theatre of extremes
GRAHAM SAUNDERS

Trans-global readings: Crossing theatrical boundaries
CARIDAD SVICH

Negotiating cultures: Eugenio Barba and the intercultural debate
IAN WATSON (ED.)

Death in modern theatre
Stages of mortality

ADRIAN CURTIN

Manchester University Press

Copyright © Adrian Curtin 2019

The right of Adrian Curtin to be identified as the author of this work has been asserted by him in accordance with the Copyright, Designs and Patents Act 1988.

Published by Manchester University Press
Oxford Road, Manchester M13 9PL
www.manchesteruniversitypress.co.uk

British Library Cataloguing-in-Publication Data
A catalogue record for this book is available from the British Library

ISBN 978 1 5261 2470 8 hardback
ISBN 978 1 5261 9123 6 paperback

First published 2019
Paperback published 2025

The publisher has no responsibility for the persistence or accuracy of URLs for any external or third-party internet websites referred to in this book, and does not guarantee that any content on such websites is, or will remain, accurate or appropriate.

EU authorised representative for GPSR:
Easy Access System Europe – Mustamäe tee 50, 10621 Tallinn, Estonia
gpsr.requests@easproject.com

Typeset by Servis Filmsetting Ltd, Stockport, Cheshire

To my father, Denis Curtin (1937–2015), who taught me the value of hard work and simple pleasures

CONTENTS

List of figures *page* viii
Acknowledgements x
Chronology xii

Introduction: Stages of mortality 1
1 Beyond the veil: sensing death in symbolist theatre 29
2 Fantastical representations of death in First World War drama 65
3 The absurd drama of modern death denial 97
4 Theatres of catastrophe after Auschwitz and Hiroshima 135
5 The drama of dying in the early twenty-first century 181
Conclusion: Unending 224

References 243
Index 254

FIGURES

0.1	The setting for *In Memory of Helen* (photo by the author)	3
0.2	Orpheus (Conor Lovett) beholds Death (Bernadette Cronin) in Steeple Theatre Company's 2000 production of *Orpheus* (after Jean Cocteau's 1950 film *Orphée*) at the Granary Theatre, Cork (courtesy of Frameworks Films)	6
0.3	Extract from *The Art of Coarse Acting* by Michael Green, © 1964 by Michael Green (reproduced by permission of Sheil Land Associates Ltd)	9
1.1	Postcard of the 'intoxication room' at the Cabaret du Néant, Paris, *c.* 1900 (author's collection)	32
1.2	Postcard of the 'vault of the dead' at the Cabaret du Néant, Paris, *c.* 1900 (author's collection)	33
1.3	John Olohan and Conor Mullen in the 1990 Abbey Theatre production of W.B. Yeats's *Purgatory* (photo by Fergus Bourke, courtesy of James W. Flannery)	60
1.4	Double transcription of a motif from Bill Whelan's music for the 1990 Abbey Theatre production of W.B. Yeats's *Purgatory*	61
2.1	Soldier-skeletons in the 1919 production of Ernst Toller's *Die Wandlung*, performed at the Tribüne theatre, Berlin (Oskar Fischel, *Das Moderne Bühnenbild* (Berlin: Verlag Ernst Wasmuth, 1923), Abb. 124)	73

List of figures

3.1 Medical misadventure in Dino Buzzati's *A Clinical Case*, produced by the Theatre of Involvement in Minneapolis, 1975 (photo courtesy of Phillip Zarrilli) — 109

3.2 The dying imagine their final judgement in the Open Theater's *Terminal, c.* 1971 (Kent State University Libraries, Special Collections and Archives) — 118

3.3 A scene from a 1957 production of Eugène Ionesco's *Amédée* by Théâtre d'Aujourd'hui at the Alliance Française, Paris (Bibliothèque Nationale de France) — 130

4.1 The superman – the representative of automatism and the usurper of power – in Józef Szajna's *Replika* (1988) (TVP Kultura) — 162

4.2 Macedonia (Vanessa-Faye Stanley) and Hitler (Alan Cox) in The Wrestling School's 2009 production of Howard Barker's *Found in the Ground* (photo by Robert Workman) — 171

5.1 Chiwetel Ejiofor as Everyman and Kate Duchêne as God in the National Theatre's 2015 production of Carol Ann Duffy's *Everyman* (© Richard Hubert Smith for NT) — 191

5.2 Patrick Godfrey in the National Theatre's 2015 production of Caryl Churchill's *Here We Go* (photo by Alastair Muir) — 207

5.3 Sharon Morgan as Rose (seated) in the 2016 production of Kaite O'Reilly's *Cosy* at the Wales Millennium Centre, Cardiff (Farrows Creative, courtesy of Kaite O'Reilly) — 220

ACKNOWLEDGEMENTS

In Eugène Ionesco's absurdist comedy *Amédée* the main characters, after much effort and consternation, manage to oust the weird, expanding dead body they have been living with and contemplating for years. Nervously and excitedly, they slide it out the window of their apartment late at night, and thus the peculiar entity is let into the public realm, where it is subsequently beheld with much curiosity, before ultimately floating off like a hot-air balloon. There are some parallels between this scenario and my experience of writing this book. Happily, though, it is not an exact match. Ionesco's characters kept the existence of their strange co-habitant a secret and had to work out what to do with it themselves. In contrast, I have been more open about my own steadily-enlarging, deathly object of fascination, and have had help in launching it into the world.

I firstly wish to thank my colleagues in the Drama department at the University of Exeter for their encouragement and assistance. I give special thanks to Kate Newey, Sarah Goldingay, Pam Woods, Konstantinos Thomaidis, Rebecca Loukes, Emily Kreider, and Kara Reilly. The College of Humanities at the University of Exeter granted me two periods of study leave to work on this project, which was hugely beneficial. My former colleague and fellow modernist-enthusiast Claire Warden gamely read the main body of this work as it took shape and provided cheery and thoughtful commentary on it. I am lucky to have such a generous scholarly interlocutor, and have incorporated many of Claire's suggestions and musings. Thanks to Audrey Keyes for helping me with various pieces of translation. I would have been stuck in the '*désert à guerre*' without her. I am deeply grateful to Kaite O'Reilly and Phillip Zarrilli for inspiring parts of this project, discussing it with me, providing research materials, and commenting on my writing. I also wish to thank the students of my 'Death in Modern Theatre' classes – at Northwestern University in 2008 and at the University of Exeter in 2015 and 2016. I have had many fruitful conversations with students about the ideas contained in this book. Thanks also to the library staff at the University of Exeter, who I think may have become a little concerned about me due to the many books on death-related topics I have ordered via interlibrary loan in recent years. I am similarly obliged to archivists at the Victoria and Albert Museum, the British Library, the Cadbury Research Library, the Bibliothèque Nationale de France, the Brooklyn Academy of Music, Kent State University Library's Special Collections, and the National University of Ireland, Galway, for helping me with my research and pointing me in the right directions. Bernie Cronin sourced a production image, upon Regina Crowley's suggestion, for which I am grateful. The 'Scenography' and 'Directing & Dramaturgy' working groups at TaPRA have provided opportunities for me to share work-in-progress; my thanks to the convenors and participants for their feedback. I am indebted to the readers engaged by Manchester University Press and to Maria Delgado and copy-editor John Banks for comments and suggestions made on the manuscript.

Part of Chapter 3 appears as 'The Absurdity of Denial: Staging the American Way of Death' in *New Theatre Quarterly* (33 (2), 2017), and is reprinted with permission here. I have also re-used some text from 'The Art *Music* of Theatre: Howard Barker as Sound Designer', published in *Studies in Theatre and Performance* (32 (3), 2012, www.tandfonline.com). Thanks to the editors of these journals and the anonymous peer reviewers for helping me to hone the ideas in these articles.

Finally, a curtain call for Valerie, Audrey, Darren, and Ian, who have supported this endeavour and cheered me on, even when family circumstances made it more difficult.

CHRONOLOGY

The following is a list of key texts and productions discussed in this book, along with selected historical events.

1874   The Paris Catacombs are opened to the public.
1882   The Society for Psychical Research is founded in London.
1885   The Société de Psychologie Physiologique is founded in Paris.
1889   Charles van Lerberghe, *The Night-Comers*.
1890   Maurice Maeterlinck, *The Intruder*.
         Paul Fort founds the Théâtre d'Art in Paris, staging symbolist plays.
         W.B. Yeats is initiated into the Hermetic Order of the Golden Dawn, a secret society devoted to the occult.
1891   Rachilde, *Madame La Mort*.
1892   The Cabaret du Néant opens in Paris.
         Max Nordau, *Degeneration*.
         Georges Rodenbach, *Bruges-la-morte*.
1897   The Théâtre du Grand-Guignol opens in Paris.
1912   Maurice Maeterlinck, *Death*.
1914   The First World War begins.
         Ernst Toller joins the German army and is sent to fight on the Western Front.
1915   Sigmund Freud, 'Thoughts for the Times on War and Death'.

	Ernst Toller is invalided and launches a peace movement in Heidelberg.
1916	Leonid Andreyev, *Requiem*.
1918	Winifred Kirkland, *The New Death*.
	A flu pandemic (the 'Spanish flu') spreads globally, killing millions.
	The First World War ends.
1919	Ernst Toller, *The Transfiguration*.
1920	Vernon Lee, *Satan the Waster*.
1921	G.B. Shaw, *Back to Methuselah*.
1922	Karel Čapek, *The Makropulos Case*.
	Karl Kraus, *The Last Days of Mankind*.
1935	The British Voluntary Euthanasia Society is founded.
1938	W.B. Yeats, *Purgatory*.
1939	The Second World War begins.
1941	The first extermination of prisoners occurs at Auschwitz I.
	Józef Szajna is sent to Auschwitz.
1945	The US detonates atomic bombs over Hiroshima and Nagasaki.
	The Second World War ends.
1953	Dino Buzzati, *A Clinical Case*.
	Eugène Ionesco, *Amédée, or How to Get Rid of It*
1955	Geoffrey Gorer, 'The Pornography of Death'.
1957	Samuel Beckett, *Endgame*.
1958	Cecily Saunders begins publishing articles about the care of the dying.
1959	Herman Feifel, *The Meaning of Death*.
1960	Herman Kahn, *On Thermonuclear War*.
	Cardiopulmonary resuscitation is developed.
1961	Samuel Beckett, *Happy Days*.
1962	Eugène Ionesco, *Exit the King*.
	Robert Ettinger publishes *The Prospect of Immortality*, popularising the idea of cryonics.
1963	Jessica Mitford, *The American Way of Death*.
1965	US marines land in South Vietnam.
1966	Tom Stoppard, *Rosencrantz and Guildenstern Are Dead*.
1967	St Christopher's Hospice is founded in London.
1968	A committee from the Harvard Medical School proposes that the non-reversible loss of brain activity should be considered the definition of death.
	Marguerite Duras, *Yes, Maybe*.
1969	Open Theater and Susan Yankowitz, *Terminal*.
	Elisabeth Kübler-Ross, *On Death and Dying*.

1970	The first issue of *OMEGA – Journal of Death and Dying* is published.
1971	Józef Szajna, *Replica I*.
1973	Ernest Becker, *The Denial of Death*.
1974	Philippe Ariès, *Western Attitudes Toward Death: From the Middle Ages to the Present*.
1975	Tadeusz Kantor, 'The Theatre of Death' manifesto. President Gerald Ford declares an end to the war in Vietnam. Buzzati's play *A Clinical Case* receives its English-language premiere in the US.
1980	The Hemlock Society, a right-to-die society, is founded in the US.
1981	Philippe Ariès, *The Hour of Our Death*.
1982	Jonathan Schell, *The Fate of the Earth*.
1984	Edward Bond, *The Tin Can People*.
1985	The first issue of the academic journal *Death Studies* is published.
1990	The legal right-to-die case for Terry Schiavo begins in the US.
1991	The Natural Death Centre, a UK-based charity, is established.
1996	The first issue of the academic journal *Mortality* is published.
2001	Howard Barker, *Found in the Ground*.
2004	The first 'death café' is held in Neuchâtel, Switzerland. Biomedical gerontologist Aubrey de Grey declares that the first human who will live to be 1000 years might already be alive.
2005	Howard Barker, *Death, the One and the Art of Theatre*. The Centre for Death and Society is founded at the University of Bath. Terri Schiavo dies, following the removal of her feeding tube.
2006	Marina Carr, *Woman and Scarecrow*.
2009	Dying Matters, a UK-based charity that helps people to talk more openly about death, dying, and bereavement, is founded. The SENS Research Foundation, dedicated to developing rejuvenation biotechnology, is founded in California.
2014	Unlimited Theatre, *Am I Dead Yet?*
2015	Carol Ann Duffy, *Everyman*. Caryl Churchill, *Here We Go*.
2016	Kaite O'Reilly, *Cosy*.
2017	The 'Doomsday Clock', overseen by the *Bulletin of the Atomic Scientists*, is set to two-and-a-half minutes to midnight.

Introduction: Stages of mortality

In memoriam

It is Saturday afternoon on 1 April 2017. I am in a private performance and exhibition space in Exeter called 'The Cart Shed', a small brick building in a courtyard tucked off a quiet, residential road.[1] The building has no signage. You would not know it is used for art events unless you were told about it. I have been invited to attend a performance created by a colleague, Pam Woods, who has called the piece a 'short little something' in memory of her partner's mother, Helen, who died two years ago on this date. I briefly reflect on the slightly comical circumstance of dying on Fool's Day. I decide not to make this a topic of conversation.

The audience comprises six people. We all know one another. The performance area has been simply arranged, creating the impression of a living room – possibly an older person's living room. There is an old-fashioned standing lamp, which is lit; some flowers; a hot-water bottle; a half-full bottle of brandy and a brandy glass on a side-table; a small electric fire that looks toasty warm; and several large, knitted jumpers (sweaters) that are variously wrapped around a low chair, suspended from the ceiling on a hanger, and hung on a wall. Pam welcomes us, thanks us for coming, and begins the piece. An audio track is played on a laptop. From a speaker on a wall comes a surprisingly deep, resonant voice of an older woman with a Northumbrian accent. This, I presume, is Helen.

I know virtually nothing about Helen. Prior to being invited to this event several days ago, I had been unaware of her existence. Now, sitting in the Cart Shed and listening to the recording, I am captivated by her vocalisations. She is 'chuntering'. Pam has taught me this word. It's a British colloquialism, meaning to mutter or mumble to oneself. I look it up in the dictionary afterward. To 'chunter' can also mean to 'grumble' and 'find fault', but that isn't what Helen is doing. On the contrary, she sounds completely cheerful and content. She's making a kind of 'mouth music' – nonsense sounds, syncopated rhythms – effortlessly and fluidly. She appears to be keeping herself happy by making these sounds, and they are delightful to hear. (You can listen to an excerpt of Helen's vocalisations on SoundCloud.)[2] Her voice fills the space. I later learn she was unaware she was being recorded. She was not self-consciously performing at the time, but she is figuratively performing for us now. I think of Winnie, from Samuel Beckett's play *Happy Days*, chattering away, despite being half-buried (and then nearly fully buried), grave-like, in a mound of earth. 'Oh this is going to be another happy day!' Winnie exclaims (1963: 14).

Pam shares the space with Helen's voice. She listens to it along with us, reacts to it, moves in sympathy with it. She unfolds jumpers that Helen knitted for her son, Ian (Pam's partner), who is also in attendance. Pam holds the jumpers close and puts them on, somehow managing to wear several of them at once. The mood is playful. We laugh at a funny sound or sentence Helen has uttered and smile along with Pam. A bird warbles, but I can't tell if the sound is on the recording or from outside. A clock ticks. My sense of time and place blurs slightly. Ian's voice is heard on the recording, asking Helen if she is content; he encourages her to have another drink. Helen accepts, and gently drifts along a stream of consciousness. '*Lovely boy ... Oh, get off my bloody toe! ... Oh dear, that's nice, isn't it? Very nice. Sitting on the grass and then waiting for the flowers to bloom. ... Y'see, I can't see now. Oh, well. It doesn't matter. You can put the eyes in my eyes. ... Fair enough, fair enough. And I'm goin' home now. So, good night, good night ...*' Pam drinks some brandy and raises a glass to Helen, who keeps chuntering to herself, merrily.

I find all this quite moving. I notice my breathing has become shallow and more rapid. This surprises me. I am not usually emotionally affected by performance so readily. Why should I be feeling sad about Helen? I didn't know her. And she sounds like she lived to a

Introduction 3

0.1 The setting for *In Memory of Helen* – a private performance piece devised by Pam Woods in memory of Helen Cumming (1916–2015)

good age. This must be the result of tiredness, I tell myself. I hadn't sleep well the night before, and it's the end of what has felt like a long academic term. But there's more to it than that. I am specially primed to be affected by this performance, I reason. After all, I've been thinking about death and theatre for a while now, and have recently begun work on a new chapter of this book. Moreover, it has not been long since my father died, and it occurs to me I might be having a ripple effect of grieving – one of those sudden emotional swells that can overwhelm, though I had thought such disturbances had passed. Yes, this must be it. I had, to some extent, swapped Helen for my father – Helen, whom Pam is *not* performing, but whose voice is resounding in the space, and whose empty garments are laid out on the floor, with no body inside them, as though the owner had been raptured (see Figure 0.1). I had effected 'surrogation', Joseph Roach's term for the process through which culture reproduces and re-creates itself. 'In the life of a community', Roach writes, 'the process of surrogation does not begin or end but continues as actual or perceived vacancies occur in the network of relations that constitute the social fabric' (1996: 2). Surrogation also works on an individual level. After my father's death, lines from Patrick Kavanagh's poem 'Memory of My Father', which I had studied at school, had rattled around my brain:

> Every old man I see
> In October-coloured weather
> Seems to say to me:
> 'I was once your father.'
>
> (Martin, 1969: 194)

Additionally, several weeks prior to attending the performance in memory of Helen, I had heard, for the first time, an old reel-to-reel recording of my father in which he converses with my siblings and me when we were children. Perhaps, during the performance in memory of Helen, I had subconsciously been thinking about this other recording, which I had listened to closely, repeatedly, for several days, captivated by this sonic record of my distant, personal past. In my acts of listening I resembled Beckett's Krapp, playing back old tape recordings of himself and saying 'Spooool!' with a '[*happy*] *smile*' (1957: 12).

After the performance, we talked about Helen, and then, sipping prosecco, delicately discussed the topic of death, sharing our thoughts and concerns. Pam said she was 'holding the space' for Helen during the performance. Technically, of course, Helen was not present. She was not there. However, in a way, she was also 'not not there', to riff on Richard Schechner's formulation of the liminal, double-negative state of the actor in performance ('not me ... not not me'). Actors performing characters are 'not themselves', Schechner writes, 'nor are they the characters they impersonate' (2002: 64). Instead, they are something (or someone?) in-between. Similarly, this piece had – in a manner of speaking – conjured Helen (back) into being through a combination of factors: the recording of her voice; the inclusion of items of clothing she had made; the arrangement of the performance space; Pam's sensitive playing of that space as she responded to her invisible 'scene partner'; and a small audience of sympathetic, engaged attendants. *This is what theatre can do*, I reminded myself, *and this is why you're writing this book.*

This piece, touching in its simplicity, illustrates how theatre allows us to memorialise the dead and make them feel present to us, even if we are generating this feeling ourselves.[3] Theatre can help us to fulfil a psychological – and maybe a spiritual – need to connect to the dead, and, by extension, to contemplate death and ponder our mortality. This may seem like a grand or even pretentious-sounding pronouncement to make, especially in the context of a short, simple piece performed once for a small audience of invited guests. Nonetheless, obscure, 'poor theatre'-style work can be noteworthy and revealing (see Grotowski, 1969). The small-scale, semi-ritualistic, and bare-bones aesthetic of the performance in memory of Helen resembles this type of theatre. Moreover, this piece achieved in miniature what many dramatists and theatre-makers strive to effect through more compositionally dense and intricate means – namely, to evoke the dead and provoke reconsideration of personal mortality. There is a nexus between theatre and death: an interchange of absence and presence, 'ghosting' from the past in the present, conjuring of the inanimate through the animate, and reminder of our mortality in moments of experiencing live performance with people who are with us – and sometimes remembering people who have 'passed' – as time slips by. Some people appreciate this about the art form; others shy away from it. Notably, there is a long list of dramatists and theatre-makers from the late nineteenth century onward – artists who have been called 'modern' or 'modernist' – who have experimented with the 'deathly' dynamics and potential of the live theatrical event.

This book addresses the topic of how the dead are memorialised in theatre, but this is not its sole focus. Rather, it investigates how a range of Western dramatists and theatre-makers from the late nineteenth century onward have explored historically informed ideas about death and dying in their work, often by way of formal invention, symbolism, and fantasy. My goal is to analyse representation of death and dying in drama and theatre from this period by finding salient points of connection between plays, productions, and sociohistorical contexts. I consider how modern dramatists, theatre-makers, and audience members use theatre to meditate on the end of life, querying how this functions and what it means. First, though, the theoretical nexus between theatre and death, adumbrated above, must be fleshed out.

Theatre: a deathly art?

Theatre is more commonly associated with liveliness than with death or dying. If one were playing a word association game, and one person said 'theatre', the other person would probably not say 'death' or anything like it (unless one were morbidly inclined, or writing a book on the subject!). And yet, the language of death is part of the performance vernacular. An actor who breaks character is said to have 'corpsed' (in British slang). A performer may be encouraged to 'knock 'em dead'. An actor or stand-up comedian who performs badly may be said to have 'died' onstage. If they perform well, they might claim to have 'killed it'. A remounting of a production is called a 'revival'.[4] Furthermore, on the level of content, death and dying feature throughout world drama, both as theme and plot point, but then death may be thought to underlie lots of culture in one way or other, so can one say it has a unique association with theatre?[5]

There is a long-standing tradition in Western theatre of presenting death in character form as part of a dramatis personae. (*Alcestis*, by Euripides, is an early example.) Granted, personification of death – as a skeleton, or a shrouded figure with a scythe, for instance – features in other art-forms too, including film.[6] However, in theatre one can be in a shared space with an embodiment of death. It is qualitatively different to encounter a personification of death by a human performer in theatre than in a piece of visual art or in a literary work. In the latter cases, 'Death' does not have real flesh and blood. 'Death' does not breathe. 'Death' cannot literally return your gaze if you look at her or him. When 'Death' appears before us in theatre, we encounter an uncanny spectacle: a corporealisation of an abstraction – a living, breathing memento mori. This can provide a special thrill (see Figure 0.2). When an actor portrays Death, their sex and gender are typically mapped on to the character,

0.2 Orpheus (Conor Lovett) beholds Death (Bernadette Cronin) in Steeple Theatre Company's 2000 production of *Orpheus* (after Jean Cocteau's film *Orphée*) at the Granary Theatre, Cork, directed by Regina Crowley

or otherwise inform how the character is interpreted, thus potentially making the idea of death seem (more) human and familiar. Acting the role of Death invariably involves using social conventions, cultural associations, performative actions, and ideological formations relating to sex and gender – reinforcing or subverting them.[7] Characterising death in drama as a sexed or gendered entity is not incidental and should not simply be dismissed as an inevitable feature of using human actors. Embodying death does 'cultural work' and may be ideologically loaded. One might expect that the act of personifying death in character form would have permanently fallen out of fashion at some point, given its ostensible preposterousness and association with fairy-tales and superstition, but death continues to appear in personified form in theatre into the twenty-first century. This device has – quite literally – got legs.

Nevertheless, presenting death and dying onstage can be contentious and difficult to achieve satisfactorily. In some quarters, representations of death and dying in theatre are regarded dubiously or wryly. In a treatise on drama published in 1668, John Dryden advises against representing dying onstage, because such efforts invariably miss the mark and prompt unwanted laughter:

> I have observ'd that in all our Tragedies, the Audience cannot forbear laughing when the Actors are to die; 'tis the most Comick part of the whole Play. All *passions* may be lively represented on the Stage ... but there are many *actions* which can never be imitated to a just height: dying especially is a thing which none but a *Roman* Gladiator could naturally perform upon the Stage when he did not imitate or represent, but naturally do it; and therefore it is better to omit the representation of it. (1971: 39–40)

Hearing a verbal report of death works better, Dryden suggests, so long as the report does not offend one's sensibilities (presumably by its length or content). He continues: 'When we see death represented we are convinc'd it is but Fiction; but when we hear it related, our eyes (the strongest witnesses) are wanting, which might have undeceiv'd us; and we are all willing to favour the sleight when the Poet does not too grosly impose upon us' (*ibid.*: 40).

Dryden's comments about the difficulty of performing dying onstage, and the adverse reactions it may provoke, still have purchase centuries later, especially in the context of realist theatre, in which mimetic failure may diminish or suspend the reality effect.[8] It can indeed be amusing, and even fascinating, to observe an actor play dead by appearing not to breathe, or by visibly breathing despite their character's death, then perhaps surreptitiously rising and exiting during a blackout, or otherwise being dragged off by an actor or stagehand.[9] In his spoof book on amateur acting, Michael Green advises actors to be sure to die in a comfortable position and avoid being shown 'dead' onstage for too long (see Figure 0.3): 'My advice to the aspiring body is to die behind something and then have a good sleep. If one is in view there is always the danger of heavy breathing or even a sneeze, apart from the strain of having to lie still' (1964: 56).

Tom Stoppard makes the actor's craft of dying part of the comic fodder and philosophical exploration of death in *Rosencrantz and Guildenstern Are Dead* (1966). The character of the Player says '[there's] nothing more unconvincing than an unconvincing death', but claims dying is what actors do best; it is their 'talent' (1967: 55, 60).[10] Guildenstern dismisses the idea that actors know anything meaningful about the 'real' nature of death, which he conceptualises in terms of non-appearance:

> ... you can't act death. The fact of it is nothing to do with seeing it happen – it's not gasps and blood and falling about – that isn't what makes it death. It's just a man failing to reappear, that's all – now you see him, now you don't, that's the only thing that's real: here one minute and gone the next and never coming back – an exit, unobtrusive and unannounced, a disappearance gathering weight as it goes on, until, finally, it is heavy with death. (*ibid.*: 61–2)

Guildenstern decries the actors' efforts at portraying death, but he still falls for the Player's performance of dying after Guildenstern stabs him with what turns out to be a prop knife. In this play, Stoppard celebrates theatrical conventions of dying while broaching a conceptual understanding of death as a state of non-existence, which is more difficult to grasp and thus harder to represent.

Aesthetic considerations (vis-à-vis taste) and practical challenges have not prevented dramatists from scripting scenes involving dying characters and dead bodies, or from treating the topic of death. Some have taken this to an extreme: for example, in Eugène Ionesco's *Jeux de massacre* (*Killing Game*, 1970), characters drop dead in huge numbers over the course of the play because of an epidemic. The stage is rife with corpses.[11] But even in genres where onstage death is rare, such as Ancient Greek tragedy, verbal reports of death are delivered. Death is still 'present' in these plays even if a character's final moments are not shown (see Macintosh, 1994).

Theorists writing in the late twentieth and early twenty-first centuries have noted theatre's 'deathly' aspects. Herbert Blau was a major proponent of the idea that theatre is intimately and profoundly connected

Introduction

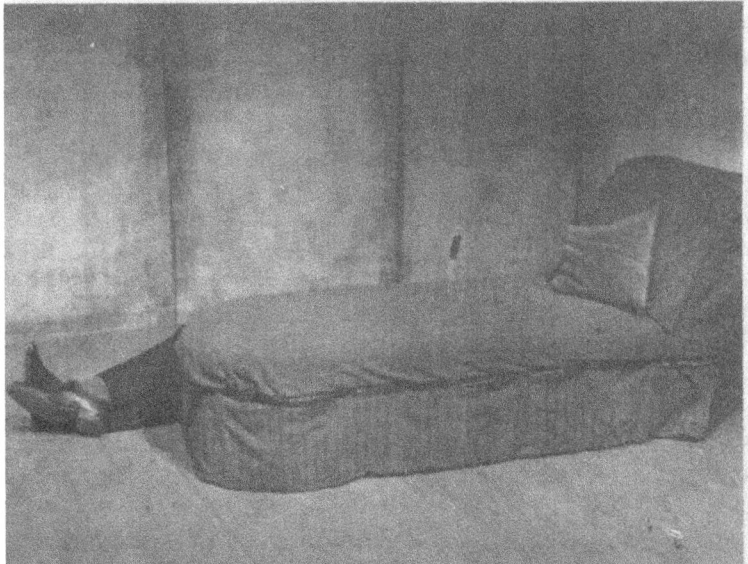

Above:
Wrong way to die. This pose is impossible to hold. Also the knife will slowly teeter to the floor.

Below:
Right way to die. All is ease and comfort.

0.3 Extract from *The Art of Coarse Acting* (1964) by Michael Green

with death and dying. He makes numerous observations of this kind in his writings, repeatedly returning to the idea that, as a living being, the actor in performance is metaphorically 'dying' – is subject to the passage of time – in front of one's eyes, thereby affecting one's perception of the art-form. He considers the spectator's awareness of the actor's mortality a 'universal' of performance, despite 'the myriad of ways in which the history of performance has been able to disguise or displace that elemental fact' (1990b: 267). Blau suggests one may be captivated by the act of witnessing the (mortal) human actor in theatre, even if this is not thematically foregrounded in the performance. 'When we speak of what Stanislavski called Presence in acting', writes Blau, 'we must also speak of Absence, the dimensionality of time through the actor, the fact that he who is performing can die there in front of your eyes; is in fact doing so. Of all the performing arts, the theater stinks most of mortality' (1982: 83). Arguably, circus, with its 'death-defying' (and, sometimes, death-causing) aerial feats, or high-risk performance art, where a performer can literally die in front of your eyes, might more readily be considered the performing art most redolent of mortality, but Blau is referring to theatre's ability to connote mortality ideationally and sensorially in its basic apparatus. Per Blau's proposition, theatre does not have to feature death-defying feats for it to evoke mortality powerfully; theoretically, it can do so if participants are suitably mindful of it.[12]

Blau highlights the bodily reality of a performance event where people are co-present in a shared physical space. 'In the theater, if we think about it, we breathe each other, giving and taking life', Blau muses (*ibid.*: 86). Blau worked with actors from the experimental group KRAKEN on psychophysiological exercises that aimed to heighten consciousness of their biology and mortality, instructing them: 'You are living in your breathing. Stop. Think. You are dying in your breathing. Stop. Think. You are living in your breathing. You are dying in your breathing. You are living in your dying, dying in your living' (*ibid.*). For this to count as theatre, an actor had to *show* these ostensibly oppositional states 'through the radiance of inner conviction' (*ibid.*). Elsewhere, Blau writes about (imaginatively) seeing the famous Italian actor Eleonora Duse (who died in 1924, two years before Blau was born) convey 'dying' in performance via facial expression and conscious intent. Blau does not say Duse, in his imagining, was performing a character who was dying; Duse ostensibly conveyed the *idea* of her own dying, in passing, through her self-awareness and technical skill:

> I have always retained (from I know not where) an image of [Duse] in perfect stillness, then something passing over her face like the faintest show

of thought, not the play of a nerve, *only thought*, and you would suddenly know she was dying. I mean dying right there, *actually*, articulating the dying, with a radiance of apprehension so breathtaking that, in the rhythm of your breathing, you could hardly escape your own death. (1990b: 267)

Blau appears to be writing speculatively here.[13] This is closer to performance fiction than performance analysis, and it might be thought to indicate how meaning is *projected on to* a performer, in line with one's own ideas and fancies, rather than what a performer might aim to communicate. Yet, this does not invalidate the impression that theatre can evoke intimations of mortality through imaginative encounters between performers and audience members.

Blau says there is something in the 'Imaginary' of theatre that 'makes death *present*', if only notionally, and it is the actor's 'vocation' to make this happen (1990a: 137, 138). Interestingly, he believes the 'smell of mortality' (a phrase he borrows from *King Lear*) may be detected in theatre even in the absence of an onstage performer: 'you can smell it in the wings, that smell of mortality' (2011: 100). Apparently, the mere suggestion of bodily presence in theatre is enough to prompt consideration of mortality. For Blau, mortality functions as a type of theatrical dark matter. He calls it 'the unseeable substance of theater, there, not there, which in the consciousness of its vanishing endows it [theatre] with Life' (*ibid.*). This is a curious, seemingly contradictory proposition, recalling Peggy Phelan's (1992) much-debated ontology of performance based on ephemerality and disappearance.

The connections Blau makes between theatre, death, and mortality also involve consideration of theatrical '*ghostliness*': an uncanny impression on the part of spectators that '*we are seeing what we saw before*', even if attending a production for the first time (1990b: 259, 260). Blau posits 'ghostliness' as another universal of performance. Scholars have since queried the significance of 'ghosts' (both supernatural and metaphorical) in theatre using various theoretical lenses (see Luckhurst and Morin, 2014). Marvin Carlson has analysed how theatre is figuratively haunted by the 'ghosts' of previous characters, plot points, gestures, scenographic items, spaces, performer personae, and so forth. (I experienced the 'ghosting' of Beckett characters in the performance piece discussed at the beginning of this chapter.) In his study of theatre as a 'memory machine', Carlson examines how 'ghosting' – the return of something one has encountered before in a subsequently altered context – operates distinctively in theatre. He affirms Blau's proposal that 'ghostliness' (or ghosting) is a universal aspect of theatrical performance, saying: 'Everything in the theatre, the bodies, the materials utilized, the language, the space itself, is now and has always been haunted, and that haunting has been an essential part of the theatre's meaning to and reception by its audiences in all times and all places' (2001: 15).

Alice Rayner has a different take on theatre's ghosts. In a book that conceptualises ghosts as 'death's double', Rayner argues for preserving a non-rational understanding of a ghost as something that originates in a 'realm of uncertainty': '[A] ghost appears only from an oblique perspective and emerges only from the side-ways glance at the void of death or the blanks in memory. ... Theatre's ghosts, when they are present, induce ... something close to the fearful astonishment or even vertigo in the radical unknowing and lack of explanation for what appears' (2006: xxii–xxiii). In her study, Rayner explores how theatre makes familiar elements (e.g., curtains, lighting) uncanny and is haunted by disappearance and the presence of loss.

In a paper given at Northwestern University in 2008, Rayner spoke about attending a production of *Rosencrantz and Guildenstern Are Dead* decades earlier and having an existential realisation at the end of the play when the protagonists disappeared onstage, signifying their death.[14] At this moment, Rayner remarked, she recognised herself as a being who was aware of death – as someone who, in the future, would be gone. Rayner is not alone in describing theatre as 'a human space where we humans encounter not only the dead who have gone before but also the images of our own mortality' (2006: xii). Hélène Cixous defines theatre as 'the stage where the living meet and confront the dead, the forgotten and the forgetters, the buried and the ghosts, the present, the passing, the present past and the passed past' (2004: 28–9). Howard Barker envisions theatre as being 'situated on the bank of the Styx (the side of the living). The actually dead cluster at the opposite side, begging to be recognized. What is it they have to tell? Their mouths gape ...' (2005: 20). In their study of opera as an 'art of dying', Linda Hutcheon and Michael Hutcheon hypothesise that 'when people go to the theater, at times and in part, they find themselves participating in a ritual of grieving or experiencing their own mortality by proxy through an operatic narrative. ... [They] can feel both identification and distance as they – safely – rehearse their own (or a loved one's) demise through the highly artificial, conventionalized form of opera' (2004: 10–11). Admittedly, one does not need to attend theatre to have an existential experience of this sort, but it is still significant that theatre can facilitate contemplation of mortality and consideration of the dead in various ways through its modus operandi. Theatrical *deathliness* may be thought to shadow theatrical *liveliness*.[15]

Scholars have probed theatre's deathly connections – its capacity to make death and dying uniquely apparent through performance. What they have not done in depth or at length is to examine how and why Western dramatists and theatre-makers from the late nineteenth century onward have used theatre's ability to 'make death present' (i.e., metaphorically, experientially, conceptually, etc.) to engage thematically with death-related historical events, social practices, and cultural phenomena, as well as contemporaneous attitudes toward human mortality. That is what this book sets out to accomplish.

Death and dying: in context

Death is a fact of life and dying is universal, but understanding of death and dying and the ways we respond to these phenomena are historically and culturally informed. They are largely – but not totally – period- and context-specific.

Take definitions of death. In the first *Encyclopaedia Britannica*, published in 1768, death was defined as the separation of the soul and the body (Dennis, 2014: 156). In contrast, the most recent online edition refers to multiple definitions of death, in line with modern scientific understanding of death as a process – with organs losing function at different rates due to lack of oxygen – and not as a single moment. Modern scientific definitions of death include clinical death (the cessation of heartbeat and respiration), which is not permanent and may be reversed; brain death (irreversible brain damage and permanent non-functionality), determined by unresponsiveness to external stimuli, no bodily movement or independent breathing, no automatic reflexes, and no recorded electrical activity in the brain (a.k.a. the Harvard criteria of 1968); and cellular death. The latter type of death results from one of three mechanisms: necrosis, where cells die due to being deprived of nutrients and energy (e.g., by the interruption of blood flow); autophagy, where a cell consumes all or part of itself in an effort to 'generate useful nutrients during times of scarcity'; and apoptosis, where a cell is directed to self-terminate because internal damage has been detected (Warraich, 2017: 13). Death is therefore a multiform phenomenon that can be framed and determined in different ways.[16] A doctor's pronouncement of a person's death ('calling' the time of death) may be considered a performative utterance. Determining the point at which the death of a human being has occurred can be a contestable issue: it relates to how death is biologically understood, legally defined, and is also dependent on the cultural and spiritual beliefs of those involved. Dixie Dennis observes:

> By and large, in the United States and other developed countries, brain death is accepted as the definition of death, even if the heart continues to beat by way of artificial means for some time afterward. Yet, in some countries, Japan, for example, brain death is not widely accepted. In the United Kingdom, it takes the independent judgement of two physicians before someone can be declared dead. In Islamic doctrine, death is not complete as long as the spirit continues in any part of the body. Among persons of the Hindu faith, birth, death, and rebirth (i.e., reincarnation) are cyclical, meaning persons are born to die but die to be reborn. (2014: 159)

Death and dying can mean different things to people, depending on their understanding of these phenomena and on the circumstances in question. This seems self-evident and uncontroversial, but it is easily overlooked or ignored, especially in large-scale theorisation and general studies of the subject.

Conceptions of death and dying in modernity, or in any sociohistorical or cultural context, are always potentially multiple and discrepant. Tony Walter, a sociologist, remarks: 'too many [sociological studies of death] refer to "modern society", as though they are all the same, which in the area of death they manifestly are not' (2008b: 327). He cautions against assuming an absolute distinction between modern ways of death and those of traditional societies, observing that 'there are in fact wide variations in how all kinds of societies deal with the deaths of their members. In the modern urbanised world, for example, Americans, Irish and Japanese regularly view human corpses at the wakes of colleagues and neighbours; the English do not' (*ibid*.: 326). Representatives from the US-based Association for Death Education and Counseling highlight individual variation in death, dying, and grieving practices: 'Individuals experience dramatic life events on their own terms ... within the "micro-culture" of themselves and their own understandings and assignments of meaning. We believe that it is not uncommon for one's own reactions and understandings to match imperfectly with whatever cultural norms one's group(s) may dictate' (Chapple *et al.*, 2017: 219).

Furthermore, our understanding of, and attitude toward, death and dying typically alters over the course of our lives as we gain life experience and endure loss; in this, we are united by awareness of our mortality (part of the 'human condition') and by the emotional and psychological difficulties of confronting death – both our own and that of others. In one way of thinking, we can experience death only by proxy through witnessing other people's deaths. We can experience *our own dying*, but (probably) not *our own death*. Yet, there are forms of death other than biological death: for example, in the modern West, 'social death' has been recognised since the late 1960s. This refers to 'the process of marginalization and isolation experienced by the long-term sick and dying, whereby they are rendered socially dead even before actual physical death occurs' (Brennan, 2014: 386). Unfortunately, this type of death *can* be experienced, though, happily, it can also be reversed or ameliorated.

Recognising the variety of ways death has been conceived and rationalised (or not) throughout history means recognising its constructed nature. Death is a reality, of course, but, in a way, it is also a fiction, in that it is creatively (re)interpreted. Michael Neill, a literary scholar, calls death a 'fiction of a particularly fluid kind. For "death" is not something that can be imagined once and for all, but an idea that has to be constantly reimagined across cultures and through time; which is to say that, like most human experiences that we think of as "natural", it is culturally defined' (1997: 2). Sandra M. Gilbert, also a literary scholar, makes a similar observation in her study of modern dying and grieving practices. She writes: 'Each death changes the world even while each way of dying, each different imagination of death, has itself been changed by the world's changes. There's a sense, then, in which we might say history makes death, even while there's also a corresponding sense in which death makes history' (2006: 104–05). 'Death makes history' in the sense that accounts of the deaths of individuals and groups can form part of a historical study. This is fairly straightforward. 'History makes death' is a trickier formulation. It signals the way in which historical studies of death retrospectively construct (or retrieve?) its past meanings.

The French social historian Philippe Ariès is probably the most well-known historian of death. Ariès's short study *Western Attitudes Toward Death* (1976) and its much longer follow-up *L'homme devant la Mort* (1977, published in English translation as *The Hour of Our Death* in 1981) are landmark texts in the historiography of death, and have been the subject of much scholarly debate. As the title of his earlier book indicates, Ariès outlines Western attitudes to death from the 'Middle Ages' (his term) to the 'present day', identifying and explaining various '*mentalités*' – 'mental lives and attitudes that tacitly shaped the daily lives of particular groups or whole societies' – largely associated with historical periods (Bleyen, 2009: 66). Ariès identifies collective attitudes to death from the perspective of the *longue durée*, using a purposely wide field of vision to gain historical perspective. 'If [the historian] confines himself to too short a time span, although it may seem long according to classical historical method, he runs the risk of attributing originality to phenomena that are really much older', he remarks (1981: xvi–xvii). In Ariès's estimation, changes in attitudes to death take place very slowly. They may appear almost static over long periods of time, unnoticed by contemporaries, and yet 'sometimes, as today, more rapid and perceptible [changes]' occur (1976: 1). Ariès suggests attitudes to death can be characteristic of certain epochs but can also be continuous between them (i.e., they may relate to the sensibility of an earlier age) (Dollimore, 2001: 121). He does not suppose attitudes collectively change all at once or are ever entirely uniform, which would, indeed, be unusual.

Ariès begins with 'tamed death' in Europe in the early 'Middle Ages'. Here, death, following early Christian teaching, was 'both familiar and near, evoking no great fear or awe' (1976: 13). Death was a 'public ceremony' with 'no theatrics', a 'ritual organized by the dying person himself', at which parents, friends, neighbours, and children were present (*ibid.*: 12, 13). There was harmonious 'coexistence of the living and the dead' (vis-à-vis burial sites) and felt connection – perceived oneness – between this world and the next (*ibid.*: 13, 14). Ariès detects a shift in the eleventh and twelfth centuries from the traditional 'familiarity' with death, which implied 'a collective notion of destiny', to a preoccupation with 'one's *own* death' and posthumous survival, in keeping with humanist individualism. 'In the mirror of his own death each man would discover the secret of his own individuality' (*ibid.*: 51–2). For members of the elite, death was imagined as a mortal enemy – something to be feared, resented, and rigorously prepared for via *ars moriendi* (art of dying), overseen by the priesthood. Accordingly, burial was relocated into the church itself.

By the end of the sixteenth century, death 'gradually began to be surreptitious, violent, and savage', arousing strange curiosities, fantasies, and eroticism, despite the age of Enlightenment (1981: 608). Ariès subsequently sketches a cultural preoccupation with 'the death of the other person', beginning in the eighteenth century, giving rise to a romantic, rhetorical treatment of death: 'Like the sexual act, death was henceforth increasingly thought of as a transgression which tears man from his daily life, from rational society, from his monotonous work, in order to make him undergo a paroxysm, plunging him into an irrational, violent, and beautiful world' (1976: 57). Attention was switched from the deceased to the mourners, prompting elaborate death rituals and mourning behaviour. Consequently, 'the fear of death ... was transferred from the self to the other, the loved one' (1981: 610).

Ariès's final outlined attitude to death in the West concerns the 'modern' era, in which death has become 'shameful and forbidden'

(1976: 85). It is to be avoided, if possible: made taboo, hushed up, euphemised, distanced, denied, made 'invisible', kept private but away from the home, yielded to the authority of medical and mortuary professionals. 'Death in the hospital is no longer the occasion of a ritual ceremony, over which the dying person presides amidst his assembled relatives and friends. Death is a technical phenomenon obtained by a cessation of care, a cessation determined in a more or less avowed way by a decision of the doctor and the hospital team' (*ibid.*: 88). Ariès's disapproval of the 'modern' Western attitude to death, and his preference for an earlier, simpler, less managed outlook and set of social practices, are plain in his writing.

Ariès's history of death in the West is intriguing and insightful, but problematic. It is too reliant on generalisation and speculation. It pays insufficient attention to cultural, geographic, and religious differences; economic factors; women's mortality; demographic trends; changes in medical science; mass persecutions throughout history; and other major historical events (such as the World Wars).[17] Understandably, Ariès had to be selective in his approach. His scholarship reveals, but it also obscures.

I have taught an undergraduate seminar on death in modern theatre on several occasions and have always included an excerpt from Ariès's work. Typically, some students will object to Ariès's 'blanket' pronouncements on modern society and find fault with his conclusions. They will say how, in their experience, death is not 'denied' or considered 'shameful' today (overlooking the fact that Ariès was writing in the 1970s, decades before they were born). Yet, other students will rush to defend his thesis, saying it articulates something they perceive to be true, and will relate feeling ostracised when they were grieving, linking this to social discomfort with bereavement, for example. Ariès's work is thus valuable as a provocation, and not just in a pedagogical context.

Ariès's scholarship demonstrates how 'history makes death', indicating the value of this enterprise, while also signalling the need to qualify and supplement it – or perhaps even to correct it. As Jan Bleyen remarks, 'death cannot be understood to have had one linear narrative of downfall', recalling Ariès's implicit valorisation of the 'familiar' death of the early medieval period and dismissal of the 'unfamiliar', 'hidden' death of the modern era. '[Death] does not have one history, but rather it has multiple histories' (2009: 68). Scholars working in various fields have attended to death's multiple histories in different contexts, including engagement with mortality in artistic work. This book contributes to this endeavour and takes inspiration from Ariès's work by outlining *a* history of death in modern theatre – a history that, surprisingly, has not yet been told.

Connecting theatre studies and death studies

This book connects theatre studies with 'death studies' – 'an umbrella term for research spanning all aspects of death, dying and bereavement, including end-of-life care' (Borgstrom and Ellis, 2017: 93). Death studies is a multidisciplinary field of study, including psychology, sociology, history, anthropology, philosophy, literary studies, clinical medicine, and palliative care (Brennan, 2014: xviii). It has flourished in the academy since its beginnings in the 1950s, and now has journals and research centres devoted to it.[18] The fact that scholars from a diverse range of disciplines are drawn to researching death is not surprising. As Elisabeth Bronfen and Sarah Webster Goodwin observe, 'death is not a topic like any other. For one thing, it is genuinely of universal interest. Every discipline is pertinent, every scholar has a body of reflections to draw on, every reader has experiences to bring to bear on the scholarship of death' (1993: 3). Correspondingly, Walter believes death studies is not a discipline unto itself: 'It has no distinctive theories or methods, that is to say, one's mind does not have to be disciplined in a way specific to death studies in order to study death, hence, the social study of death is best conducted by scholars trained in one or more existing disciplines, whether history, sociology, religious studies, English literature, archaeology, or whatever' (2008b: 329).

Theatre scholars have typically written about aspects of death tangentially rather than as a main objective. There are relatively few monographs specifically focused on death and dying in drama and theatre, and fewer still that consider the work of multiple dramatists or theatre-makers in a comparative manner.[19] Notable examples include Fiona Macintosh's (1994) comparative analysis of death and dying in ancient Greek and modern (i.e., early twentieth-century) Irish tragic drama; Michael Neill's (1997) study of mortality and identity in English Renaissance tragedy; and Mischa Twitchin's (2016) theoretical investigation into 'the uncanny in mimesis' in Tadeusz Kantor's 'theatre of death'. Thérèse Malachy's short study *La mort en situation dans le théatre contemporain* (1982) is perhaps the closest antecedent to *Death in Modern Theatre*. Malachy treats the work of four dramatists who wrote in French – Michel de Ghelderode, Jean-Paul Sartre, Beckett, and

Ionesco – and provides literary analyses of their plays. For Malachy, 'contemporary theatre' is characterised by death as a morose state of being – an overarching, morbid disposition she traces to the aftermath of the Second World War. In her view, death 'is no longer an end ... it is rather a category, or even a condition' (1982: 30). Malachy's morbid diagnosis of 'the spirit of the age' is instructive, but her study is limited in scope and presupposes a single, unifying mindset with respect to how death is conceived in 'contemporary' theatre.

Rather than propose a grand narrative about death in modern theatre, a narrative that would purport to encompass and explain the ways in which modern dramatists and theatre-makers have engaged with death and dying in their work (e.g., the 'death of God', or another concept of this sort), this book offers a series of micro-narratives, foregrounding death's variable, historically contingent, and socioculturally inflected meanings in a broadly chronological series of investigations. Beginning in the late nineteenth century and ending in the early twenty-first century, I examine how dramatists and theatre-makers explore contemporaneous ideas about death and dying in their work, using theatre's ability to 'make death present' in a unique manner. I do not aim to catalogue *all* the ways death and dying feature in drama and theatre from the late nineteenth century onward; such a task would be impossible. Instead, I adopt a period-specific approach, considering how and why death and dying are represented at certain historical moments using dramaturgy and aesthetics that challenge audiences' conceptions, sensibilities, and sense-making faculties. In some chapters, I examine the work of artists who were part of a movement, or whose work has aesthetic affinity; in others, I analyse the work of artists who were (or are) contemporaneous but do not have a shared style. In all cases presented here, dramatists and theatre-makers engage with one or more aspects of death in modernity, exploring issues of social, cultural, historical, personal, and/or philosophical significance.

Chapter outlines

We begin in the late nineteenth century. Chapter 1 explores the role death played in the cultural imaginary of the *fin de siècle*, when spiritualism and other death-related pursuits were in vogue, particularly in bohemian Paris. Spiritualists claimed to be able to contact the dead, thus proving that death did not mean the end of life but simply marked a transformation from a corporeal to a non-corporeal state of being. I relate this to representations and evocations of death in symbolist drama and theatre, outlining how symbolist dramaturgy and *mise-en-scène* made it possible to 'admit' death as paradoxical presence in theatre – as something that could be sensed but not readily defined or contained. Short plays discussed in this chapter include Rachilde (a.k.a. Marguerite Vallette-Eymery)'s *Madame La Mort* (*Madame Death*, 1891), Charles van Lerberghe's *Les flaireurs* (*The Night-Comers*, 1889), Maurice Maeterlinck's *L'intruse* (*The Intruder*, 1890), and Leonid Andreyev's *Requiem* (1916). The chapter ends with an analysis of W.B. Yeats's symbolist-inspired play *Purgatory* (1938).

Chapter 2 swaps the cultural fascination with death in the *fin de siècle* for the reality – and 'unreality' – of death in the years surrounding the 'Great War' of 1914–18. The war made death seem newly strange, affecting how it was represented and understood. The devastation wrought by the war, the scale of the conflict, and the types of death it caused challenged conceptions of 'the real', inflecting it with perceptions of the 'unreal'. This chapter analyses plays written during and immediately after the First World War that represent death in a 'fantastical' manner and on a grand scale, abstracting it. I focus on three plays: Vernon Lee (a.k.a. Violet Paget)'s allegorical satire *Satan the Waster* (1920), Ernst Toller's expressionist drama *Die Wandlung* (*The Transfiguration*, 1919), and a section of Karl Kraus's monumental documentary drama *Die letzten Tage der Menschheit* (*The Last Days of Mankind*, 1922). These dramatists strove to capture something of the 'shock' of the war – its disruption of the status quo and conventional understanding of mortality – through their depictions of death.

Chapter 3 confronts the phenomenon of death denial, which has been closely associated with Western societies in the twentieth century, despite global conflicts and repeated incidences of mass death. Death denial is a psychological impulse and a cultural attitude that banishes thoughts about death and disavows the reality of personal mortality. This chapter surveys theories of death denial and analyses examples of drama and theatre from the 1950s to the 1970s that expose its potentially damaging effects on the individual and society. My four case studies are Dino Buzzati's *Un caso clinico* (*A Clinical Case*, 1953), the Open Theater's *Terminal* (1969–1971, text by Susan Yankowitz), and two plays by Eugène Ionesco, *Le roi se meurt* (*Exit the King*, 1962) and *Amédée, ou Comment s'en débarrasser* (*Amédée, or How to Get Rid of It*, 1953). I situate these examples in relation to the 'death awareness movement', which began in the 1950s and advocated for transparency about death and dying. I argue that these pieces offer mordant social commentary by challenging prevailing orthodoxies through the presentation of absurd, theatrically arresting, and sometimes morbidly funny scenarios.

Chapter 4 sheds light on the shadows cast by the Holocaust, the dropping of the atomic bomb, and the prospect of future nuclear devastation in various 'theatres of catastrophe' from the mid-twentieth century to the early twenty-first century, investigating how plays and performance pieces explore conceptions of death relating to these events and to possible futures stemming from them. The plays discussed in this chapter (some in passing, others at length) are Samuel Beckett's *Fin de partie* (*Endgame*, 1957) and *Happy Days* (1961), Marguerite Duras's *Yes, peut-être* (*Yes, Maybe*, 1968), Edward Bond's *The Tin Can People* (1984), Józef Szajna's *Replika* (*Replica*, 1971–-88), and Howard Barker's *Found in the Ground* (2001). These pieces approach the spectres of the Holocaust and/or death-by-nuclear-attack obliquely, only ever alluding to historical events or evoking them in fantasy.

Chapter 5 concerns the drama of dying in the early twenty-first century: a time of increased public awareness about issues relating to death and dying, but also of great private uncertainty and worry about the end of life – specifically, the form it will take, its duration, and the degree of agency one will have. Due to the interventions of modern medicine, which continually work to extend life, dying in the early twenty-first century can be a protracted process, and may be burdensome both for the dying person and for care-givers. Achieving a 'good death' (whatever that might be) is not guaranteed or always readily accomplished. This chapter surveys contemporary attitudes toward death and dying and investigates how they are dramatised and staged in Carol Ann Duffy's *Everyman* (2015), Marina Carr's *Woman and Scarecrow* (2006), Caryl Churchill's *Here We Go* (2015), and Kaite O'Reilly's *Cosy* (2016).

The Conclusion considers the future of death, which involves its possible elimination due to advances in medical science, and addresses the way in which resuscitation science is challenging death's ostensible fixity and irreversibility. Examples of human longevity and immortality in modern drama are briefly discussed, and a short account is given of a piece of devised theatre by Unlimited Theatre, which premiered in 2014, entitled *Am I Dead Yet?* The chapter ends with a combination of performative writing and critical commentary that reflects on the whole study.

Death in Modern Theatre thus examines various 'stages of mortality' from the late nineteenth century onward, tracing contextualised ideas about death and dying across the 'long' twentieth century, as explored in examples of modern drama and theatre. I take a leaf out of Ariès's book by surveying changing attitudes to death over an extended period (though I fall far short of the millennia he covers!). I depart from Ariès (and from Malachy) in forgoing the use of a single, overarching *mentalité* of death in modernity, instead advancing a more complicated, plural, mosaic-like impression of how death and dying have been understood since the late nineteenth century. Ariès nonetheless allowed for the possibility of attitudes to death being continuous between epochs; on a smaller scale, this is borne out here too. There are lines of continuity and overlap between the various 'stages of mortality' outlined in this book; the aspects of death in modernity analysed here are not wholly discrete or compartmentalised.

The phrase 'stages of mortality' refers to theatrical presentation and exploration of death and dying. It also nods to Elisabeth Kübler-Ross's famous theoretical model of the 'five stages of grief' (denial and isolation; anger; bargaining; depression; acceptance): in her view (and contrary to popular misconception), the stages 'do not replace each other but can exist next to each other and overlap at times' (1970: 236). The possibility of non-linear ways of comprehending mortality is less neat than one might prefer, but is possibly more true to life, which makes it an apt model for historiography. Relatedly, the five chapters following in this book have their own discursive frameworks, so can be read out of order, although the later chapters will be more resonant if one has read what has preceded them.

This study does not aim to be comprehensive: although it includes consideration of major topics and is intentionally wide-ranging, there are many other subjects that could be factored into this history (e.g., AIDS, 9/11), just as there are many other modern plays about death and dying that are not discussed here or are only briefly mentioned. Obviously, one can't cover everything, and it's an enormous topic. I invite other scholars to supplement or revise this history. Even still, readers may wonder why I have chosen to focus on one play over another, or one dramatist or theatre-maker over another. Why not discuss Sarah Kane's play *4.48 Psychosis* (2000) in Chapter 5, for instance? My selection of case studies is driven by several factors: the extent to which a play or performance piece engages thematically with the subject of each chapter; the insight it offers into the chapter topic; the degree and type of provocation it provides; its resonance, or complementarity, with other examples I have chosen; the language in which a play is written or translated; the availability of relevant archival material; and the overall mix of examples chosen. To my mind, *4.48 Psychosis* does not engage with the specific end-of-life issues that are the subject of Chapter 5 as well as the four plays featured here. O'Reilly's *Cosy* engages the topic of assisted suicide, but the topic of personally conducted suicide, which Kane's play raises, is a distinct issue and could form the basis of a different study altogether. Moreover, Kane's work has also already received a lot of critical attention.

I have tried to get a mix of well-known and lesser-known plays from an international range of dramatists and theatre-makers. I do not attend at length to certain modern theatre artists whose work often engages with the theme of death, such as Beckett and Kantor, as scholars have already written about them in depth (e.g., Barfield et al., 2009; Twitchin, 2016). Regarding gender representation, the fact that the dramatists whose work is discussed in Chapter 5 are all female is largely coincidental. I did not intend to focus on female dramatists when planning this chapter. Rather, I became taken with each of the plays in question, detecting points of contact between them as well as potentially fruitful avenues for critical investigation. This is how I proceeded throughout: endeavouring to select plays that illuminate the topic under survey, especially when grouped in certain configurations. This approach has the advantage of creating novel combinations of artistic work, going off the 'beaten track', on occasion, and forging unexpected lines of connection between modern dramatists and theatre-makers.

On 'modern theatre'

This book uses the term 'modern theatre' to refer to the work of dramatists and theatre-makers from the late nineteenth century onward that is self-reflexively 'modern', in that it responds – directly or indirectly – to 'current' events, phenomena, attitudes, concerns, etc., or those of the recent past. This framing is in line with recent scholarship.[20] Marshall Berman's conception of the destabilising quality of being modern informs my usage of this term. 'To be modern', he writes, 'is to experience personal and social life as a maelstrom, to find one's world and oneself in perpetual disintegration and renewal, trouble and anguish, ambiguity and contradiction: to be part of a universe in which all that is solid melts into air' (1988: 345). This conception of 'being modern' recurs throughout the chapters that follow in relation to death and dying.

Conceived in a flexible, relational manner, the term 'modern' is a perpetually moving target. The modernity of the late nineteenth century is obviously different from the historical situation of the early twenty-first century, but there are correspondences too, which a focus on mortality can bring to light.[21] '[Modernity] is a creative self-destruction', observes Décio Torres Cruz:

> [Each] modern creation that appears destroys its preceding tradition, and generates a new one, which, in its turn, will be obliterated by another new tradition in an endless series of interruptions and returns. ... ['Modern'] is always dependent on a time reference: yesterday's modern is not the same as today's, and today's modern will not be the same tomorrow. ... Like the phoenix, the 'modern' resists death and always reappears, soaring over the ruins and the dust of time and chaos. (2014: 9–10)

The 'modern' may resist 'death' in the sense of continually being renewed, but artistic work, such drama and theatre, may be deemed 'modern', in part, because of the way it treats the subject of death, as this study shows.[22]

In this book, 'modern theatre' serves as an umbrella term for a variety of plays and performance pieces, but the emphasis is on work that is on, or near, the avant-garde side of the aesthetic spectrum. I am interested in work that seeks to challenge audiences' ideas about mortality through some combination of form, content, and presentational approach. This includes work that has been called 'modernist', but extends to examples from the later twentieth and early twenty-first centuries that are differently 'modern', but no less challenging in terms of the ideas and/or the aesthetic experiences they can provide. This accords with recent developments in modernist studies, in which modernism's temporal and cultural or geographic boundaries have been expanded, reaching forward and backward in time (see Friedman, 2015). Theorising multiple modernisms and multiple modernities has become a vital part of modernist scholarship, as has deconstructing the highbrow/lowbrow cultural divide. Plays that are not compositionally experimental or avant-garde can also provide valuable insight into culturally and historically located conceptions of death and dying; nonetheless, I have opted to focus more on work that has clear disruptive potential, complicates conceptions of death and dying, and can rattle readers and audience members by what it communicates and how it communicates it. This gives the study necessary coherence and facilitates lines of contact between the plays under consideration.

Methodology

Scholars working in the multidisciplinary field of death studies use their own disciplinary methods and knowledge from other disciplines to investigate a wide array of topics associated with death and dying. That is how I proceed in this book. I provide close readings of dramatic texts and performance analyses informed by scholarship from various fields – chiefly history, sociology, psychology, and philosophy. I use information and concepts from these sources to illuminate plays and productions, with the aim of advancing original interpretations of them. I also draw on non-scholarly historical texts, and refer to other examples of art or performance from a specific period or milieu to supplement my analyses. Close reading is therefore coupled with a commitment to historicise and theorise texts.[23] My production analyses are enriched by reference to archival documents, including reviews, audio-visual recordings, rehearsal notebooks, programmes, promotional material, and so forth. I include consideration of my own experience as an audience member, when relevant. In the cases of plays written in a language other than English, I primarily work with translations, either previously published or my own, and am alert to the semantic differences that can arise. I address the methodological challenge of interpreting phenomena that may be culturally discrepant in different national contexts (such as attitudes toward mortality) by foregrounding this fact, and not assuming transhistorical or trans-cultural universalism; instead, I situate cultural texts and performances in their sociohistorical contexts. When analysing plays in performance, I may refer to original production contexts and/or to later productions in a different cultural context, depending on what a production may 'offer' the investigation, and on the quantity and quality of information I have obtained. I use production analysis to assist interpretation of a play, gain insight into a specific example of its theatrical interpretation, and assess the significance of its 'revival'. The last objective is a complicated but potentially instructive undertaking for death-themed drama, as stages of mortality (i.e., historical attitudes toward death and dying, and theatrical exploration of end-of-life) involve both continuity and change, as this study will show.

Envoy

Static theatre –
all is silent ... all is still ...
A noise. Death steals in.

Notes

1 Events at The Cart Shed are organised by Peter Hulton and Dorinda Hulton.
2 Listen to an excerpt of the recording by searching for 'Helen, chuntering' on SoundCloud or by using this link: https://soundcloud.com/a-curtin/helen-chuntering/s-4kY2U. I am grateful to Pam Woods and Ian Cumming for making this recording available.
3 Other examples of autobiographical, devised theatre about the death of a family member include Complicite's *A Minute Too Late*, which premiered in 1984 and was reperformed in 2005; *Have I No Mouth*, by the Dublin-based company Brokentalkers, which premiered in 2012; and *So It Goes*, by the British theatre company On The Run, which premiered in 2014.
4 'Drama is like palaeontology', writes Kirsten Shepherd-Barr. 'We study the fossils (play texts) that remain after the full dramatic experience (the performance) has *died*' (2016: 3, my emphasis).
5 As Elisabeth Bronfen and Sarah Webster Goodwin remark: 'much of what we call culture comes together around the collective response to death': Bronfen and Goodwin (1993: 3).
6 Some famous filmic examples: *Der müde Tod* (*Weary Death*, a.k.a. *Destiny*, 1921, directed by Fritz Lang); *Death Takes a Holiday* (1934, directed by Mitchell Leisen); *Orphée* (1950, directed by Jean Cocteau); and *Det sjunde inseglet* (*The Seventh Seal*, 1957, directed by Ingmar Bergman).
7 'Probably without exception, at least in Western culture, representations of death bring into play the binary tensions of gender constructs, as life/death engages permutations with masculinity/femininity and with fantasies of power' (Bronfen and Goodwin, 1993: 20). See also Guthke (1999).
8 Case in point, the subheading of a 2011 *Guardian* blog post on 'what makes a good stage death': 'A really convincing theatrical death is better left unseen' (Soloski, 2011).
9 Tim Etchells writes about watching a performer play dead in *A Cursed Place*, a production based on Georg Büchner's *Woyzeck*, directed by Pete Brooks in 1993: 'one of the performers/characters lay still and silent – "dead" on the floor. I lost the play for a moment then, only watching the contradictory breathing of the corpse, the rise and fall and sound of her breath. ... I liked to watch her then because her part in the play was finished and she had nothing whatever to tell me' (1999: 115–16).
10 Indeed, actors have been famed for their prowess at, or commitment to, dying (in character) onstage. The London-born actor J. Hudson Kirby (1810–1848) inspired the New York audience catchphrase 'wake me up when Kirby dies', which came to be applied to any supreme effort by an actor (Hendrickson, 2000: 684). One might also, in this context, think of Bottom's lengthy death throes when performing as Pyramus in the play-within-the-play in Shakespeare's *A Midsummer Night's Dream*.

11 This play also features a personification of death in the guise of a very tall, black-robed, hooded monk who shadows the action – a possible allusion to the robed figure of death in Bergman's *The Seventh Seal* (1957).
12 The practice of actors literally dying during a performance might also be considered in this context. The Dublin-based 'Centre for Dying Onstage', a research project initiated by Krist Gruijthuijsen and developed by Kate Strain, has a website (www.centrefordyingonstage.com) that catalogues 'unexpected deaths that have occurred during moments of performance in the public domain'. See also Dent (2001) and Ward (2010). David Barnett (2017) surveys the phenomenon of the 'last-gasp monologue' that intimates the imminent death or unconsciousness of the performer. Jody Enders writes about the medieval legend of a performance of the biblical drama of Judith and Holofernes that took place in Tournai, France, in 1549, in which 'the "actor" playing Judith actually beheaded a convicted murderer who had briefly assumed the "role" of Holofernes' (1999: 203). The veracity of this legend is unclear.
13 Might Blau have seen Duse in the 1916 silent film *Cenere*, directed by Febo Mari, or did he just imagine seeing her perform? Rosalia, the character Duse plays in this film, dies at the end.
14 Alice Rayner, 'Now You See Me. Now You ...', *Theatre: Crossroads of the Humanities*, Northwestern University, 11–12 April 2008.
15 One could make a parallel here between the ways in which theatre and history, or theatre and the past, are connected. Rebecca Schneider remarks: '[Just] as theatre may not be entirely real, so too may it not be entirely, or only, live. A repeated gesture, an aged object, a clichéd phrase, an old letter, a footprint, a way of walking – all of these things, material and immaterial, might drag something of the no longer now, the no longer live, into the present, or drag the present into the no longer now' (2014: 45). Schneider uses the term 'inter(in)animate' to refer to passageways between 'then' and 'now' (*ibid.*).
16 '[There] is no uniform way to define irreversible brain death', writes Sam Parnia, who notes that one of the biggest differences is between the United Kingdom, where a person is classified as dead if their brain stem is dead, and the United States, where brain death refers to the death of the whole brain (2014: 267–8).
17 For a discussion of Ariès's work in relation to that of another French historian of death, Michel Vovelle, see Kselman (1987).
18 *Mortality*, *OMEGA – Journal of Death and Dying*, and *Death Studies*. The Centre for Death and Society, founded in 2005, is located at the University of Bath.
19 There are edited book collections on death in theatre: e.g., Gritzner (2010) and Perdigao and Pizzato (2010). The Fall 1997 issue of the *Journal of Dramatic Theory and Criticism* was devoted to the theme of representing death in theatre. *Performance Research* 15 (1) (2010) has the theme of 'memento mori'. Modernist literary scholars writing about death have either

mentioned theatre in passing, as in the case of Friedman (1995), or not at all, as in the case of Sherman (2014). For examples of books focused on themes of death and dying in the work of a single author (in these cases, Beckett), see Barfield *et al.* (2009); White (2009).

20 Karoline Gritzner's *Adorno and Modern Theatre* (2015) analyses the work of Edward Bond, David Rudkin, Howard Barker, and Sarah Kane. Kirsten Shepherd-Barr's *Modern Drama: A Very Short Introduction* '[spans] a period from roughly 1880 to the present' (2016: 2). The journal *Modern Drama* treats literature of the past two centuries, according to the current description on the journal's website. In his *History of Modern Drama*, volume two, David Krasner proposes that 'modern drama circa 1960–2000 was co-constituted by modernism past (pre-1960) and postmodernism' – but he still uses 'modern drama' as an overall descriptor (2016: 31).

21 The term 'modern' is admittedly problematic, as Graham Ley observes: 'That modern drama might begin with Ibsen, yet somehow antedates the motor car, the aeroplane, and the telephone is more than a little perverse in terms of an effective nomenclature, but the tradition persists, even into the hyper-reality of a new millennium' (2014: 157).

22 And what of postmodernism? Julia A. Walker and Glenn Odom note that this concept has 'fallen into critical disuse since the new modernist studies (NMS) found evidence of its stylistic traits within works traditionally identified with classic high modernism' (Walker and Odom, 2016: 131). Additionally, Jean-Michel Rabaté remarks: 'It seems today that modernism has absorbed most of the twentieth century, that it goes back deep into the nineteenth century and that it has moreover swallowed postmodernism. This notion [postmodernism], which emerged in the 1980s, has surprisingly lost all of its purchase, in a sudden disaffection that some have found disappointing' (2013: 11).

23 As Alan Ackerman notes: 'Close reading is entirely compatible with the drive to historicize' (2012: 15).

1

Beyond the veil: sensing death in symbolist theatre

Picture something, if you will. It is the early 1890s, and you are attending a performance of symbolist drama in Paris, presented by Paul Fort's Théâtre d'Art. A gauze scrim has been placed behind the footlights, veiling the stage. This material object dematerialises the scene of performance, casting it in a mysterious, murky light. The scrim makes the actors resemble shades. From your perspective, the actors are beyond the veil; figuratively, they are 'beyond' the mortal world. You are intrigued and captivated. You sense something larger-than-life, something otherworldly …

The phrase 'beyond the veil' is biblical in origin. In Exodus, instructions are given for the use of a piece of precious cloth to separate the innermost sanctuary, which contained the divine presence, from the rest of the Jewish Temple in Jerusalem. The Gospel of Matthew notes how the veil of the temple was 'rent in twain from the top to the bottom' upon Jesus's death (27:51). A veil erected in a place of ritual, such as a temple or a theatre, therefore has mystical connotations, which the symbolists were keen to exploit. Many symbolists sought 'to catch some far-off glimpse of that spirit which we call Death', to quote Edward Gordon Craig, who had links with this movement (1911: 74). Disaffected with what they perceived as drab, enervating reality, symbolists sought spiritual rejuvenation in imaginary, mythological realms that could be intuited by artful arrangement (or derangement) of the senses and by veiling the scene of performance.

It is little wonder that death was a favourite theme of the symbolists, who evoked it in a range of art-forms, including theatre. In the *fin de siècle*, spiritualism was in vogue, and so the subjects of mortality and the afterlife were addressed with renewed interest. Spiritualists claimed to be able to contact the dead, thus proving that death did not mean the end of life but simply marked a transformation from a corporeal to a non-corporeal state of being. Scientists endeavoured to ascertain if there was any truth to spiritualists' supposed abilities to contact the dead. In this way, the *meaning* of death was contested and put into flux. Symbolists tapped into these metaphysical concerns and called attention to the ambivalent presence of the dead in everyday life. Death haunts their art, and theatre provided a way for them to test out their ideas about that which lies 'beyond the veil'.

This chapter explores cultural fascination with death in the *fin de siècle*. I outline how symbolist dramaturgy and *mise-en-scène* made it possible to 'admit' death as paradoxical presence in theatre – as something that could be sensed but not readily defined or contained. Audiences of symbolist theatre were invited to perceive death not only in embodied form as a personified character but as a stage presence, as something that could be sensorially detected, like a spirit in a séance, though with terror and uncertainty in lieu of spiritual assurance. I theorise how the symbolists marshalled the power of theatrical atmosphere to help them achieve this end. This chapter primarily concerns symbolist drama written in the 1890s and the early twentieth century, relating it to bohemian culture and social anxieties. Short plays discussed include Rachilde's *Madame La Mort* (*Madame Death*, 1891), Charles van Lerberghe's *Les flaireurs* (*The Night-Comers*, 1889), Maurice Maeterlinck's *L'intruse* (*The Intruder*, 1890), and Leonid Andreyev's *Requiem* (1916). The chapter ends with an analysis of W.B. Yeats's symbolist-inspired play *Purgatory* (1938). Yeats titled his 1922 autobiographical work *The Trembling of the Veil* after a statement made by the symbolist poet Stéphane Mallarmé in the 1890s. Mallarmé, in Yeats's words, said his epoch was '*troubled by the trembling of the veil of the temple*' (1922: v). What might this mean? This chapter investigates the 'trembling of the veil' made by these deathly plays on the page and in performance. But first, let's go on a jaunt.

The cabaret of nothingness

One of the curiosities of the red-light district of Paris in the *fin de siècle* was the Cabaret du Néant (the Cabaret of Nothingness), situated at 34 Boulevard de Clichy in Montmartre. Founded in 1892 by a magician called Dorville, the Cabaret du Néant was one of three death-themed venues he operated. The other two were the grandiosely titled Cabaret du Ciel (Cabaret of Heaven) and the Cabaret de l'Enfer (Cabaret of Hell), located on the same street as the Cabaret du Néant.

An evocative account of these cabarets is provided in a work of tourist literature from the period entitled *Bohemian Paris of To-day*, written by American author W.C. Morrow (based on notes by Edouard Cucuel). Morrow ostensibly relates Cucuel's experiences as an American art student living in Paris. In the penultimate chapter, Cucuel and his friend Bishop take a visiting American writer, A. Herbert Thompkins, for a night out on the town. Instead of going to the opera, as Thompkins expects, Cucuel and Bishop take him to Montmartre on a 'tour of discovery', intending to 'introduce him to certain things of which he might otherwise die in ignorance, to the eternal undevelopment [*sic*] of his soul' (1899: 253, 251). Following an uplifting visit to the Cabaret of Heaven, which features a man dressed as Dante, a lantern projection of St Peter's head, a bevy of gyrating angels, and a shrine containing an immense golden pig, the pair lead Mr Thompkins to the Cabaret du Néant. The entrance is draped with black cerements with white trimmings, like that which 'hang before the houses of the dead in Paris' (*ibid.*: 364). Patrolling it is a solitary pallbearer with a black cape and top hat. Inside, the trio find a chamber dimly lit by wax tapers and a chandelier made of human skulls attached to bones clutching candles. Wooden coffins, resting on biers, are ranged about the room (see Figure 1.1). The walls are decorated with skeletons in grotesque attitudes, battle pictures, and guillotines in action. The trio, noting what appears to be the distinct odour of a charnel house, find an empty coffin-table and order drinks from a *garçon* dressed in the garb of a hearse-follower. They sit in the cabaret's gloomy atmosphere for a while. Thereafter, the master of ceremonies invites the guests to enter a passage lined with bones, skulls, and fragments of human bodies, at the end of which is the *chambre de la mort*. Inside, they are seated upon rows of small caskets and behold an upright, coffin-shaped opening in the wall (see Figure 1.2). Presently, a greenish-white light illuminates the coffin-shaped hole, revealing a young woman robed in a white shroud. She smiles at the audience and

1.1 Postcard of the 'intoxication room' at the Cabaret du Néant, Paris, c. 1900. Note the coffin-tables and the skull-and-bones chandelier. One of the signs on the wall says 'To be or not to be'.

looks at them saucily. Her smile soon fades as a voice from the depths charges her to compose her soul for the end. A grisly transformation occurs. Morrow details the macabre spectacle:

> Her face slowly became white and rigid; her eyes sank; her lips tightened across her teeth; her cheeks took on the hollowness of death – she was dead. But it did not end with that. From white the face slowly grew livid ... then purplish black. ... The eyes visibly shrank into their greenish-yellow sockets. ... Slowly the hair fell away. ... The nose melted away into a purple putrid spot. The whole face became a semi-liquid mass of corruption. Presently all this had disappeared, and a gleaming skull shone where so recently had been the handsome face of a woman; naked teeth grinned inanely and savagely where rosy lips had so recently smiled. Even the shroud had gradually disappeared, and an entire skeleton stood revealed in the coffin. (*ibid.*: 272)

But the show isn't over yet. The voice in the darkness addresses the skeleton, informing the audience that death is not final for everyone: 'The power is given to those who merit it, not only to return to life but to return in any form and station preferred to the old' (*ibid.*). The young woman is bid to return if she thinks she deserves to, and if she wishes. Lo and behold, the process of bodily decay slowly reverses and the skeleton becomes a living person again – but not the young woman of before. Instead, the rotund body of a banker appears in her place. He promptly

1.2 Postcard of the 'vault of the dead' at the Cabaret du Néant, Paris, c. 1900

steps out from the coffin-shaped hole in the wall, to the audience's amusement. The trio later exit and set out to visit the cabaret of hell. Mr Thompkins, the narrator notes, 'seemed too weak, or unresisting, or apathetic to protest. His face betrayed a queer mixture of emotions, part suffering, part revulsion, part a sort of desperate eagerness for more' (*ibid.*, 276, 279).

The attraction/revulsion felt by Mr Thompkins is presumably what enticed patrons to the Cabaret du Néant. The cabaret offered patrons a morbidly amusing, potentially unnerving social entertainment capped with techno-wizardry; the schlock factor was likely a draw as well. Picture postcards corroborate Morrow's account of the cabaret's distinguishing features and unique selling points. The cabaret was overloaded with deathly signifiers, which furnish Morrow's thick description. It is hard to imagine patrons taking the cabaret's offerings seriously. However, despite its gore, the cabaret provided an oddly comforting take on death, courtesy of the stage illusion at the end. Patrons could enact a sped-up version of their own final bodily decay. (What fun, eh?) They could imaginatively and performatively undergo transformation into a corpse and then 'magically' be restored to their former selves (via a Pepper's Ghost-type effect involving canny lighting and a second, hidden coffin complete with skeleton, shown via a glass reflection). Those attending could witness a person's 'death' and know this event did not necessarily mark the end of life, but rather foreshadowed possible reincarnation. Conceivably, the repetition of this trick could have made death seem less frightening, despite the surface horror of 'corpsification'.[1] The cabaret sought to unnerve *and* console patrons – a good business strategy.

The Cabaret du Néant was not the only venue that provided spectacles of death in 1890s Paris. Oscar Méténier founded the Théâtre du Grand-Guignol in 1897, inspired by the naturalist aesthetic of the Théâtre Libre. The Grand-Guignol, also located in the Pigalle area of Montmartre, offered audiences a 'slice of death' – a counterpart to the naturalists' 'slice of life' – in presentations of heightened horror (throat-slitting, beheading, and the like), reportedly causing audience members to become nauseous or lose consciousness (Hand, 2010: 73).[2] Nor were Parisians restricted to *stage* renderings of mutilation, death, and decay. They could observe actual human corpses at the Paris Morgue, which was purpose-built to allow public viewing of unidentified dead bodies. The morgue became a tourist attraction, receiving up to ten thousand visitors per day (Kosmos, 2014: 464). Additionally, the Catacombs of Paris, opened to the public on a regular basis in 1874, allowed access to the remains of an estimated six million people contained in its ossuaries (*ibid*.: 465). In the late nineteenth century, when symbolist theatre emerged, the subject of death was hardly taboo. Quite the opposite: in Paris, death was an object of fascination; there was an appetite for death-themed attractions. However, some cultural commentators thought this morbid sensibility was indicative of widespread cultural decadence and social decline.

Degeneration

The Hungarian-born social critic Max Nordau was one of the principal architects of this vision. Nordau's book *Degeneration*, first published in 1892, is a sprawling, venomous denunciation of the *fin de siècle* and the artwork it inspired. The book caused a sensation upon its release, as well as strident backlash and criticism. Nordau contended that rich inhabitants of great cities and certain types of modern artists were social degenerates who were contributing to the decline of humanity by their morose dispositions and moronic activities. Nordau diagnosed the spirit of the age as being weak and sickly, in a state of nervous exhaustion, overcome by malaise, and in love with death. The mood of the *fin de siècle*, he writes, is 'the impotent despair of a sick man, who feels himself dying by inches in the midst of an eternally living nature blooming insolently for ever' (1993: 3). Nordau believed an unhealthy, defective subset of humanity was responsible for the temperamental funk he poetically calls the 'Dusk of the Nations' (*ibid.*: 6). Degenerates, in Nordau's estimation, crave fads and sensations, or else they are overwhelmed by sensation and indulge in melancholia. They are weak-willed, mentally deficient, aimless, unable to concentrate, overemotional, and hysterical. They are fatigued and incapable of doing work or bonding with their brethren in a common cause. (I know the feeling.) They are fearful of the world around them and the unknown spectres it contains. They are predisposed to reverie and easily become entranced with specious mysticism and fuzzy thinking. They are to be pitied and disdained, these mental drifters. (Reader: focus.) Nordau suspects that modern urban life is responsible for increased signs of degeneracy in culture and society. He writes:

> The inhabitant of a large town, even the richest, who is surrounded by the greatest luxury, is continually exposed to unfavourable influences which diminish his vital powers far more than what is inevitable. He breathes an atmosphere charged with organic detritus; he eats stale, contaminated adulterated food; he feels himself in a state of constant nervous excitement (*ibid.*: 35).

Following Nordau's spook-train of thought, is it any wonder that world-weary Parisians would seek such morbid pleasures as the Cabaret du Néant?

Nordau gets out his rhetorical knives for the exemplars of social degeneracy and cultural decadence, which are legion, in his opinion. Mysticism is one of his chief bugbears. He lambastes exponents of a state of mind 'in which a man fancies that he perceives inexplicable relationships between distinct phenomena and ambiguous formless shadows' (*ibid.*: 57). Nordau explains mysticism as the result of weakness of will and incapacity to organise thoughts in an orderly, rational manner. Unsurprisingly, Nordau derides symbolist artists and the work they produce. He contends they show 'all the signs of degeneracy and imbecility: overweening vanity and self-conceit, strong emotionalism, confused disconnected thoughts, garrulity … and complete incapacity for serious sustained work' (*ibid.*: 101). He criticises them for being 'vague often to the point of being unintelligible', and pious to boot (*ibid.*). Maurice Maeterlinck's work is exemplum 'of an utterly childish idiotically-incoherent mysticism'; his poetry demonstrates 'the workings of a shattered brain' (*ibid.*). In his insult-laden screed, conducted over hundreds of pages, Nordau ironically comes off seeming as hysterical as the 'degenerates' he feverishly castigates. Nordau's study is of particular interest for its attempt to articulate and explain an aspect of the late nineteenth-century Zeitgeist: namely, its deathly tenor. Nordau's understanding of why modern artists were preoccupied with death and dying is biased, but his sweeping polemic nevertheless indicates the cultural vibrancy and breadth of this interest. As it happens, the symbolists did not need Nordau to sound out deathly inclinations and fantasies in modern life. They were already attuned to these dynamics.

Envisioning death: *Madame La Mort*

Symbolist artists envisioned death in various ways. Some used traditional iconography. Death is depicted as a violin-playing skeleton in Arnold Böcklin's *Self-Portrait with Death as a Fiddler* (1872) and in August Brömse's series of paintings *The Girl and Death* (1902), which borrows from the medieval tradition of the Dance of Death. Jaroslav Panuška's drawing *Death in the Alley* (1900) shows a white-robed skeleton standing ominously alongside a bird that looks like a raven – a familiar deathly icon. Some depictions of death by symbolist artists have an abstract, quirky tone. Max Klinger's *Death Pissing* (c. 1880) features a skeleton improbably urinating into a lake. Panuška's watercolour *Death Looking into the Window of One Dying* (1900) portrays a blue, humanoid creature peeping into someone's home. Odilon Redon imagines death as a green corporeal figure, incompletely rendered, rising out of a purplish whirlpool in *The Green Death* (1905).

Female personifications of death are prevalent in symbolist art. Gustave Moreau's 1865 painting *The Young Man and Death* depicts death as a beautiful, mostly naked, young woman with closed eyes, hovering behind a shirtless young man in a near embrace. The image is inescapably sensual. Carlos Schwabe portrays a female angel of death dressed all in black, kneeling above a gravedigger in an open grave in *The Death of the Gravedigger* (1895–1900). Jacek Malczewski presents female angels in the style of classical Greek statues or goddesses in his 'Thanatos' paintings of 1898–99. His 1902 painting *Death* shows an agrarian scene featuring a woman with a scythe gently closing an old man's eyes.

Rachilde's play *Madame La Mort* also envisions a female personification of death. However, Rachilde complicates a trope often used in a straightforward fashion by male artists. Moreover, Rachilde's play offers subtle critique of decadent aesthetes with death wishes – a type of degenerate scorned by Nordau. *Madame La Mort* focuses on a rich layabout, a malcontent who actively seeks to end his own life. Paul Dartigny is an idle, nervous, world-weary decadent who has become satiated with life and wishes to seek out death, which he believes takes female form, and so he commits suicide by poisoning one of his own cigars. The first and third acts of the play are realist in style; the second act shifts to symbolism. In Act 2, Dartigny ostensibly encounters death in the form of a veiled woman who claims dominion over him. Interestingly, Rachilde neither romanticises Dartigny nor valorises his deathly interests. Other characters in the play point out his failings to his face, behind his back, and over his corpse. Jacques Durand, Dartigny's bourgeois spongerfriend, tells him he has an imaginary illness and talks gibberish. He is blunt with him.

> Listen, my dear Paul, at bottom you are an egotist: you give because you don't need anything, you don't like women any more because you had a lot of women, you don't like society anymore because you were part of it whenever you wanted. ... My friend, your misfortune is that you squandered your wealth to gain knowledge instead of living an honest life. (Rachilde *et al.*, 1998: 130)

Doctor Gaudin, from whom Dartigny steals poison, calls him a madman and a neurotic, exclaiming 'Only demented poets commit suicide with poisoned cigars! ... How the fin-de-siècle mocks us with this business!' (*ibid.*: 136). This may be an intended laugh-line on Rachilde's part – a jab at cultural conventions she was employing but also subverting. Upon finding Dartigny's dead body, Lucie, his erstwhile paramour or courtesan, offers a frank assessment of him:

> Dear Paul! He was really demented. There is no reason to lie about it any more, it was almost ridiculous ... He saw everything in black! ... And the manias, the egotism! (158)

Dartigny takes little notice of criticisms of his character and death wish. He is entirely absorbed in his morbid fantasies.

These come to the fore in Act 2 when a vision of Lucie as a symbol of light or life faces off with 'the veiled woman' for possession of Dartigny's body and soul. Dartigny finds all this terribly thrilling and erotic to boot. The allegorical women fight over him (a cliché male fantasy). The veiled woman wins the war of wills and words, and draws Dartigny to her. Dartigny, eager to intermix *eros* and *thanatos*, tries to pump her for information (she tells him nothing) and insinuate intimacy between them. The veiled woman is indifferent to his advances and remains inscrutable. She is a cipher, apparently even to herself. In this instance, there may be nothing beyond the veil.

DARTIGNY: At last, can you tell me who you are, you, Death?
THE VEILED WOMAN (*in a very hollow voice*): I do not know. (149)

Dartigny, instead of being frustrated by the veiled woman's obliqueness, is transported by it and drifts off into an ecstatic sleep of death. This is perhaps unsurprising; she is his fantasy, after all. (Note how 'Madame *la mort*' sounds like 'Madame *l'amour*'.)[3]

When the Théâtre d'Art presented this play in 1891 many reviewers thought the final act, in which Dartigny's body is discovered, was unnecessary (Lively, 1998: 18). They seem to have missed the point. Act 3 establishes the 'reality' of the situation and casts doubt over the previous act. Dr Godin, examining the corpse, explains the effects of the poison Dartigny took, which include hallucinations of sight and hearing. This puts the veiled woman's metaphysical veracity into question. Unlike personifications of death in other symbolist plays, such as Hugo von Hofmannsthal's *Der Tor und der Tod* (*Death and the Fool*, 1893) or Arvid Järnefelt's *Kuolema* (*Death*, 1903), here, the veiled woman may well just be a phantasm conjured by a dying man, a proverbial dagger of the mind. Dartigny ostensibly achieves his desire of making off (if not making out) with a female embodiment of death, but it is equally possible he simply imagined his dream coming true. Rachilde undercuts the symbolic legitimacy of the veiled woman – a dubious vision of death as a mysterious female seductress, a blank cipher on to whom male desire is projected – taking a pot-shot at existing conventions and exposing male fantasy. Dartigny's associates do not take him seriously, so why should we? Rachilde's character description insinuates the veiled woman is a psychic apparition, not a 'real' incarnation of death. 'She does not look like a ghost', we are told; 'she is not returning from the dead, she has never existed. She is an image, not a living being' (Rachilde *et al.*, 1998: 122). Rachilde dramatises a fantastical, possibly sham, encounter between a decadent and a female personification of death. She thereby implicitly critiques the decadent mindset and the longing for death it promotes. Nordau did not suppose symbolist art could be critically astute, self-reflexive, or do anything other than promote the supposedly corruptive, escapist spirit of the age. He was wrong.

Rachilde participates in the symbolist envisioning of death, but puts this practice under scrutiny. Symbolist art (including poetry and literature) often romanticises death, foregrounding its imagined aesthetic features. The desire for death was frequently expressed in beautiful, flowery language, as in Charles Baudelaire's poem 'Semper Eadem' from *Les fleurs du mal* (*The Flowers of Evil*, 1857):

Be still, O soul, with rapture ever rife!
O mouth, with the childish smile! Far more than Life,
The subtle bonds of Death around us twine.

Let – let my heart, the wine of falsehood drink,
And dream-like, deep within your fair eyes sink,
And in the shade of thy lashes long recline!

(1909: 28)

This is highly reminiscent of the end of Act 2 in Rachilde's play, when Dartigny embraces sleep/death in the form of the veiled woman:

> THE VEILED WOMAN (*sweetly*): Come, the hour is here, the nuptial bed is ready. Sleep, my unhappy lover. (*She wraps him in her arms and in her veil.*)
> DARTIGNY (*faintly*): Let us sleep … together, is it not … together …
> THE VEILED WOMAN (*softly, spreading out once and for all the folds of her veil*):
> Forever. (Rachilde *et al.*, 1998: 150)

Rachilde invokes the (male) fantasy of bonding with death in romantic slumber; however, the play's quasi-realist frame invites us to be wary of this impulse and those who harbour it. Even still, the play's symbolist second act encourages reflection on the hidden, unknown aspects of life – whether that is the unconscious or some other realm.

Deathly atmospheres

As well as personifying death, symbolists also strove to evoke death incorporeally through atmosphere and staging (as at the Cabaret du Néant). Georges Rodenbach's novel *Bruges-la-morte* (1892), later adapted into a play called *Le mirage* (*The Mirage*, 1901), evokes death for the protagonist, a grieving widower, in the atmosphere of Bruges.[4] Hugues, the protagonist, sees, hears, and feels multiple resemblances between his state of mind, his memories of his dead wife, and the city:

> Bruges was his dead wife. And his dead wife was Bruges. The two were united in a like destiny. It was Bruges-la-Morte, the dead town entombed in its stone *quais*, with the arteries of its canals cold once the great pulse of the sea had ceased beating in them. … The closed houses exhaled a funereal atmosphere, window-panes like eyes clouded in death throes, crow-steps tracing stairways of crepe in the water. (2007: 60)

This novel conjures death as an intangible presence in the reader's imagination. Unlike literature or visual art, theatre can evoke atmosphere not just in the perceiver's imagination but also in the performance itself, which is dramaturgically shaped, technologically mediated, and collectively constructed. It can situate the audience in an actual atmosphere, not just a depicted atmosphere. Theatre, like music, creates atmosphere as a matter of course. In this respect, it can figuratively bring death into the room – even if no one can see it for sure, or at all.

Presentations of symbolist texts by the Théâtre d'Art (led by Paul Fort) and the Théâtre de l'Œuvre (led by Aurélien Lugné-Poe) in Paris in the late nineteenth century strove to evoke perceptual realms through stylised, oblique, potentially multisensory or synaesthetic modes. For aesthetic and economic reasons, staging by these companies was often minimalist. Symbolist playwright Pierre Quillard's dictum '[the] spoken word creates the scenery along with everything else' suggests scenography was verbally constituted, as in English early modern theatre (quoted in Boyer, 1998: 91). Quillard explains: 'The stage scenery must be an ornamental pure fiction that perfects the illusion through analogies of colour and lines with the drama. Most often, a backdrop and a few drop curtains suffice to give the impression of the infinite multiplicity of time and place' (*ibid.*: 91). In addition to the aforementioned scrim, symbolist theatre-makers experimented with dim lighting; shadows; tableaux vivants; artistic backdrops that explored colour and form abstractly (painted by members of the 'Nabi' school); a mostly bare stage; statuesque poses by actors; slow, ritualistic movements and gestures; liturgical-style vocal delivery; mask-like make-up; full-length costumes that obscured the actor's physical distinctiveness; and, in the Théâtre d'Art's notorious production of Paul Roinard's *The Song of Songs* in 1891, the creative use of scent in performance (Deák, 1993: 156–83; Fleischer, 2007). These components of symbolist scenography are well established in the critical literature, and it is also commonly known that they were not always successful; indeed, some of the symbolists' efforts to 'dematerialise' the theatre space, such as the aforementioned attempt at scent design, misfired. Still, the symbolists' ideas about the creation of mysterious, otherworldly theatrical atmospheres through scenography, acting style, and dramatic design deserve fuller attention, particularly as they relate to theatrical presentations of death.

Personifying death suggests that death is motivated, has an agenda, and might perhaps be bargained with or avoided for a while, which is purely fanciful.[5] In contrast, death presented as an atmosphere is much more ambiguous and difficult to fathom. It is like the weather. It defies fixity. It is transitive, porous, affective. It cannot simply be seen but appears to hang in the air, so to speak, and inflect the perceptions of those who are located in it and who give it shape. As modernity is characterised by epistemological crisis, ontological doubt, and breakdown of traditional meaning-structures, then death conceived as atmosphere rather than as a bogeyman (or bogeywoman) may be a more resonant means of evocation. A hallmark of being modern in the *fin de siècle*, one might say, was the attempt, or maybe the willingness, to encounter and make sense of death as a pervasive atmosphere. The Cabaret du Néant offered patrons a kitschy atmosphere of death, replete with recognisable depictions of mortality and items associated with it. The Grand-Guignol, inspired by naturalism, staged death overtly and made it grossly apparent. Symbolist dramatists and theatre-makers sought to make death atmospherically perceptible through the art of suggestion. *That which is imagined* is often more frightening than *that which is seen*.

Phenomenological enquiries into the nature of atmosphere illuminate the symbolists' endeavours in this area. They indicate why atmosphere was such a powerful incentive for symbolist theatre artists, who struggled to evoke esoteric ideas and impressions, given the material realities of theatre, including the involvement of human performers.[6] Atmosphere is a nebulous concept, which makes it appropriate for symbolism. It is a 'quasi-thing', according to Tonino Griffero, 'a *je-ne-sais-quoi* perceived by the felt-body in a given space. ... [It is a] spatialised feeling, a something-more in an affective and corporeal sense, rather than in an abstractly semantic sense' (2014: 7, 6). In other words, atmosphere, conceived phenomenologically, is something one perceives sensorially, first and foremost. It operates on an *affective* level. It is never something that is simply 'out there', separate from one's perception of it; it is the sensing of atmosphere that gives it shape (much like sound, in one way of thinking, is the result of the human perception of vibration).

Gernot Böhme also grapples with the quasi-thing-like abstraction of atmospheres – their peculiar quality of being *between* things and perceiving subjects. He writes:

> [Atmospheres] are neither something objective, that is, qualities possessed by things, and yet they are something thinglike. ... Nor are atmospheres something subjective, for example, determinations of a psychic state. And yet they are subjectlike, belong to subjects in that they are sensed in bodily presence by human beings and this sensing is at the same time a bodily state of being of subjects in space. (1993: 122)

Even if atmospheres operate indeterminately between the perceiver and the thing(s) perceived, they are still tied to environmental and spatio-temporal conditions; they do not simply float free from the circumstances of their perception.

Atmospheres are contingent on a host of factors, including interpersonal dynamics. Ben Anderson, meditating on the phenomenology of Mikel Dufrenne and others, observes that '[atmospheres] are perpetually forming and deforming, appearing and disappearing, as bodies enter into relation with one another. They are never finished, static, or at rest' (2009: 79). They are, additionally, 'a kind of indeterminate affective excess through which intensive space-times can be created', like those intensive space-times of theatrical performance, for instance (*ibid*.: 80). Anderson describes atmospheres as 'collective affects that are simultaneously indeterminate and determinate'; they are 'a class of experience that occur before and alongside the formation of subjectivity, across human and non-human materialities, and in-between subject/object distinctions'. As such, he writes, 'atmospheres are the shared ground from which subjective states and their attendant feelings and emotions emerge' (*ibid*.: 78).

Phenomenologies of atmosphere draw attention to an important aspect of human experience that often gets overlooked, even though it can strongly influence our perceptions and dispositions (the same is true of soundscapes). Phenomenology reveals atmosphere as not simply a fancy, a trick of the mind or body, but rather a complex, shifting intersubjective perception shaped by environmental factors: thing-like but immaterial. Atmospheres are real, but one can't necessarily see them – or rather, potentially everything one sees, and hears, and feels, or otherwise senses can give rise to one's perception of an atmosphere, though we may not be consciously aware of this process or how it works. We enter into atmospheres. We detect them. (As comedian Russ Abbott once sang, 'I love a party with a happy atmosphere …').[7] We can change atmospheres, either intentionally or accidentally, but they can also change us without our knowing. Atmospheres can undermine our ontological security and our ability to make sense of the world.

It is not surprising, then, that symbolist theatre artists were drawn to atmosphere as a dramatic concept and a staging principle. Atmosphere theoretically occupies a liminal terrain. It exists between ontological states. It subsumes and captivates the human subject. It is worldly but also conceivably otherworldly or numinous. It relies on sensory perception and imaginative engagement over a literal presentation of things. It cannot be absolutely determined but retains a mysterious, irrational quotient, a 'something-more' or 'something-else' that can be intuited but ultimately remains obscure and ambiguous. In Böhme's view, the art of theatre scenography is a paradigm for the aesthetics of atmosphere; scenographers create 'tuned spaces' to which audiences react and adjust (2013: 5). If symbolists could harness theatre's aptitude for creating a certain kind of atmosphere, then its problematic materiality would matter less. Abstract ideas could be 'floated' in performance. Furthermore, for symbolists interested in depicting death as a force to be reckoned with, an abstract presence rather than an embodied personification, the ambiguous constitution of atmosphere offered a powerful vehicle for achieving this aim.

Acousmatic death: *The Night-Comers*

Charles van Lerberghe, a Belgian symbolist who was a coeval of Maeterlinck, explored this territory. His play *The Night-Comers*, written in 1889 and first performed by the Théâtre d'Art in 1892, predates several plays written by Maeterlinck in the 1890s that treat death, including *Les aveugles* (*The Blind*, 1890) *Intérieur* (*Interior*, 1891), and *La mort de Tintagiles* (*The Death of Tintagiles*, 1894). In these plays, the fictional environment becomes a character of sorts; it threatens the wellbeing of the human characters who populate it. The action is relatively 'static' (Maeterlinck's descriptor of symbolist theatre), but the atmospheres they conjure are dynamic and charged. They focus attention on things the characters detect, or think they detect, in their surroundings. On the page, these plays are flush with scenographical possibilities; as performance scores, they provide templates for potential theatrical atmospheres.

In *The Night-Comers*, van Lerberghe connotes death as a semi-personal, semi-abstract force. There is no character called Death (or something analogous) in the play. Instead, a series of offstage voices purporting to be harmless, real-life people are implicit proxies for death. The play, dedicated to Maeterlinck, has a fable-like quality. It concerns a girl living with her mother in a poverty-stricken cottage during a stormy night. There is a series of knocks on the door and repeated requests for entry: first from a poor man asking for alms, then from a man bringing linen, and subsequently a man with a coffin who attracts a crowd. The girl adamantly refuses entry to these people; her mother, who is ailing, wants her daughter to open the door for the visitors. The mother apparently becomes delusional near the end and thinks the Virgin Mary is at the door. Thereafter, a 'frightful rattle begins in the old woman's throat' (1895: 70). Outside the door a different sort of noise erupts as the antagonistic crowd, led by the mysterious voice, begins to break down the door, which eventually yields, ending the play. The breaking of the door and '*a rush of cold air*' into the house, extinguishing two tapers, symbolise the mother's death, or are else implicitly coincident with it (*ibid.*: 71).

The play's conceit is that the voices seeking entry are all one and the same: they are incorporeal manifestations of death, cunningly presented in different guises. While the play's quasi-realist tone makes it possible to conceive the offstage voices as being innocuous (i.e., not symbolic), this interpretation would be a stretch, given the dénouement. It is hard to imagine why a crowd of people would break down the door otherwise. Besides, they call out 'That corpse! That corpse!' while the mother is still alive, presaging her death (*ibid.*). It is also telling that no one physically enters the stage or house when the door collapses; only an atmospheric disturbance is described. Van Lerberghe strongly indicates that death is the supernatural visitor on the scene. The first voice announces himself as 'the man who … you know quite well'; he refuses to give the girl his name, telling her 'it should not be spoken' (recalling the ancient Jewish prohibition against speaking or writing God's name) (*ibid.*: 62). The girl later articulates her fears, accusing the voice of malevolent intent. 'Do you come to kill my mother, you there? … Do you bring death to us?' (70). The voice does not answer her question, except perhaps in its subsequent actions.

The most compelling feature of *The Night-Comers* is the prominence given to the offstage voices. Van Lerberghe treats these as *acousmatic* entities, meaning that the sources of the sonic or atmospheric phenomena remain unseen. This is a play about the potential danger of unknown, outside elements and the ability of external forces to impinge on domestic and personal security. Van Lerberghe alludes to death via a series of incorporeal voices, seemingly human and personable, but very probably of otherworldly origin. He positions them offstage, beyond the sight of the audience, in the virtual void. In this way, he makes the darkness of the theatre seem terribly ominous.

Spectral death: *The Intruder*

Maeterlinck takes van Lerberghe's treatment of death as an incorporeal stage presence one step further in his play *The Intruder*, written one year after *The Night-Comers* but staged by the Théâtre d'Art several months before it in 1891. Maeterlinck removes personality and characterisation from his symbolic representation of death altogether. He invokes death solely as an atmosphere, an implied force. The audience principally becomes aware of death as the eponymous intruder from the characters' comments about what they can see, hear, and sense around them. Like *The Night-Comers*, it is possible to interpret *The Intruder* as a realistic series of events, but it is quite apparent that death is the spectral force on the scene. Unlike many of Maeterlinck's plays, which have mythological settings and appear not to have anything to do with modernity, this play is '*set in modern times*', per the stage directions (1985: 52). *The Intruder* is indeed a modern play about death, despite its lack of references to the modern world. It is modern in its sensibility.

The play is set in a sombre room in an old chateau. Inside, a family pass an unsettled evening. The mother is offstage, sleeping, recovering from a recent, difficult childbirth. The grandfather, who is blind, frets about her and becomes increasingly apprehensive. He communicates his general uneasiness to the rest of the family, who try to assuage his concerns and privately dismiss them as a product of his age and physical condition, but the seeds of doubt are sown. 'Do you not feel anxious?' he asks them, inadvertently priming them to feel anxious, generating an atmosphere of profound unrest in which seemingly innocuous occurrences acquire portentous meaning (*ibid.*: 55). Very slowly, Maeterlinck builds up a feeling of terror, like the script of a horror film. The grandfather says he is no longer able to hear the nightingales. One of the daughters supposes there must be someone in the garden, which made the birds stop singing. They hear a scythe being sharpened outside. Could it be the gardener about to mow the lawn? The grandfather imagines he hears the scything sound coming from *inside* the house. They think they hear someone enter the house. The maid tells them no one has come in. The grandfather senses his daughter has taken a turn for the worse. He becomes convinced that someone else is sitting among them. As the clock strikes midnight '*a sound is heard, very vaguely as if someone was getting up in haste*' (65). Moments later, a sister of mercy appears and wordlessly makes the sign of the cross, thereby announcing the death of the mother. The family silently enters the 'chamber of death' leaving the grandfather literally and figuratively in the dark.

The Intruder is an ostensibly simple play. Maeterlinck employs conventional tropes, yet the dramatic construction is deft. It is a taut depiction of psychological unrest building into terror. Maeterlinck puts the reader or spectator in the position of the blind grandfather: we too have things explained to us and cannot be sure of their veracity. Most of the sounds referenced in the play come from reported speech. These are things the characters supposedly hear, but we cannot. The play's sound world, primarily constructed from reports made by the characters, serves to create a theatrical atmosphere in which the supernatural visitation is made possible. The grandfather is brought to the realisation (accurate or not) that death is sitting among them because the family has (inadvertently) tracked the supposed intruder's movements from the garden into the house. The grandfather makes them complicit in his mindset. They in turn feed his anxieties. Collectively, the characters generate the atmosphere of doom that hangs over the play. The grandfather orchestrates the deathly tenor of the scene with the other characters' assistance, despite the uncle's and the father's attempts at rationalisation. From the audience's perspective, it does not matter if we cannot see or hear the things mentioned in the play. In fact, it may not even matter if these things are real or imagined; they are verbalised and thereby put into the air as speech. Consequently, they contribute to the play's atmosphere, which *is* shared with the audience.

In accordance with phenomenological theories of atmosphere cited earlier, Maeterlinck's play, considered as drama, describes a scenario in which an atmosphere is created through 'spatialised' feelings as the characters project themselves into their environment and try to decipher it. They alternate between semantic determinations (attempts at rational explanation, such as the gardener mowing the lawn) and affective-corporeal responses (the grandfather's feeling of dread), ultimately privileging the latter. They create an 'intensive space-time', operating as a collective sensory unit that traverses 'human and non-human materialities' (e.g., their observations about the natural world) (Anderson/Dufrenne). This results in the perception of a 'quasi-thing' – the presence of the intruder, which is 'a something-more, a *je-ne-sais-quoi* perceived by the felt-body in a given space' (Griffero), which the grandfather intuits but does not name; we take it to mean death.

The metatheatrical irony of Maeterlinck's play is that when it is performed there *is* something out there in the dark (most likely), invisible to the characters in the scene – namely the audience, figurative inhabitants of another realm who form a kind of spectral entity. In this regard, the audience notionally resembles the 'theatrical dark matter' at the heart of this play. This is Andrew Sofer's term for invisible phenomena, 'felt absences' that 'continually structure and focus an audience's theatrical experience' (2013: 4). 'Materially elusive though phenomenologically inescapable, dark matter is the "not there" yet "not not there" of theatre', Sofer writes, reformulating Richard Schechner's classic 'not me … not not me' model of acting (*ibid.*: 4). Maeterlinck conjures death as theatrical dark matter in his play, making it indirectly present to the audience through vocal suggestion, verbal description, and the collective creation of atmosphere. The audience can apprehend the conjoint, paradoxical absence-presence of death along with the grandfather. Moreover, the absence-presence of the audience (present in the theatre but absent from the fictional world of the play) gives this phenomenon a special charge.

The Théâtre d'Art's production of this play was rehearsed in a makeshift fashion and produced with limited resources, but was still critically well received, in general, though some audience members reportedly did not appreciate the symbolist acting style and bid the actors to speak louder, prompting disagreement (Deak, 1993: 159–62). The set consisted of a table with a single lamp, which provided the sole lighting; when this lamp went out, the rest of the play was conducted in (virtual?) darkness. František Deak notes that at the end of the play, when the sister of mercy appeared, she was upstage and lit from behind, appearing 'to the actors on the stage and to the audience as a phantom' (*ibid.*: 160). The symbolist acting style (typified by stillness, gestural restraint, and liturgical-style speaking) worked to create the impression of a certain type of stage presence, ghosted by absence. Franc Chamberlain observes: 'The actors in Fort's productions needed to maintain their significatory function, but without drawing attention to themselves. They did not perform their absence but were made absent by the scenography; the attempt was to make the actor less substantial rather than less significatory' (1997: 34). Reviews indicate the audience for this production was not all on the same wavelength as Fort and his collaborators, but the aesthetic provocation was still made: theatrical atmosphere had metaphysical possibilities the symbolists could harness.

The terror of the empty space: *Requiem*

Leonid Andreyev's play *Requiem*, an example of Russian symbolist drama, both complements and extends earlier symbolist attempts to evoke death atmospherically in theatre. *Requiem*, written between 1913 and 1916, was first performed, after Andreyev's death, at the Komissarzhevsky Theatre in Moscow in December 1916. Andreyev dramatises the power of theatre to present things that are not there, except in the audience's imagination. He makes death the implicit subject of the drama by fine-tuning theatrical atmosphere so that uncanniness takes centre stage.

The play takes place in the void. Surprisingly, this void contains the replica of a small theatre, complete with stage, backstage, and seating area. The latter is filled with puppet spectators who surround the small stage in a semicircle. Sitting on imaginary chairs, *'they watch relentlessly with painted eyes, they do not move, they do not breathe, they keep totally quiet. The glare from the footlights is reflected on their dead rouged faces, it gives them an illusion of life; wavering, it appears to make them waver'* (1985: 211). The theatre has been purpose-built at the instigation of an unnamed royal who is alternately designated 'the man in the mask' and 'his highness'. He wishes a private performance to be staged in this theatre for an undisclosed reason. Andreyev's play consists of conversations about this enterprise between the people involved as well as glimpses of the symbolist-style play-within-the-play.

The manager shows the man in the mask a parade of the actors who are costumed and made-up for performance. A young couple dressed in romantic medieval costumes slowly pass across the stage *'with a gliding step'*, *'their faces deathly and strangely immobile, like those of corpses'*; another actor *'floats'* over the stage like a *'ponderously moving statue'* (*ibid.*: 218, 219). These directions recall the highly restrained, hieratic style of symbolist acting undertaken by the Théâtre d'Art and the Théâtre de l'Œuvre. The man in the mask enquires of the manager why the actors walk with such a strange step, like ghosts. 'They *are* ghosts', the manager tells him. 'They are asleep and dreaming' (219). Like the puppet audience, the actors in this theatre simultaneously resemble both the living and the dead. After the procession of somnambulant ghost-actors, the man in the mask takes over as apparent director of the proceedings, unnerving the manager. There appears *'the vague, undulating image of a woman who was once beautiful'* (220). This apparition may be the manager's wife, who he has previously said is dead. It is unclear whether this apparition is 'real' or not, or why the man in the mask would want to show it to the manager. Andreyev seems more interested in creating unnerving and atmospheric scenes and impressions than presenting a realistic narrative. After the man in the mask leaves, the manager is left alone in the theatre. He soliloquises on his existence and on the space around him, saying: 'I love the stage, when it is still empty, but the lights are already on; I love the empty ballroom before the beginning of the ball; I love the lowered curtain, downcast eyes, unspoken speech' (223). Andreyev evokes the significatory potential and mysterious quality of an empty theatre space.

'What happens inside a theatre when nothing is happening?' asks theorist Augusto Corrieri. 'In a state of suspended functionality, the presumed emptiness of the auditorium might offer a renewed scene of possibility: curtains, walls and seats hold a certain potential – a promissory force of sorts – and conjure up past historical realities' (2016: 2). Indeed, one may be inclined, while in an empty theatre, to think about the 'ghosts' of previous productions, about absent performers and audiences – the people who have enlivened the space in times past – and the potential of the space to bring a multitude of possible characters and imaginary worlds into being. In 2003, Hugo Glendinning and Tim Etchells initiated a project called *Empty Stages*, which documents a wide variety of performance spaces devoid of people: village halls, arts centres, pub stages, clubs, school auditoriums, disused theatres, magnificent proscenium theatres, opera houses, and so forth. The project showcases the 'magic' of empty theatres and performance spaces as well as their unnerving quality. Looking at the *Empty Stages* images, one is encouraged to project life into them to offset the void they connote. Nick Kaye notes: 'Laden with their meaning-making function, yet seemingly absent from the performance of this meaning, these images invoke their own uncanny double – becoming "meaningful" in their very lack of signification; "present" in their emphatic assertion of absence as the object of attention' (2012: 250). This resembles what Paul Fort, Lugné-Poe, and others were trying to achieve with their symbolist productions: evoking abstract, spiritual ideas by dematerialising the scene of performance, including the actor's presence.

Andreyev's metasymbolist drama features ghostlike actors and characters that question their own reality. Sitting (alone) in the theatre, the manager says to his audience of painted spectators: 'Who knows – perhaps I died a long time ago, and all this is only the fantasy of my dead brain ... or the void that it has peopled' (1985: 211). In a performance of Andreyev's play, an audience of real-life people would, of course, be present, observing the replica theatre on the stage with its 'shadow' audience of puppets. What would a living audience make of its puppet doppelgängers? The 'dead' atmosphere of the replica theatre with its inanimate puppet-audience would presumably be enlivened by the presence of an actual audience in the theatre-outside-the-theatre, but this would depend on the quality of their engagement. As Erika Fischer-Lichte states, the 'self-referential and ever-changing feedback loop' of theatrical performance 'is generated and kept in motion not just through visible and audible actions and attitudes of actors and spectators but also through the energy circulating between them. This energy is no phantasm ... but it is indeed physically perceptible' (2008: 38, 59).

In *Requiem*, Andreyev imaginatively restages symbolist aesthetics, reproducing key stylistic elements and thematic concerns. In this way, he harnesses the potential of theatrical atmosphere to confront the reader or spectator with mortality allusively and affectively. The stylistic self-referentiality does not undercut the play's dramatic power. *Requiem* offers a devastating, nihilistic take on human life. The play ends with the manager crying out into the darkness of the theatre, bewailing his isolation and his precarious existence:

> And who am I? (*Silence.*) Oh, how desolate the night is. Never since the world began has there been such a desolate night as this, its gloom is frightful, its silence fathomless, and I am utterly alone. I listen for a door to bang. No, not a sound. So many doors, but no one comes, no one calls, and no voice of any living creature. (*Cries out loudly.*) Mercy! Mercy! (1985: 223)

The play's nihilistic tone accords with accounts of Andreyev's personality and attitude toward death. In Maxim Gorky's reminiscences of his friend, Andreyev emerges as an often-morose figure, obsessed with his own mortality and the apparent meaninglessness of life. Gorky relates how he once heard Andreyev sobbing while telling his son a bedtime story about how death stalked the earth and mowed down little children. The boy was understandably frightened. Gorky writes: 'Great was the force of [Andreyev's] imagination; but notwithstanding the continuous and strained attention which he gave to the humiliating mystery of death, he could not imagine anything beyond it, nothing majestic or comforting – he was after all too much of a realist to invent comfort for himself even though he wished it' (1934: 140). Andreyev, 'too much of a realist', nevertheless experimented with symbolism, exploring its potential to 'go beyond' surface reality – to dig deeper, to peek 'behind the veil', as it were. *Requiem* suggests there is nothing beyond the veil, nothing after death – there is only the void. This raises some pressing questions. What did symbolist theatre convey about death on a philosophical level? How were the symbolists' conceptions of death, and consequently their theatrical aesthetics, historically informed? Uncovering the connections between symbolist theatre and spiritualism will help to answer these questions.

Symbolism and spiritualism

The symbolists were not alone in their fascination with atmosphere, or in using it to intimate the otherworldly. 'The enlivening problem for modernist artists', says Steven Connor, 'was how to write, paint, photograph, compose, from within the condition of the atmosphere' – an atmosphere telegraphy, telephony, and radio waves had electrified, giving rise to new perceptions about what the air might contain and communicate (2006). Connor argues that the 'cultural atmospherics' of the late nineteenth and early twentieth centuries were typified by 'modernist haze': artistic explorations of interference and disturbance, virtual noise, mixed registers and channels, the in-between, the nebular, the obscure (*ibid.*). The symbolists' hazy theatrical performances (enabled by the gauze scrim, for instance) exemplify this. Significantly, atmosphere was crucial to spiritualist practitioners as well. Spiritualist mediums required a 'good' (i.e., a supportive) atmosphere in the room to 'contact' the dead, and, even then, they would have to 'tune in' to the 'right vibrations', distinguishing signal from noise (Doyle, 1930: 18; Lachapelle, 2011: 109). Séances were, of course, a form of theatre, or at least they relied on performative behaviour in addition to participants' belief (or suspension of disbelief).

Spiritualism emerged in the US in the late 1840s and in Europe the following decade. Spiritualists claimed to be able to contact spirits using an intercessor and manifest them by various means (e.g., the formation of 'ectoplasm', an invisible force). The popularity of spiritualism was buoyed by the rise of spirit photography in the 1860s, which appeared to capture spirits in photographic form (recalling the superstition that photography might capture part of the soul) but was really a hoax – the result of superimposition or double exposure (see Chéroux *et al.*, 2005). Nordau, true to form, branded spiritualism a parody of mysticism. In *Degeneration* he comments sneeringly: 'A Society has been formed which has for its object the collecting of ghost-stories, and testing their authenticity; and even literary men of renown have been seized by the vertigo of the supernatural, and condescended to serve as vouchers for the most absurd aberrations' (1993: 214). Nordau does not specify which society he had in mind. In 1885, the Société de Psychologie Physiologique was created in Paris, which aimed to investigate séances and the subconscious mind (Lachapelle, 2011: 30). Three years earlier, a group of Cambridge dons helped found the Society for Psychical Research in London. These societies were serious about their work. If spiritualist practices could be scientifically validated, it would, of course, mean corporeal death did not mark the end of human life. One would not need to believe in an eternal soul as a matter of religious faith alone. Modernity would have 'conquered' death, so to speak. Furthermore, it might be confirmed that, in the words of noted French spiritualist Allan Kardec (writing in 1850), '[incorporeal] beings people space. They surround us constantly, and unknown to them, exert a great influence over men' (quoted in Ragon, 1983: 15). Like dark matter in the universe (or in the theatre, to use Sofer's analogy), invisible phenomena might be shown to have mysterious and powerful effects. Atmosphere thus acquired another potential current of meaning.

Scholars have only begun to examine the influence of spiritualist practices on symbolist theatre; traditionally, the spiritual and occult aspects of modernism have been swept under the rug.[8] Serena Keshavjee observes how the 'ephemeral' performance style of Loïe Fuller (sometimes claimed as the inventor of symbolist dance) was likened to spiritualist materialisations. She argues that photographs and prints of the dancer relied on the formula developed by scientific and spiritualist photographs to depict ghosts: 'Fuller is depicted as someone who is able to move so quickly that she transforms herself, ectoplasm-like, into different forms' (2006: 38). Keshavjee also highlights the fact that artists associated with Paul Fort's Théâtre d'Art, including Maeterlinck, were knowledgeable about spiritualism and attended séances (*ibid.*: 65). She notes that 'the subject matter of symbolist drama, the stylised acting, and the nebulous imagery of the prints, as introduced by [Paul] Gauguin's drawings [in the magazine *Le Théâtre d'Art*] all borrow formal elements from séances and the photographs that circulated widely of mediums and ghosts' (*ibid.*). Although Rachilde declares the veiled woman in *Madame La Mort* is not a ghost, Keshavjee remarks: 'everything about her description in the published version of the play utilizes the qualities of spectral materializations documented in popular Spiritualist journals' (*ibid.*: 63). Does this mean, however, that symbolist theatre replicated the *ethos* of spiritualism? Or did symbolist artists just borrow from its discourse and stylistic repertoire? Maeterlinck's work, for example, does not fully chime with spiritualist tenets, even if it evoked its atmospherics in performance.

Maeterlinck's philosophical writings demonstrate his knowledge about spiritualist and supernatural matters, but they also reveal his independence of thought. He did not simply adhere to spiritualist thinking. In his 1912 study *Death* (revised and expanded as *Our Eternity* in 1913), Maeterlinck advances his own conception of mortality. Maeterlinck hypothesises that, when we die, our consciousness merges with a universal consciousness, where it is continually transformed: '[Our] spiritual being, liberated from its body, if it does not mingle at the outset with the infinite, will develop itself there gradually, will choose itself a substance [in the universe] and, no longer trammelled by space and time, will grow without end' (1912: 63).[9] Maeterlinck's account of human mortality, while eccentric and contestable, is ultimately uplifting. Death is not something to be feared, he maintains; rather, it is 'a glorious adventure', 'a form of life which we do not yet understand' (*ibid.*: 54). Notably, Maeterlinck suggests death entails a radical transformation of personal identity, which puts him at odds with exponents of spiritualism.

Maeterlinck acknowledged this difference of opinion in his 1914 study *The Unknown Guest*, which is devoted to the consideration of various supernatural phenomena. Maeterlinck uses the metaphor of 'the unknown guest' as a catch-all descriptor and unifying principal for diverse phenomena, 'phantasms of the living and the dead' that may be subconsciously perceived (1914: 4). We may be able to apprehend aspects of 'the unknown guest' (i.e., the supernatural), Maeterlinck supposes, but we do not have the means to grasp its meaning fully. Maeterlinck echoes Kardec when he states: 'It is quite possible and even very probable that the dead are all around us, since it is impossible that the dead do not live' (*ibid.*: 312). While Maeterlinck accepts that communication with the dead might be possible, he takes issue with the 'narrow and pitiable interpretation' of life-after-death propounded by spiritualists. He writes:

> [Spiritualists] see the dead crowding around us like wretched puppets indissolubly attached to the significant scene of their death by the thousand little threads of insipid memories and infantile hobbies. They are supposed to be here, blocking up our homes, *more abjectly human than if they were still alive*, vague, inconsistent, garrulous, derelict, futile and idle, tossing hither and thither their desolate shadows, which are being slowly swallowed up by silence and oblivion, busying themselves incessantly with what no longer concerns them. (*ibid.*: 313–14, my emphasis)

Maeterlinck thus rejected one of the key propositions that attracted people to spiritualism: the idea that you would continue to be yourself after you died. As a spirit who materialises in a séance in Sir Arthur Conan Doyle's spiritualist-propaganda novel *The Land of Mist* (1926) announces: '[Death] is nothing. You are no more changed than if you went into the next room. You can't believe you are dead' (1930: 77). Maeterlinck did not suppose posthumous existence could be this banal; he had grander, more ambiguous, notions about human destiny.[10]

Spiritualism alleviated anxieties about death by ostensibly contacting the afterlife and rendering it (more) comprehensible and familiar to human understanding. As Alan Friedman remarks, spiritualism 'promulgated a harmonizing Einsteinian vision of nature and the supernatural'; spiritualists 'appropriated scientific materialism to depict the afterworld and express assurance in our ability to know and contact it' (1995: 142). Helen Sword concurs, saying spiritualism sought to 'allay ontological uncertainties' and 'slay … that biggest bogey of them all,

Death' (2002: 162, 47). However, unlike the spiritualists, Maeterlinck heralds the inevitability of ignorance with respect to humanity's ultimate destiny. Certain things *cannot* be known, Maeterlinck claims, and this gives him solace. He surmises: 'It is very probable ... that no one in this world, or perhaps in the next, will discover the great secret of the universe. ... We have not only to resign ourselves to living in the incomprehensible, but to rejoice that we cannot go out of it. ... The unknown and the unknowable are necessary and will perhaps always be necessary to our happiness' (1913: 257). Maeterlinck espoused epistemological uncertainty about the nature of life-after-death – not whether there *is* such a thing but what form it will take. He shared neither Andreyev's nihilism nor the spiritualists' confidence about the posthumous endurance of individual consciousness or personal identity.

Maeterlinck's philosophical writing shows he did not merely replicate spiritualist beliefs but had his own ideas about metaphysical matters. His symbolist plays reflect this independence of thought (cf. Rachilde's satirising of decadence in *Madame La Mort*). Productions of symbolist theatre by the Théâtre d'Art and the Théâtre de l'Œuvre may have aped the visual and performative stylistics of spiritualism (e.g., séances, spirit photography, ectoplasmic materialisations), but this does not mean the plays reinforced spiritualist philosophy. Spiritualism's positivist bent, which connected it to scientific naturalism, was anathema to the symbolists. Symbolist theatre artists appropriated spiritualist ideas for their own ends. They used theatre to generate imaginative possibilities and create a space for dreaming; they did not advance assurances about the afterlife. Indeed, the theatrical dream worlds presented by Maeterlinck and other symbolist artists were generally not reassuring, especially in relation to death; they more closely resembled nightmares. Symbolist artists did not present a single, stable conception of death, but rather a hazy continuum of impressions – assorted takes that illustrate lack of knowledge and certainty in this matter, as well as an overwhelming sense of human frailty in relation to an unknown and unknowable metaphysics.

This is what makes symbolist theatre recognisably modern: its embrace of radical uncertainty. As Maeterlinck writes in his essay 'The Modern Drama' (included in the 1904 collection *The Double Garden*): 'There still abides with us, it is true, a terrible unknown; but it is so diverse and elusive, it becomes so arbitrary, so vague and contradictory, the moment we try to locate it, that we cannot evoke it without great danger' (1904: 124). In tapping into this 'terrible unknown' and presenting it onstage using spiritualist-inspired aesthetics, Maeterlinck and other symbolists worked to unsettle audience members, challenging their perceptions of death and their ontological security. This made their art subversive and a target of attack from social commentators such as Nordau. The symbolists exploited theatre's 'deathly' potential – its ability to infuse presence with absence, and vice versa. As Alice Rayner remarks, theatre is 'a ghostly place in which the living and the dead come together in a productive encounter' (2006: xii). The final play to be discussed in this chapter further exemplifies this proposition.

The ambiguity of the in-between: *Purgatory*

Purgatory, which Yeats wrote the year before he died (in 1939), synthesises and redeploys key elements discussed throughout this chapter. Yeats was deeply involved in the occult. He was knowledgeable about theosophy, magic, spiritualism, Celtic folklore, and Hindu mysticism, and was, for a time, a member of the Hermetic Order of the Golden Dawn, a secret magical society (see Harper, 2006: 144–66). Unsurprisingly, his plays are suffused with supernatural elements. Like Maeterlinck, Yeats had his own ideas about séances and how they functioned. In the introduction to a 1934 edition of his spiritualist-themed play *The Words upon the Windowpane*, he remarks:

> I consider it certain that every voice that speaks, every form that appears, whether to the medium's eyes and ears alone or to some one or two others or to all present, whether it remains a sight or sound or affects the sense of touch, whether it is confined to the room or can make itself apparent at some distant place, whether it can or cannot alter the position of material objects, is first of all a secondary personality or dramatisation of the medium's. (Fitzgerald, 2002: 235)

Yeats acknowledges that séances can involve dramatisation and trickery in some cases, but he also postulates that mediums might be able to channel spirits in an unknowing fashion (like Maeterlinck's idea of the 'uninvited guest'). The capaciousness of Yeats's esoteric interests and his recognition of potential crossover between the phenomenal and the numinous, the artificial and the real, the theatrical and the uncontrived inform his drama.

Yeats presents death in *Purgatory* as a liminal, paradoxical state-of-being – a half-life, a ghostly presence both characters and audience members may perceive. His depiction of death differs from that of Rachilde, van Lerberghe, Maeterlinck, and Andreyev, and is also of a different order from the kitschy fare offered by the Cabaret du Néant. However, the proposals Yeats makes in *Purgatory* resonate with aspects of the symbolists' work, and indeed with the programme of entertainment offered by the Cabaret du Néant. *Purgatory* suggests the dead continue to have a spectral existence the living may apprehend. In depicting the presence of the dead in the world of the living, Yeats dislodged a cornerstone of modernity: one of the rationalising projects of the European Enlightenment and a legacy of urbanisation and concomitant efforts to improve sanitation and hygiene. Joseph Roach explains:

> Under a regime of newly segregationist taxonomies of behaviour in several related fields of manners and bodily administration, the dead were compelled to withdraw from the spaces of the living: their ghosts were exorcised even from the stage; their bodies were removed to newly dedicated and isolated cemeteries. ... As the place of burial was removed from local churchyard to distant park, the dead were more likely to be remembered (and forgotten) by monuments than by continued observance in which their spirits were invoked. (1996: 50)

Rather than banish the dead, Yeats staged their spirits, thereby confirming their continued importance – in Ireland, at least. Invoking a traditionally medieval, Christian, and specifically Catholic concept (purgatory), Yeats's play illustrates intercourse between the living and the dead – something the Protestant Reformation quashed and modern burial practices diminished.

In *Purgatory*, an old man has brought his sixteen-year-old son to the ruins of the old man's childhood home. It is the anniversary of the old man's parents' wedding night. The old man relates how his (own) mother married against her family's wishes. His mother died giving birth to him (i.e., to the old man) and his father subsequently neglected him. When the old man was sixteen, his father burned down the house while inebriated. The old man stabbed his father and left him to burn. The old man believes his mother is now in purgatory: she is one of those souls who 'come back / To habitations and familiar spots. / ... Re-live / Their transgressions, and that not once / But many times' (Yeats and Finneran, 2002: 260). He claims to hear the hoof-beats of his ghost-father riding back from the public house where he had been carousing. The boy says he cannot hear a sound. The old man points to a spectral appearance of his mother in the ruined house. The boy says he sees nothing. The old man proceeds to observe the scene of his parents' wedding night, or else he imaginatively plays it out (it is unclear). A window in the house lights up and '*a man is seen pouring whiskey into a glass*' (*ibid.*: 264). This time the boy sees the figure too; he announces the paradoxical status of his spectral grandfather: '[a] dead, living, murdered man' (265). The old man reckons his father's apparition is a chimera dreamt up by his mother: 'There's nothing leaning in the window / But the impression upon my mother's mind; / Being dead she is alone in her remorse' (*ibid.*). Following the old man's reasoning, his mother's spirit is 'real'; she is the one in purgatory reliving her wedding night.[11] His father's apparition is cast as a figment of his spectral mother's imagination. Hoping to free his mother's soul from her apparent torment, the old man kills his son, using the same jack-knife he used to kill his father. He says he did this to end the 'consequence' of his parents' fateful union and prevent further ill effects:

> Dear mother, the window is dark again
> But you are in the light because
> I finished all that consequence.
> I killed that lad because he had grown up.
> He would have struck a woman's fancy,
> Begot, and passed pollution on.
> I am a wretched foul old man
> And therefore harmless.
>
> (266)

The old man's fantasy is short-lived. He hears hoof-beats advancing again and surmises the cycle is repeating – his mother's soul is still trapped in purgatory.

Purgatory is a peculiar play. As in Maeterlinck's symbolist drama, not much happens in it, and the major action – the old man killing his son – is somewhat perplexing. The old man's reasoning is hard to follow; his logic seems skewed. The narrative he recounts is certainly absorbing: it fleshes out the bare scene, peopling the ruined house and desolate landscape. His storytelling recreates the past; it might even make it performatively present, depending on how one interprets his speech actions. Is he witnessing his mother's purgatorial presence, observing her as she re-performs actions from her life, or is he seeing it in his mind's eye and 'speaking it' into being? The boy professes neither to see his mother's spirit standing in the window nor hear the hoof-steps of his father's horse, though he does apparently see his grandfather's spectre after the old man points him out. The stage directions state that both figures are respectively shown in the window. Does this mean they are 'really' present, or are we seeing what the old man sees, or thinks he sees?

The spectral figures are not listed in the dramatis personae. Unlike Yeats's earlier play *The Dreaming of the Bones*, which dramatises an encounter between a young, post-1916 Irish patriot and a pair of medieval Irish ghosts, the spirits in *Purgatory* do not speak; they are only shadows, stage presences. It is difficult to know what to make of them, as the old man is the one telling their story, and he may not be a reliable narrator. Why should we take his word for what happened in the past and what is now ostensibly being re-enacted (especially as he was not present at the original event)? Why should his mother be in purgatory at all? The old man insinuates she is there because of her 'transgressions', which presumably relate to her union with his father, but this is contestable. It is not clear his mother did anything wrong (even if she married out of the faith, which is a possibility). Why would her soul need to be purified? The old man says purgatorial souls 'know at last / The consequence of those transgressions / Whether upon others, or upon themselves' (260). This implies his mother's remorse stems from a chain of events (i.e., her untimely death, the old man's difficult childhood, the house burning down, his father's death, the old man's 'bastard' son) of which her marriage was the beginning, but this seems like resentful fantasy on the old man's part – what he imagines his mother must, or should, feel on his behalf. He does not account for his own actions at all. Perhaps his mother 'transgressed' in other ways that require atonement. But then why would her spirit be compelled to relive *her wedding night* in apparent torment? Something is out of kilter here. There is cause to distrust the old man's version of events. Admittedly, Yeats is not aiming at psychological realism in *Purgatory*, and the play is not a whodunit, but its narrative and dramatic ambiguities are an important part of its aesthetic design. If one queries the old man's perspective, the meaning of the scenic signs becomes more doubtful.

Consideration of the production history of *Purgatory* helps to make sense of the play and illuminates its interpretative possibilities. The original 1938 Abbey Theatre production, directed by Hugh Hunt and designed by Anne Yeats (the playwright's daughter), adopted a minimalist staging approach. In an interview conducted in 1965, Anne Yeats said of the set design for *Purgatory*: 'It really could not have been simpler. It was just a bare whitish tree in the middle of the stage and a backcloth with a window cut out of it' (Unterecker, 1965: 8). Yeats recalls: '[The] backcloth, I remember, was black and the window was dark blue – exceptionally dark. ... There was probably gauze in the window and they [the ghost figures] were probably very vague behind. I am sure there was gauze in the window' (*ibid.*: 8–9). The description of this staging resembles the symbolist theatre productions of the Théâtre d'Art, which also made a virtue of limited resources. Evidently, the production even featured a gauze veil that cast two actors as shades. The spectral elements were also *heard*. The production prompt scripts contain marginal annotations for hoof-beats, signalling the spectral arrival of the old man's father; further hoof-beats are noted at the end of the script, marking the repetition of events.[12] The first production thus appears to have closely adhered to Yeats's text and suggested stage design (see Siegel, 1986: 60–1).

Later productions have taken more liberty with theatrical interpretation. A 2004 Abbey Theatre production directed by Conall Morrison did not represent the house on stage.[13] This production had no square window, no illuminated spectral figures therein. The stage was mostly empty and suffused with haze. The two actors looked into the audience and 'saw' the house somewhere in the auditorium, which made the scene they described seem hallucinatory, despite the fact that the hoof-beat sequence was twice sounded. *Not* staging the spirits visually, or corporeally, but rather indicating their presence in the auditorium cast the audience as virtual shades, which they already resembled in the darkness.

A 1990 Abbey Theatre production of the play, directed by James W. Flannery, accomplished a similar effect using scenographical and choreographical means. Flannery introduced a silent, quasi-sculptural chorus onto the scene. They 'became' the tree and the window (Lapisardi, 1992: 40). The spirits were neither represented as shadows in the window nor left to the audience's imagination. Instead, a naked man and woman emerged from the chorus and adopted positions upstage of the old man and the boy. From the audience's perspective, the spirits were positioned behind the old man and the boy. John Olohan, as the old man, faced away from them (see Figure 1.3). This created a curious stage picture. Was the audience meant to be seeing what the old man claimed to see, although he was looking elsewhere? Olwen Fouere and David Heap, who played the spirits, were partially obscured by shadow. Their movements were slow; they mostly held static poses. Sarah-Jane Scaife, the movement director, used a Butoh-inspired style (Lapisardi, 1992: 33). Intriguingly, this made their union seem tender and beautiful, an eerie spectacle of *eros* and *thanatos*, quite unlike the impression of the couple conjured by the old man. The disjunction between the visual presentation of the spirits – slowly enacting a sensual, deathly embrace – and the old man's verbal account of them, filled with bitterness and invective, was striking. It suggested his account of his mother's supposed torment was biased and possibly false. The production thereby opened a wedge between mimesis and diegesis, between the acts of imitation or representation and the mode of narration.

The production's music contributed to the disconcerting atmosphere and further complicated the interpretation of the stage picture.

1.3 John Olohan as the Old Man (kneeling) and Conor Mullen as the Boy, now dead, in the 1990 Abbey Theatre production of W.B. Yeats's *Purgatory*

The music, composed by Bill Whelan, was mostly electronic. It did not include the hoof-beat sounds. These were left in the acoustic imaginary: sounds the old man says he hears but the audience cannot. In lieu of the hoof-beats, Whelan introduced a leitmotif consisting of a mysterious-sounding melodic phrase set over a drone. This cue suggested uncanniness and a creeping sense of irresolution.

A formal analysis of the music uncovers how it can yield this impression; furthermore, it clarifies the play's puzzling features. The interval structure of the melodic line forms what is known as a tritone. This interval, which comprises three whole tones or six semitones, can sound dissonant or unstable to the ear; one expects it to 'resolve'. The tritone acquired the nickname of '*diabolus in musica*' (the devil in music) in the later medieval period; the music theorist Guido of Arrezo designated it a 'dangerous' interval. In Romantic opera it was associated with evil. In traditional harmonic thinking, the tritone weakens the tonality of a musical passage and assists key change (Whittall, 2011). By putting the tritone at the end of a repeating phrase, Whelan suspends melodic or harmonic resolution; the listener is left 'hanging'. Harmonically, this cue presents an unresolved descent, a looped fragment that goes nowhere. This has an unsettling effect. Moreover, Whelan sets the music

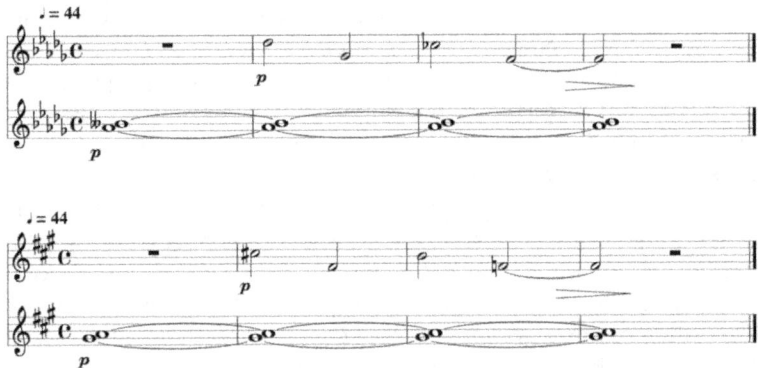

1.4 Double transcription of a motif from Bill Whelan's music for the 1990 Abbey Theatre production of W.B. Yeats's *Purgatory*. The music may be in G-flat minor (a theoretical key) or F-sharp minor, depending on how it is notated

in an enharmonic key. In twelve-tone equal temperament (the system of tuning upon which Western music has been based for several centuries), enharmonic notes differ in name but not in pitch (e.g., D flat/C sharp), at least on a keyboard instrument. Whelan's cue is either in the key of G-flat minor or F-sharp minor (differently put, it is potentially in both these keys) (see Figure 1.4). This is not incidental. G-flat minor is an obscure, theoretical key, rarely used because of its awkward configuration. Its correlate, F-sharp minor (three sharps in the key signature), has particular affective associations. In a book on musical aesthetics published in 1806, Christian Schubart says of F-sharp minor: 'A gloomy key: it tugs at passion as a dog biting a dress. Resentment and discontent are its language. It really does not seem to like its own position: therefore it languishes ever for the calm of A major or the triumphant happiness of D major' (quoted in Benson, 2007: 191). How appropriate for a musical setting of purgatory! The fact that the music occupies an indeterminate, enharmonic realm, notionally in a flat key *and* a sharp key, positions the listener in a liminal tonality. Even if one had perfect pitch (the ability to identify a note without a reference tone just by hearing it), one could not know whether this piece was in G-flat minor or F-sharp minor.[14] Whelan thereby presented the 'in-between-ness' and ontological suspension of the purgatorial state in music. The music insinuated there was something awry in the world of the play; things were, perhaps, not as they seemed. The production made it possible for audience members to experience perceptual uncertainty on multiple levels.

In Flannery's production, the doubt and questioning initially offered by the character of the boy, who distrusts the old man's words, was extended to the audience as they encountered the play. The production highlighted ambiguous and problematic elements of Yeats's play. It encouraged alternative interpretations. What if this play is presenting the purgatorial experience of the old man and *not* his mother? Perhaps the old man is the one who is unknowingly stuck in ontological limbo, revisiting his grievances and transgressions. Frederick S. Lapisardi raises this as an interpretative possibility, too. '[Are] we witnessing the old man's dreaming back after he is dead, or is he still alive and killing his son for the first time?' (1992: 34). Is the old man alive or dead? As in the 'Schrödinger's cat' thought experiment (made three years prior to the writing of this play), one cannot know for sure, and so both states are possible, like the joint tonality of Whelan's music. In this reading, *Purgatory* suggests a type of infinite regression of the dreaming dead (the old man dreaming his dead mother dreaming her husband, and so forth). In *Purgatory*, the dividing line between the living and the dead is blurred. The audience is invited into this deathly atmosphere, and rendered betwixt and between, imaginatively positioned on both sides of the metaphorical veil.

Conclusion

In the plays discussed in this chapter, death is presented as an imagined, personified character (*Madame La Mort*), an array of offstage voices (*The Night-Comers*), atmospheric presence (*The Intruder*), theatrical uncanniness (*Requiem*), and existential liminality (*Purgatory*). By prompting audiences to perceive death as paradoxical presence in performance – as something simultaneously there and not there, or only notionally apparent – symbolists engaged fundamental conceptual problems about death, such as the difficulty of grasping it intellectually, reconciling it with one's lived experience, and recognising its strange, conjoint absence-presence in our lives. Symbolist dramatists and theatre-makers explored this uncomfortable terrain, encouraging audiences to face the radical uncertainty posed by death, in contradistinction to the apparent certainties about the afterlife offered by spiritualism. This aspect of symbolist theatre makes it modern, even if the symbolists' modernity is now our yesteryear. These plays undermine security about what lies 'beyond the veil', but they still allow for possibilities about death to emerge in a dreamlike state. They are informed by the deathly tenor of the *fin de siècle* but they do not simply replicate prevailing belief systems; rather, they invite the audience to test out ideas and find their own answers. Sensing death in symbolist theatre, even if one does not fully comprehend its meaning, parallels the existential dilemmas faced by characters in the plays.

This space of ambiguity, doubt, and confusion was re-examined in subsequent explorations of death in modern theatre. Twentieth-century world events, such as the First World War, further complicated conceptions of mortality, making death seem strangely unreal. This new 'unreality' inspired dramatic representations of death that were differently fantastical, as the next chapter reveals.

Notes

1 Flash-forward to the early twenty-first century. A 2016 article in the *New York Times* reports on a recent trend in Seoul of acting out a mock funeral service as a way of better appreciating life. This involves writing a last testament, putting on a burial shroud, and lying in a coffin with the lid closed for ten minutes and imagining oneself dead. See Sang-Hun (2016).
2 'A play is a slice of life on the stage with art' (Jean Jullien, 1892). Quoted in Carlson (1984: 279).
3 Thanks to a former student of mine, Daniela Parkes, for pointing this out.
4 Eric Korngold used *Le mirage* as the basis for his 1920 opera *Die tote Stadt* (*The Dead City*).
5 '[Death] is not a thing', Guy Brown remarks, 'it is the absence of a thing: life. And life is not really a thing – it is a set of processes and functions such as moving, breathing and thinking. So death is the absence of these functions, and dying is the transition between being fully functional and the complete absence of these functions' (2008: 42).
6 'The stage is where masterpieces die', Maeterlinck wrote in 1890, 'because the presentation of a masterpiece by accidental and human means is a contradiction. All masterpieces are symbols, and the symbol never withstands the active presence of man' (Maeterlinck, 1994 [1890]: 145).
7 I must credit Claire Warden for this important reference.
8 An exception: Gerould and Kosicka (1980: 3–42).
9 Contrast with Peer Gynt's terror at the prospect of being 'swallowed up / Like a speck in a mass of strange material', 'melted down / With any Tom and Dick and Harry / And moulded fresh' in Henrik Ibsen's play. '[Naturally] we make a fight / To keep the self with which we came / Into the world', Peer Gynt tells the Button-Moulder (1936 [1867]: 228, 230, 231).
10 Maeterlinck's ideas about ultimate human destiny resemble those of G.B. Shaw. In the fifth part of Shaw's *Back to Methuselah* (1921), set in the year AD 31,920, ancient humans imagine a future, eternal existence 'when there will be no people, only thought' (1930: 253). The character of the She-Ancient imagines becoming a vortex: 'I began as a vortex: why should I not end as one?' (*ibid.*: 255).

11 Two other plays written in the late 1930s feature dead characters reliving episodes from their lives. In J.B. Priestley's *Johnson Over Jordan* (1939), the protagonist, Robert Johnson, conjures scenes from his life in a dreamlike state of posthumous existence, and must come to terms with what his death means for himself and others. In the last act of Thornton Wilder's *Our Town* (1938), the character of Emily Webb relives her twelfth birthday, fourteen years earlier, but finds the experience painful. She returns to her grave and reconciles herself to the fact of being dead. The character of the stage manager says that the dead 'gradually ... lose hold of the earth ... and the ambitions they had ... and the pleasures they had ... and the things they suffered ... and the people they loved' (1957: 81).
12 The prompt script for the Abbey Theatre's 1938 production of *Purgatory* is held at the Abbey Theatre Digital Archive at National University of Ireland, Galway.
13 My discussion of the 1990 and 2004 Abbey Theatre productions of *Purgatory* is based on video recordings held at the Abbey Theatre Digital Archive at the National University of Ireland, Galway.
14 This is true of music written in any enharmonic key; one cannot distinguish between related enharmonic keys by aural means alone.

2

Fantastical representations of death in First World War drama

A British journalist, present at a regatta featuring British and German naval ships in the port of Kiel in 1914, pondered what was to come: 'Those of us who were privileged to be present ... realised then, if never before, that when war came – should it ever come – it would be conducted under conditions *new and strange and fantastical*' (Hurd, 1914: 15, my emphasis).

A French priest, stationed at a military hospital in France during the war, recalled listening to wounded soldiers discussing their experiences: 'It seemed to me, while listening to them, that I was witnessing *unreal scenes*, conceived by some imagination, creative of *the fantastic and fabulous*' (Gaëll, 1916: 167, my emphasis).

A British soldier, posted to northern France in 1916, described a scene of conflict: '[It] was as awful a sight as could be imagined. From end to end it was covered with a thick cloud of grey smoke, lit here and there by the twinkling flashes of shell-bursts. Seen across that peaceful-looking countryside *it seemed unreal, fantastic*, but there was no one so new to warfare that he did not know what it meant' (Watts, 1930: 67, my emphasis).

Words such as 'fantastical', 'fabulous', and 'unreal' were frequently used in writing about the First World War by combatants and non-combatants.[1] This is a marker of the startling nature of the events in question. The devastation wrought by the 'Great War' of 1914–18, the number of deaths it incurred (approximately sixteen million people), and the scale of the conflict justifies the use of adjectives of this kind. Language of amazement was deployed to describe scenes that were out of the ordinary and difficult to fathom – both for those directly involved and for those on the home front. The First World War gave rise to a variety of scenarios that could be perceived as fantastical (i.e., extraordinary). These included mass death and death caused by new technologies (e.g., tanks, chemical weapons). Gas took the war 'into the realm of the unreal, the make-believe', writes Modris Eksteins. 'When men donned their masks they lost all signs of their humanity, and with their long snouts, large glass eyes, and slow movements, they became figures of fantasy, closer in their angular features to the creations of Picasso and Braque than to soldiers of tradition' (1989: 163). The war made death newly strange, affecting how it was represented and understood.

Every representation of death is a misrepresentation of death, Elisabeth Bronfen and Sarah Webster Goodwin observe, since '[there] is no knowing death, no experiencing it and then returning to write about it, no intrinsic grounds for authority in the discourse surrounding it' (1993: 4). Spiritualists might disagree with this statement, as might people who have had near-death experiences. Spiritualism, not coincidentally, enjoyed renewed popularity during the First World War, as the bereaved sought comfort by 'making contact' with the war dead. Nevertheless, Bronfen and Goodwin's claim is a useful reminder of the limits of representation concerning death, and the potentially large gap, or mismatch, between signifier and signified. In the last chapter, I proposed that one of the symbolists' innovations was the atmospheric evocation of death in theatre. Is this less of a misrepresentation than death represented in character form? The question is moot. Choice of representation is linked to the kind of death being represented, the historical circumstances in which the representation is made, and the attitude toward death of those involved in making the representation. These are foundational premises of this study.

The deathly tenor of the *fin de siècle* changed register because of the First World War, which, paradoxically, made death seem both unreal and all-too-real. Soldiers' experiences of death often confounded their perceptions, yet both they and millions of bereaved families had to cope with the fact of the deceased, as well as the destruction caused by the war. This chapter analyses examples of modern drama written during and immediately after the First World War that represent death in a fantastical manner. The corpus of plays that thematically engage with the First World War is considerable, and important historiographical work has been done, most recently in the years marking the centenary, to rediscover 'forgotten' plays in various genres, including plays by women that provide insight into a more diverse range of wartime experiences and concerns (see, for example, Maunder, 2015).[2] This chapter also features a little-known play about the First World War written by a woman – Vernon Lee [Violet Paget]'s allegorical satire *Satan the Waster* (1920) – but I have chosen this play not because of the author's sex or because the play illuminates a forgotten or marginalised part of history, but because it treats wartime death on a grand scale, abstracting it, and thereby provides insight into how the war shaped conceptions of death. I have selected my other two case studies – Ernst Toller's expressionist drama *Die Wandlung* (*The Transfiguration*, 1919) and Karl Kraus's documentary drama *Die letzten Tage der Menschheit* (*The Last Days of Mankind*, 1922) – for the same reason.

To my knowledge, these plays have not been linked before. They do not share a common aesthetic or style, though the end of Act 5 of Kraus's play, which is my focus, has an expressionist bent and so connects to *The Transfiguration*. However, all three plays involve fantastical representations of death that outline the enormity of the conflict and its challenge to conceptions of reality and mortality. Relatedly, they all depart from, or disrupt, realism by using non-realistic devices and scenarios, including personified abstractions and mythological characters, to account for wartime death. Indeed, the skeletal figure of Death-by-War is a character in Toller's drama (alongside his doppelgänger, Death-by-Peace), and death also appears in personified, skeletal form in Lee's play, though this conventional trope is adapted in both cases and made specific to the war. Kraus presents visions of real incidents from the war along with phantasmagoria near the end of his play, providing a kaleidoscopic overview of death during the war and setting it as a prelude to global apocalypse. (The short, scene-setting quotations presented at the beginning of this chapter are meant as a nod to Kraus's play.) Both Lee's play and Kraus's play were written to be read, not performed; they proffer a mental theatre, unconstrained by staging practicalities, by which the totality of the death caused by the war can notionally be apprehended. My analysis of this trio of plays, based on close readings of dramatic texts, considers how their depictions of death resonate with the kinds of death engendered by the war, and how they correspond with, and challenge, other writing from the time as well as later historiography.

The 'new death'

The First World War looms large in the history of modern death in the West. Indeed, it has overshadowed the influenza epidemic of 1918–19, which claimed many more lives (estimated in the tens of millions worldwide). Arguably, it is not just the war's death toll that distinguishes it but the *kinds* of death it produced and the responses it generated. Sociological and technological factors made the death caused by the war seem aberrant and 'new':

> The age of death [i.e., the age of the soldiers who died] disrupted expectations. Populations in the industrialized world were living longer lives, enjoying lower infant-mortality rates, and developing life-narratives in which death was increasingly the plight of the aged. The war reversed that by sending millions of young, healthy, able-bodied men to die in the prime of their lives. Death seemed new in other ways, as well. New technologies of war changed its aspects. Chemical warfare, long-range and high-volume artillery, and military aeronautics changed the face of battle and the look and feel of soldiers' deaths. (James, 2013: 17)

The British journalist quoted at the beginning of this chapter, who pondered the 'strange and fantastical' conditions in which the war might be conducted, were it to occur, ruminated over the new technologies that would be used: 'One wondered, in idle curiosity, if the submarine had really rendered the battleship obsolescent. Would the aeroplane prove the antidote to the submarine? ... Was the torpedo more potent than the gun?' (Hurd, 1914: 15). He then expressed dissatisfaction that he might never find out what would happen, saying: 'War was no doubt a terrible business, but it seemed a little disappointing that all of us who were taking part in the pageant ... would probably end our days and never know – continuing until we were old and bent to wonder, wonder, wonder' (*ibid*.). This gauche remark reflects the British romanticisation of the war and glorification of death prior to the conflict. For the soldiers who went to war, many of whom did not live to be 'old and bent', new technologies of killing, such as gas warfare, gave rise to a bleaker form of wonderment.

Tony Walter has proposed that the First World War – 'hell on earth' – ironically killed off the idea of hell down below: 'no field chaplain could even so much as hint that the brave lad he was burying might be going to the wrong place, and thereafter hell disappeared off the agenda in all but the most conservative of churches. And without hell, death lost any spiritual risk, and became a medical and psychological affair' (1994:

15). The war may have contributed to the concept of hell falling out of favour, but the war dead and their posthumous existence were nonetheless topics of philosophical speculation.

In 1918, Winifred Kirkland, an American popular writer, published a treatise entitled *The New Death*, named after what she proposed was a widely held viewpoint, a newly emerging consciousness about mortality. Kirkland states that the war had prompted international re-evaluation: death was now deliberately being thought about, and in a new and more spiritually aware fashion. 'Never before in history has death been so prominent a fact', Kirkland states (ignoring obvious examples, such as the 'black death' of the fourteenth century). She continues:

> Always before it has been possible to avoid thinking about it. To-day no one can escape the constant presence, before his mind, of dissolution. ... No one can forget them, no one can get away from them, these boys dead upon the battle-fields of Europe. ... There is not one of us who has not thought more about death within the last four years than in a whole lifetime before, and by their very intensity our thoughts are new. (1918: 1–2)

A lot of what Kirkland writes in this book is contestable. She frequently makes exaggerated and unsupported claims, and insinuates that her opinion is shared by a multitude. Nevertheless, her ideas about 'the new death' indicate how the war was thought to mark a paradigm shift in relation to attitudes toward mortality.

Kirkland's spiritual beliefs guide her understanding and interpretation of the death caused by the war. Indeed, 'the new death', as a mode of thinking, involves newfound certainty about posthumous existence – faith in the indestructability of the soul: 'With an intensity that only a world-ruin could have wrought, plain people everywhere are making trial of immortality as the sole speculation to nerve our action instantly needed, and to safeguard the future that it is our duty to reconstruct' (1918: 41). This seems like wishful thinking on the author's part, and maybe on the part of the 'plain' people she purports to represent, too. Kirkland contrasts the 'new', spiritually minded attitude toward death with what she calls 'the modern view of death, the scientific, the agnostic', about which she notes: 'its confidence that we can know nothing of life after death is as arrogant as the confidence of past ages that we can know everything' (*ibid.*: 14). Note: the modern – already out of date in 1918, in Kirkland's estimation, and replaced by a newer, unnamed sensibility!

Kirkland locates in accounts of dying soldiers an absolute faith that they are going to a better place, and testifies for them to this effect.

'[One] is overwhelmed by the impression given by all trench records: whatever else the soldier may expect of that other side, of one thing he seems absolutely assured, measureless well-being; he is going to a place that is good, and he is going with every faculty alert for new adventure' (*ibid.*: 74–5). The author paints a strangely jolly picture, suggesting that soldiers' travails were all worthwhile. She even suggests envying these seer-soldiers 'for what one might call their cosmic security, the content of the atom that perceives itself part of an indestructible whole' (*ibid.*: 83).[3] (This association would not remain felicitous for much longer.) One of Kirkland's less contentious, but still hyperbolic, claims is that the new attitude toward death is unlike the old in being the result of 'universal bereavement': 'In such vast grief, class distinctions are swept away; high and low, rich and poor, are seeking inspiration from each other in the same naked need. Even the fierce animosities of nation to nation are dulled by their shared losses. Blinded and brutalized as are the Germans, they must still love their slaughtered sons' (*ibid.*: 46).[4] While it is fair to say the bereaved of the 'Great War' endured common suffering, the historical novelty of this is questionable.

Scholars have disputed claims about the 'uniqueness' of the First World War in terms of the death and destruction it caused. John Mueller, a political scientist, points out that, when the First World War is placed in the context of the long history of human warfare, it 'was not all that unusual in its duration, destructiveness, grimness, political pointlessness, economic consequences or breadth' (1991: 3). He provides numerous examples of prior conflicts dating back to ancient times that were just as bad as it, or worse. What *is* unique about this war, he proposes, is that 'it was the first major war in history to have been preceded by substantial, organized, anti-war agitation' and that 'it followed a century that was most peculiar in European history, one in which the continent had managed, perhaps without fully appreciating it, to savour the relative blessings of substantial periods of peace' (*ibid.*: 3–4). Accordingly, Mueller notes, the experience of being plunged into the First World War came as a 'special shock' (*ibid.*: 15). A war of this kind, which was not quickly conducted, as had been expected, may have seemed especially novel, or even fantastical, to some. Mueller surmises: 'It was not the first horrible war in history, but it was the first in which people were widely capable of recognizing and being thoroughly repulsed by those horrors and in which they were substantially aware that viable alternatives existed' (*ibid.*: 12). The plays featured in this chapter, which are all anti-war, demonstrate this mode of thinking.

Kirkland's treatise about 'the new death' resonates with the 'special shock' of the war, as Mueller puts it, even if her attempt to make sense of death was fanciful, and did not consider that soldiers on the western front used mental coping strategies (including belief in an afterlife) to survive (Watson, 2006). Contrary to Kirkland's reports of soldiers experiencing spiritual revelations about death and dying, historian David Cannadine, surveying the experiences of British soldiers, observes that surfeit of death could lead to stupefaction of sympathy and numbing of the senses (1981: 203). Additionally, some soldiers, he remarks, 'found life in the trenches so ghastly that death was looked upon with selfish pleasure, as offering the certain prospect of release from earthly torment' (*ibid.*: 209). Acknowledging that the varying scenes of death experienced by the millions of soldiers who served in the First World War are not easily summarised, Cannadine states:

> [Whatever] might be the reactions to death, the reality, the presence of death, was inescapable. Any soldier would see more of it in a week at the front than he might reasonably have expected to have witnessed in a lifetime. And, at the same time, the presence of death all around him would oblige him to confront the prospect of his own death – at an age when, for civilians, death had become unlikely, and in a manner which, for those not in the trenches, was literally unimaginable. (*ibid.*: 208)

The difficulty of conceiving, processing, and representing the death caused by the war – especially on a macro level – informs the trio of plays examined here. The authors of these plays transposed the 'special shock' of war – in particular, the kinds of death it produced, along with attitudes to death and confusions between life and death – into a variety of fantastical scenarios, reconfiguring conventional tropes in the process.

Deathly personae in *The Transfiguration*

In his autobiography, Ernst Toller reflects on his experience as a soldier in the war, which included being stationed at the front. The German and French trenches were so close to one another, he says, that if the soldiers had stuck their heads above the parapet they could have spoken to one another without raising their voices. He discusses the effect that encountering dead bodies on a regular basis had on him, noting how the visages of the living and the dead resembled one another. 'When I went slipping and slithering down the trench, with my head bent low, I did not know whether the men I passed were dead or alive; in that place the dead and the living had the same gray faces' (1991 [1934]: 80). He mentions how he became inured to the sight of the dead. For him, they had 'that same unreality, which shocks without arousing pity' as waxwork figures (*ibid.*: 86). In a striking passage, he writes about cutting into the earth with a pickaxe and accidentally butchering a corpse he did not know was there. He experiences a sudden realisation about this dead man, whose entrails are now wrapped around his pick:

> [Suddenly], like light in darkness, the real truth broke in upon me. The simple fact of Man, which I had forgotten, which had lain deep buried and out of sight; the idea of community, of unity.
> A dead man.
> Not a dead Frenchman.
> Not a dead German.
> A dead man. [...]
> [It] was only then that I realized, at last, that all these dead men, Frenchmen and Germans, were brothers, and I was the brother of them all. After that I could never pass a dead man without stopping to gaze on his face stripped by death of that earthly patina which masks the living soul. (*ibid.*: 87)

This incident, and the epiphany it sparked, mirrors a scene in *The Transfiguration*, which Toller wrote between 1917 and 1919. In this scene, set in no-man's land, skeletons descend from barbed-wire entanglements and strike up a conversation with one another (see Figure 2.1). They bond over the fact that they are physically identical, with no distinguishing features or residual ties to society:

> FIRST SKELETON: Today we're no more friends and enemies,
>   Today we're no more black and white,
>   Now we're all alike.
>   The worms soon ate our colored skins,
>   And now we are all alike.
>   Gentlemen ... let's dance.
>
> (Toller, 1986 [1919]: 172)

Their dance is suitably macabre: legless skeletons pick up their shinbones and rattle them together, making ghoulish body-percussion. One of the skeletons in their company is revealed to be a thirteen-year-old girl, who apparently died as the result of being gang-raped. The character of the First Skeleton falsely equates this crime with the outrages suffered by the soldier-skeletons. The scene ends with the soldier-skeletons '[*dancing*] *vigorously round and round the skeleton of the girl*' in apparent unity (*ibid.*: 174). There is correspondence between Kirkland's remarks

Fantastical representations of death 73

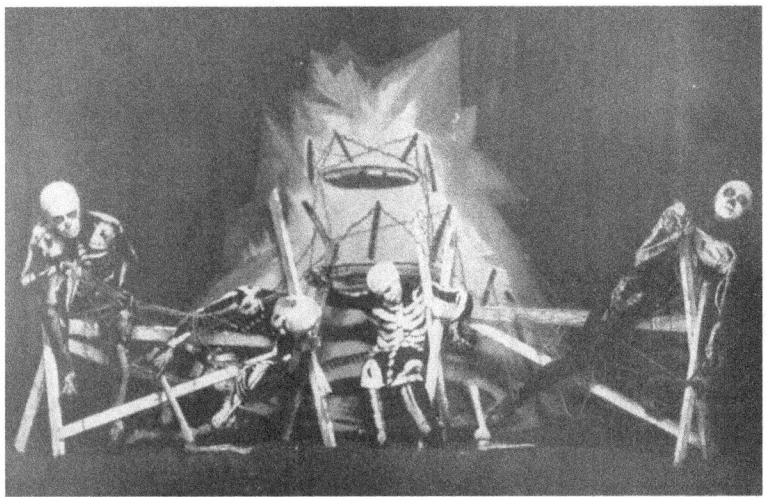

2.1 Soldier-skeletons entangled in barbed wire in the 1919 production of Ernst Toller's *Die Wandlung*, performed at the Tribüne theatre, Berlin

about universal bereavement caused by the war and Toller's vision of a brotherhood of the dead.

Toller's play focuses on a German-Jewish soldier, Friedrich (a version of Toller), who goes on a spiritual and political journey of enlightenment. As an alienated German Jew, Friedrich is keen to demonstrate his patriotism. He begins as an enthusiastic participant in the war effort but, because of his wartime experiences, becomes disaffected and champions international brotherhood instead. The skeleton scene presents Toller's vision of humanity shorn of individuating categories, such as those fostered by nationalism. His autobiographical epiphany finds dramatic form as a grotesque dance of death, one of several nightmarish scenes in the play that exist 'on the borderline between reality and unreality', as stated in a textual preamble (158).

The character of Friedrich curiously morphs into other people during periodic 'unreality' scenes, taking on their features, as though in a dream. Friedrich is not the only shape-shifter. As stated in the dramatis personae, Death appears 'as the Enemy of the Spirit in the Guise of a Soldier, a Professor, a Judge, and a Night Visitor' (*ibid.*). Friedrich, or Friedrich's persona, encounters Death as one of these characters at various points. Toller indicates that the character of Death has '*a skull for a head*', but other characters – including Friedrich – apparently perceive him in whatever guise he has adopted (just as they also accept Friedrich in other guises) (177). The play's expressionist dream-logic enables these identity shifts. The meaning of Death's designation as 'the enemy of the spirit' is not immediately apparent. The 'spirit' may refer to the anti-war, socialist movement that Friedrich spearheads toward the end of the play – the spirit of regeneration that Toller and other German expressionist artists hoped the war would produce.

In Friedrich's/Toller's imagining, Death sadistically infiltrates society and works to achieve nefarious ends. For instance, Death in the guise of a medical professor delights in the practice of working on soldiers who have been multiply amputated, transfiguring them with artificial prostheses (including, it is suggested, refashioned genitalia). This might be regarded as a positive development given the circumstances, but Toller does not present it as such. Instead, he depicts these mechanical 'cripples' (his word) as distraught freaks who are the grotesque joint-products of modern medicine and modern warfare. Maud Ellmann notes that '[technological] innovations in weaponry in World War I meant that bodies could be blown to buggery more thoroughly than ever before' (2013: 261). Postwar modernist literature and visual art are, consequently, replete with 'images of dismemberment' (*ibid.*: 257). Toller's play also features fragmented bodies. A spinal patient who describes himself as a 'living lavatory' with bowels 'blown to bits' longs for death, but it is denied him:

> When I came to, the doctor said to me:
> The bullet grazed your spine,
> But we have saved you.
> If that man knew what was in store for me
> He was a devil.
> The only kindness he could do for me
> Would be to drug me into sleep and death.
>
> (Toller, 1986 [1919]: 178–9)

Another soldier speaks of having been buried alive in an attack, swallowing earth, and eating his way to air and earth before passing out:

> FOURTH SOLDIER: Was it all that earth
> That makes me tremble so?
> Did I return to earth too soon?
> And am I paying for it now?
> Or is Earth having her revenge
> For my escape?
>
> (179–80)

The theme of dead soldiers coming back to life as 'living corpses' crops up in multiple First World War plays, for example in Hans Chlumberg's

Wunder um Verdun (*Miracle at Verdun*, 1930) and Irwin Shaw's *Bury the Dead* (1936). Perhaps the most famous example of the spirit-revenant, the ghost-soldier, is in Abel Gance's silent film *J'accuse* (1919, remade in 1938), in which soldiers on a battlefield rise from the dead and return, ghostlike, to their homes. These zombie-like beings have paradoxical ontology that reflects strange confusions between life and death triggered by the war. Toller's play is shadowed by this spectre, too. In presenting a deathly force that masquerades among the living, and dismembered, traumatised members of the living who align themselves with the dead, *The Transfiguration* offers a disturbing vision of interchange between life and death.

This vision is also common in written reminiscence about the First World War (e.g., Toller's comments in his autobiography about how the faces of the living and the dead resembled one another). Allyson Booth, surveying 'modernist writing' by both combatants and civilians, observes that in this writing

> life and death are not perceived as linear, sequential experiences; the latter does not usurp the former. Rather, the two states exist in an unpredictable relation to each other, sometimes fluctuating back and forth, sometimes holding each other in tense balance. Only rarely does either life or death appear fully in control, its opposite fully repressed, enough under wraps to be safely ignored. Most of the time, each looms over the other. (1996: 53)

The war created situations where the living and the dead were lumped together and potentially doubled one another. Death could not be kept at a safe remove; rather, it was perceived as being coterminous with the living. Booth highlights the 'weird blends of life and death' that appear in soldiers' descriptions of their wartime experiences: soldiers with corpse-like faces; soldiers whose bodies were indistinguishable from the muddy landscape around them; soldiers who did not know whether they were alive or dead; impressions of the 'aliveness' of a corpse; joking interactions with dead bodies; situational intimacies between soldiers and corpses; fears of being buried alive and thereby becoming a 'conscious corpse'; soldiers presumed dead turning up alive; and so forth (*ibid.*: 54, 61). She concludes: 'The war undermined (quite literally) a soldier's confidence in the stability of death and of a corpse's embodiment of death; the modernist imagination participates in that disturbing disinterment by investigating how the instability of death alters our concepts of the self' (*ibid.*: 63). Toller's play dramatises this mutual 'looming' of life and death, muddying distinctions between the two and inflecting scenes set outside the war zone with the same deathly atmosphere.

Friedrich's flitting between personae, Death's appearances in various guises, soldier-skeletons who dance and talk – Toller's play reflects the uncanny fusion, or crossover, of the animate and the inanimate instantiated by the war.

Toller employs conventional iconography about death (e.g., the dance of death, death represented as a skeleton), but he is careful to situate it in a contemporary context. This is signalled in a dramatic prologue set at night in a vast military cemetery. This scene features a debate between two symbolic personifications of death: Death-by-War (*Kriegstod*) and Death-by-Peace (*Friedenstod*), who appear as differently costumed skeletons. Death-by-Peace wears a top hat and carries a brightly coloured silk handkerchief, whereas Death-by-War wears a steel helmet, is decorated with medals, and carries a human thighbone as a Field Marshal's baton. Death-by-Peace professes to admire the precise order of the military cemetery, where graves are arranged in companies and further divided into sections for enlisted personnel and officers. Death-by-War trumpets his prowess. He calls the dead soldiers up on parade: skeletons dutifully arise from the graves, use the crosses that mark their graves as military arms, and follow the commands given to them, including rolling their skulls. Death-by-Peace is initially impressed, and contrasts the order manifested in the work of Death-by-War with the 'pure chaos' of his own domain, but later changes his mind and rebukes his alternate and all he represents. '[Such] discipline as yours/ Is foreign to our world', Death-by-Peace tells him, and declares that Death-by-War has been vanquished – made subservient to the desires of military men:

> Just one small paradox
> To bring this little interview
> To a successful close ...
> *You are a modern Death,*
> *A product of the times,*
> Comparable to the futile living of today
> Where everything is rotten under tinsel.
>
> (1986 [1919]: 163, my emphasis)

Death-by-War is piqued by Death-by-Peace's stinging critique, but is unable to mount a self-defence. 'It seems to me/ I'm just about played out!', he exclaims (*ibid.*: 163).

As a 'modern death' – albeit one in an old representational form (personification-as-skeleton) – Death-by-War is humanly empowered, which is what Death-by-Peace finds objectionable. (Recall Mueller's point about social awareness of the non-necessity of the conflict prior to the outbreak of war.) Death-by-Peace's excoriation of Death-by-War signals Toller's critique of how modern warfare dehumanises people and systematically organises their extinction, foreshadowing later catastrophes, such as the Holocaust. For Death-by-Peace, the application of organisational method is anathema to Death's modus operandi, which he claims is innately chaotic and mercurial. Making death subject to humanly conceived and executed plans via military-industrial design and subsequent burial protocol is a travesty, Death-by-Peace suggests; it is altogether too neat, too orderly, and too mechanical. In comparison, the historical record indicates that soldiers were also struck by the precariousness of their existence. Cannadine quotes a British soldier: 'On occasion, life was seen as a gamble with "the twin gods of war, Mr Luck and Mr Death"' (1981: 209). However, soldiers also experienced a sense of fatalism and of being caught in an imprisoning system. In a scene in *The Transfiguration* set in a travelling troop train, nameless soldiers decry their abject, mechanised status and lament being stuck in a repetitive cycle of hopeless action. A shadowy, silent soldier with Friedrich's features is also present, as is a shadowy death-figure with a skull for a head:

> FIRST SOLDIER: How long must we rattle through the night,
>   Lurching, lurching in the grinding of machinery,
>   Tortured machinery?
> SECOND SOLDIER: Time without end and space without end,
>   Days, weeks, nobody can tell. ...
> FIRST SOLDIER: Endlessly we journey.
> SECOND SOLDIER: Endlessly the engine roars and groans.
>   (Toller, 1986 [1919]: 167–8)

Toller expresses a similar sentiment in a passage from his autobiography, using a mechanical metaphor in relation to soldiering: '[Life] had become hell, death a bagatelle. We were all of us cogs in a great machine which sometimes rolled forward, nobody knew where, sometimes backwards, nobody knew why. We lost our enthusiasm, our courage, the very sense of our identity; there was no rhyme or reason in all this slaughter and devastation; pain itself had lost its meaning; the earth was a barren waste' (1991 [1934]: 90).

In *The Transfiguration*, Death-by-War represents a 'modern death, a product of the times', which, although dehumanising, is human-engineered. Mervyn F. Bendle, a historian, suggests the First World War enacted a new episteme: the industrialisation – the 'Fordism' – of death. For Bendle, the First World War represents 'the transformation of death into a large-scale technical and industrial process with human beings coming to figure as mere resources for warfare, labour, experimentation and even recycling in the case of hair, tallow, tooth fillings and skin, before being disposed of as refuse – also on an industrial scale' (2001: 350). The industrialisation of death conducted via military practices led to dehumanisation as well as 'the demystification, desacralization and banalization of the singular value of human life', Bendle writes. Thus 'traditional epistemes derived predominantly from religious, philosophical, mythological and traditional sources' were displaced and the human spirit was impoverished by reducing human beings to the 'status of mere components and functions to be administered' (*ibid.*: 350, 353). Toller dramatises this new episteme of death, foregrounding it in a philosophical debate between rival personifications of an abstraction. Ironically, he uses traditional iconography associated with death to highlight an aspect of modernity relating to industrialised killing, which he then critiques.

Toller's use of the iconography of Death as a skeleton, a familiar figure in expressionist visual art and film, recalls older ways of thinking about mortality and juxtaposes them with the reality of the present-day. Death-by-Peace informs Death-by-War of his modernity, and, unbeknownst to him, of his altered status as handmaiden to the military-industrial complex. Toller's fantastical, historically mindful representations of death in *The Transfiguration* as ideologically opposed personifications, dancing skeletons, and spectral personae further show how creative redeployment of conventional iconography was part of modern dramatists' arsenal in responding to the death engendered by the First World War. Indeed, the use of existing cultural tropes and older modes of expression, if artfully effected, may work to register the 'special shock' of the war by their ostensible incongruity, their apparent misalignment with the times, as demonstrated by the next example.

The choreography of Death in *Satan the Waster*

Vernon Lee's *Satan the Waster* is notably different to Toller's expressionist drama in terms of style and tone. Indeed, this eccentric text is compositionally *sui generis*. Nevertheless, its conceptual ambition in striving to encapsulate the death caused by the war through figuration and abstraction links it to Toller's play. That old bogeyman – death as a personified skeleton – features in both plays, but Lee's text is replete with character abstractions and offers an even wider perspective on the wastage of war.

Satan the Waster presents a modern writer using an old literary mode (the allegory) and the stylistics of a medieval morality play to satirise the events of the First World War. Lee, an English author best known for her supernatural fiction, was an ardent pacifist. Her oeuvre demonstrates crossover between late Victorianism and modernism. Kirsty Martin remarks: 'Vernon Lee was on the edge of modernism, her work falling within both the nineteenth and the twentieth centuries, and her work intimates the need for characteristically modernist modes of writing' (2013: 10). This little-known play is an expansion of one of her earlier works: an illustrated, dialogue-heavy prose text published in 1915 entitled *The Ballet of the Nations*. This work (sans illustrations) is folded into *Satan the Waster*, which adds a lengthy dramatic prologue and epilogue, totalling 110 pages in all, as well as a fifty-page introduction and 190 pages of notes, authored by Lee. As Heinz Kosok remarks, 'it can only be described as a whale of a play', especially when the supplemental, discursive material is taken into account (2007: 93). I will focus on the play itself, and specifically on Lee's figurative evocations of death as personification and choreography.

Satan the Waster is a closet drama in which a performance is discussed and staged, but it is chiefly *described* to the reader. This is likely because of the unstageable aspects of the performance. Satan has invited Clio, the muse of history, to attend a new ballet staged by Satan's ballet-master, Death, at a variety theatre Satan manages, called The World. The Ballet of the Nations is an allegory of the war. The corps de ballet is comprised of the members of the warring nations; the neutral nations join Clio, the Sleepy Virtues, and a chorus of the Ages-to-Come in the audience. The orchestra comprises a selection of human passions, including Idealism, Love of Adventure, Pity, Indignation, and Heroism; the passions are collectively known as patriotism and spur on the dancers. Joining the orchestra are Madame Science, who wears a laboratory smock and uses spectacles, and Councillor Organization, who resembles a clerk in a public office. Madame Science's instrument is a gramophone; Organization's is a miniature pianola.

Despite the play's tongue-in-cheek quality, the comical aspects belie the seriousness of the enterprise. The critical apparatus that buttresses the play-text testifies to this. But what about using mythological characters, including the ruler of hell, in a drama about the First World War? Previously, I cited Walter's thesis that the First World War contributed to a decline of belief in the concept of hell, as well as Bendle's proposition that the war displaced 'traditional epistemes derived predominantly from religious, philosophical, mythological and traditional sources'. Lee's play ostensibly jars with these pronouncements, yet the way in which she employs mythological characters suggests playful revision and ironising on her part. Consequently, her play may be thought to cast mythology and metaphysics in a more modern light. Lee's 'present-day morality play' (the subtitle of the 1915 publication of the *Ballet of the Nations*) may seem straightforward on first perusal, but it is quite complicated, and, while its modernism is not immediately apparent, it later becomes evident.

Consider the ways in which death is inscribed within the play. Death is most obviously represented in personified form as a ballet-master. Casting death in this role is quirky, although the physical form Ballet Master Death takes is familiar: he is a skeleton, dressed in loose black evening clothes. Death's agedness is commented on in the drama, like how the 'modern' Death-by-War is juxtaposed with the implicitly older Death-by-Peace in Toller's *The Transfiguration*. In Lee's drama, Satan tells Clio (in confidence) that his nephew, Ballet Master Death, is getting old, signalling acknowledgement of the history of this trope on Lee's part. In her introduction to the text, Lee references medieval masques and Holbein's woodcuts in relation to Ballet Master Death (1920: vii). Satan says Death is 'still pretty spry, but tabetic [emaciated] and threatened with creeping paralysis' (*ibid.*: 20). Death's antiquity and ailing health are periodically highlighted. The character is resolutely anti-modern: he rails at the appearance of Science and Organization on the scene, referring to them as '[spies] in the service of Life and Progress'; this prompts Satan to call him a 'senseless old relic of the Stone Age' and Science to remark on his 'very interesting primitiveness' (37, 38). Satan elsewhere characterises him as an 'old-fashioned scarecrow' and 'a preposterous, indecent anachronism' (110). After the exertion of the ballet, Death is described as the worse for wear: '[*The*] *natty BALLET MASTER has turned into a tattered tramp: his bones have worked his evening suit into rags, his wig has fallen off, and through the rents of his once smart waistcoat and shirt there is a glimpse of something far worse than a mere skeleton*' (107). What is this mysterious thing worse than the skeletal form of death but contained within him? We are left to wonder.

Intriguingly, Satan informs Clio that Ballet Master Death is not death itself, but a kind of avatar or proxy (just as the Ballet of the Nations is only an artistic representation of the war). Ballet Master Death is Satan's minion, manipulable as a marionette, to Death's chagrin. Clio had assumed the Ballet Master was an immortal power, but Death informs her that he is a mortal entity that can, and will, die. The Ballet Master is to be distinguished from 'the other Death', the 'true one', whose name and functions the Ballet Master merely usurps (21). (Reader, I hope you're following this!) Satan elaborates on the nature of the 'true' death:

> He has been my enemy since the beginning. Like me, he is an archangel, but mightier. Great Natural Death, twin of sleep and foster-brother of Love. He was born, by virgin birth, of Life herself, to be the marshal of Life's triumphal progress. He is not often seen of men, although he works ubiquitously among inanimate things, and his serene face shines through the autumn woods. ... Yet, at times, poets and sages have caught glimpses of his tender eyes. (21–2)

This image of natural death as a comforter to humankind, as distinct from the destructive and cynical force represented by Ballet Master Death, parallels the double personification of death in *The Transfiguration*. Both Toller and Lee use personifications of death in a self-reflexive, knowing manner, complicating simple identification. At the end of Lee's play, Heroism, who is blind, is shocked to discover Ballet Master Death as the conductor of the Ballet of the Nations. Heroism had been motivated by a 'purer' vision of death. He exclaims: 'Whose is that hideous braggart voice which calls upon me in the name of death? For that is not the voice, those cannot be the words, of him I have so loved. ... Where is the Death I loved and followed so faithfully – the true, pure, lovely Death? Oh, horror, horror, horror! (108–9). Heroism figuratively sees the light. His misapprehension is understandable. In *Satan the Waster*, Lee presents death in ways that make it difficult to comprehend fully, or to 'see' truly. Death is personified but it is also theatrically suggested, albeit through verbal description.

This is achieved by the centrepiece of the play, the Ballet of the Nations, which presents the death caused by the war as an allegorical dance. Ballet Master Death calls the ballet 'the vastest and most new-fashioned spectacle of Slaughter and Ruin I have so far had the honour of putting onto the World's Stage' (41). In his address to the performers he provides few directions, indicating that the human passions, under the banner of patriotism, will manifest violence as a matter of course, and that the Dancing Nations will either follow the regulation steps or improvise around them. 'The ground plan of our Ballet is so simple', he tells the performers, 'that no rehearsals have been necessary, and its variety arises out of the ever-increasing number and incompatibility of the allied dancers and their characteristic manners' (42). The Orchestra of Patriotism is instructed to ignore 'the dissonances and conflicting rhythms produced by the contradictory parts of ... fellow-performers' as 'such incoherence conduces to the volume and impressiveness of the patriotic whole' (*ibid.*). Death's comments present the war as a ridiculous folly: familiar patterns of action fuelled by base human passions, clouded judgement, and misunderstanding.

The ballet is primarily presented to the reader through Clio's oral account of the stage action. Lee occasionally interposes some stage directions indicating what the performers are doing, but the muse of history is the chief communicator of the event: she declaims what she is writing after she has watched what has happened on the stage. This puts the reader at several removes from the 'performed' action. Additionally, Satan does not permit Clio to hear the music of the Orchestra of Passions, save for the voice and drum of Heroism, explaining to her that, if History knew 'the true strains which set and keep the Nations dancing, the folly and the frenzy which move those limbs, there would soon be an end to your well-deserved popularity' (40–1). Consequently, Clio's perception of the dance is constrained, which means the reader's is, too. The impression of the Ballet of the Nations one may mentally conjure is principally derived from Clio's circumscribed viewpoint.[5] This makes for a curious reading experience. Lee keeps the theatrical spectacle notional.

Clio's account of the Ballet of the Nations means that diegesis supplants mimesis. Lee may have contrived this to make her allegory more comprehensible on the page. Rather than attempt to provide choreographic and musical scores for the ballet, Lee just has Clio describe the stage action; the reader may then decode the allegory and make the connection to the historical actors and events. The war is transformed into a symbolic stage spectacle, which Clio relays in elevated, poetical language, veering into purple prose. For instance, she describes how the 'blue solemnity' of the 'deep summer starlit vault' (i.e., the summer of 1914) is rent by 'the fitful track of rockets, and the luminous fans of searchlights and the Roman candles and Catherine-wheels of far-off explosions' (50). She subsequently notes 'masses of flame-lit smoke and poisonous vapours, rising and sinking, coming forward and receding like a stifling fog', in addition to 'the leaping flame of an exploding magazine' and an overhead fluttering and whirring of 'great wings, which showered down bomb-lightnings' (*ibid.*). (Compare with the British soldier's description of the seemingly unreal battle quoted in the introduction to this chapter.) Death's masquelike production would surely provide significant technical challenges, and would be a costly venture to boot. Interestingly, in an author's note addressed to potential stage managers '*other than Satan*' (har har), Lee makes it clear that *should* the play be performed, no attempt should be made to stage the ballet (57). She writes:

The stage upon the stage must be turned in such a manner that nothing beyond the footlights, the Orchestra and the auditorium shall be visible to the real spectators, only the changing illumination which accompanies the Ballet making its performance apparent. Similarly ... none of the music must be audible, except the voice and drum of Heroism. Anything beyond this would necessarily be hideous, besides drowning or interrupting the dialogue. (*ibid.*)

Lee states that staging the ballet would be 'hideous' for aesthetic reasons; she privileges language and textuality over embodied practice and the art of theatre. This is suggestive of anti-theatrical prejudice and modernist anti-theatricality – the way in which certain types of modernist drama and theatre interpose mimesis with diegesis in an effort to circumscribe theatricality (see Puchner, 2002). Still, despite the directive to tell rather than show, the fact that *Satan the Waster* uses theatre as a metaphor for the death and destruction caused by the war is culturally significant.

Paul Fussell devotes a chapter of his classic study *The Great War and Modern Memory* to the connection between theatre and war, which, he notes, was deeply embedded in contemporaneous modes of thinking and discourse about the First World War. Conceiving the war as theatre may have functioned as a mental coping strategy. Fussell proposes that the 'unthinkable' nature of military situations encourages participants to adopt a theatrical frame of reference. He writes:

[It] is impossible for a participant to believe that he is taking part in such murderous proceedings in his own character. The whole thing is too grossly farcical, perverse, cruel, and absurd to be credited as a form of 'real life'. Seeing warfare as theatre provides a psychic escape for the participant: with a sufficient sense of theater, he can perform his duties without implicating his 'real' self and without impairing his innermost conviction that the world is still a rational place. (1975: 192)

Fussell contends that, if soldiers in general are like actors, British soldiers were more like actors than soldiers of other nationalities. He provides copious examples, drawn from memoirs and other sources, of British soldiers using theatrical metaphors to describe their wartime experiences. Some soldiers demonstrate impressive technical knowledge of stage engineering: 'In describing the view from the forward trench they speak of cycloramas, backcloths, and drop-scenes, just as if they were stage managers weary with expertise' (*ibid.*: 202). He hypothesises that the 'vividness of the sense of role enjoined by the British class system' coupled with 'the British awareness of possessing Shakespeare as a major national asset' are the two main reasons for the British tendency to 'fuse memories of the war with the imagery of theater' (*ibid.*: 197). Additionally, theatrical devices, such as a set of exhibition trenches specially dug in Kensington Gardens, were used to edify people on the home front and to stimulate morale (although the reality of the trenches was far different). Lee's use of a play-within-a-play in *Satan the Waster* speaks to the psychological and cultural importance of theatre, especially for the British, in making the war more bearable and comprehensible. However, Lee's text problematises these functions. It subverts aesthetic ideals and reveals the danger of becoming caught up in misguided fantasy about the war.

Take the ostensible mismatch between ballet and the material reality of combat in the First World War, which was as far from notions of aesthetic beauty as one could imagine.[6] This gives Lee's play satirical bite. The Ballet of the Nations begins as a graceful and refined affair. Clio describes choreography involving one of the very little dancing nations (presumably meant to represent Belgium):

> [As] it stood there, at the western side of the stage, two or three of the tallest and finest dancers danced up in a graceful step, smiling, wreathing their arms and blowing kisses, all of which is Ballet language for 'Don't be afraid; we will look after you'. And danced away, wagging their finger at one of their *vis-à-vis*, who was also curtseying and smiling in the most engaging manner on the other side. (Lee, 1920: 48)

After the conflict commences, these graceful steps are abandoned and the movement of bodies on the stage becomes positively grisly: a monstrous, bloody spectacle – endurance art *avant la lettre*. Clio describes the nations performing Death's dance as 'a living jelly of blood and trampled flesh'; they continue to dance, even upon their stumps, provided a nation's Head (i.e., its government) remains unhurt. Clio notes: 'Death could keep up the Dance regardless of the condition of the Dancers, and of the condition also of the stage, which was such that, what between blood and mud and entrails and heaps of ravaged properties, it became scarcely possible to move even a few yards to and fro (*ibid.*: 51–2). Clio suggests the ballet becomes increasingly graphic as the nations continue to dance (i.e., to 'fight'). The performance aesthetic comes to resemble Grand Guignol (or, more latterly, a slasher film):

> THE MUSE (*writing*): Yet, dance they did, chopping and slashing, blinding each other with squirts of blood and pellets of human flesh. And as they appeared and disappeared in the moving wreaths of fiery smoke, they lost more and more of their original shape, becoming, in that fitful

> light, terrible uncertain forms, armless, legless, recognizable for human only by their irreproachable Heads, which they carried stiff and high even while crawling and staggering along … until they became … mere unspeakable hybrids between man and beast: they who had come on to that stage so erect and beautiful. (52)

The symbolic register of the performance appears to collapse, or is altered by the emergence of 'the real'. As the Ballet of the Nations proceeds (as described by Clio), it appears increasingly avant-garde: it may even rupture the structure of representation altogether, akin to a literal version of Antonin Artaud's theatre of cruelty, as the dancers are mutilated and bleed upon the stage.

This has allegorical resonance. It relates to how the reality of the war upended Romantic ideals about the magnificence and glory of battle, the beauty of heroic death for one's country, and other chivalric beliefs, which were deeply instilled in British society (more precisely, in the Edwardian public school code) before the war (Jalland, 2010: 16). The slasher-ballet in Lee's text transforms beauty into ugly brutality, as the ideals of classical and Romantic ballet morph into riotous choreography that pulsates with barbarous, dangerous energy – like Igor Stravinsky's modernist masterpiece *The Rite of Spring*, which premiered in Paris in 1913, the year before the outbreak of war. Eksteins connects the aesthetic provocation of Stravinsky's ballet – including 'the overt hostility to inherited form; the fascination with primitivism and indeed with anything that contradicts the notion of civilization; the perception of existence as continuous flux and as a series of relations, not as constants and absolutes' – to the German idea of war as a 'spiritual necessity' (1989: 52). For Germany, Eksteins writes, the war was 'a quest for authenticity, for truth, for self-fulfilment, for those values, that is, which the avant-garde had evoked prior to the war and against those features – materialism, banality, hypocrisy, tyranny – which it had attacked', and which were primarily associated with England (*ibid.*: 92). Lee uses theatrical performance in the Ballet of the Nations to evoke Romantic ideals and classical tradition as well as avant-garde, disruptive forces. Rather than privilege the traditional or the modern, or take the side of one 'dancing nation' over another, Lee's *immorality* play suggests that the bodies of the dancing nations are all deluded; they are dancing mindlessly, naively, unaware of the nefarious figures behind the scenes who are responsible for stage-managing the performance and setting it in motion. Unlike Toller's *The Transfiguration*, in which human actors are seemingly autonomous and have taken charge of 'modern death', here Ballet Master Death is the chief choreographer of this hellish theatre of war, and government heads dance to his tune. Hell-on-earth is executed in the *theatrum mundi* of Satan's stage, but all is not as it seems.

In the epilogue to *Satan the Waster*, Satan – or rather, Lee – performs a *coup de théâtre* and reveals the artifice of the preceding ballet, dismantling the fantastical representation of death in the Ballet of the Nations, which an absorbed and duped Clio has mistaken for reality. '[My] ballet, as I heard you recording it, was not the real thing, though you thought it was', Satan tells Clio (Lee, 1920: 67). Satan directs Clio's attention to a magic-lantern screen, upon which he projects scenes from 'reality' that he has 'cinematographed and gramophoned' (thus effecting a 'talkie' before the advent of sound cinema) (*ibid*.: 63). Clio is nonplussed and irked by the disjointed, non-linear, seemingly random scene fragments; she complains that they do not appear to have anything to do with the Ballet of the Nations. Satan, amused by her reaction, changes the gearing of his 'magic apparatus' and makes the recorded acts and words dramaturgically coherent, as though he were editing a documentary film about the war. There follows a lengthy montage of scenes about the prewar years, documenting exchanges conducted in a newspaper office, a French bourgeois family home, a committee-room of the International Armament Trust, and so forth. The mechanism by which these scenes are conveyed is, of course, fantastical (Satan as a spy-on-the-wall documentarian using modern technology), but the scenes themselves are not – especially when compared with the Ballet of the Nations or, indeed, with the mythological figures of Satan, Clio, and Death.[7] Satan proceeds to show Clio scenes from 'reality' (heated exchanges between heads of nations, diplomats, and the like), which he instructs her to imagine 'taking place behind the World's Stage when the Ballet [was] already raging' (95). Thus, Lee proffers a 'realistic' docudrama as a counterpart to the theatrical presentation of war in the Ballet of the Nations. Satan remarks: 'This contradiction between the visible effects [i.e., the Ballet] and the hidden cause is … one of my finest bits of poetic irony' (106).

A metatheatrical irony of Lee's text is that theatre is associated with artifice and falsity whilst cinema is associated with truth and verisimilitude, although her text is generically a closet drama. Lee's decision to write this play as a closet drama with a play-within-a-play, followed by what is effectively a film-within-a-play, suggests artistic grappling, on her part, with the limitations of theatre as an art-form for conveying the scale of the war and the death and destruction it caused. The fantastical scenario she concocts theoretically allows her to have her proverbial cake and eat it too, but the convoluted construction indicates uncertainty about mimesis. Could the scale of the war, and the totality of the death it encompassed, be effectively staged, or even adumbrated in theatre? Notably, there are no scenes in the filmic portion of Satan's recordings of 'real' wartime events that directly correspond with the bloody, messy choreography of the Ballet of the Nations (with stumpy dancers chopping and slashing at one another, etc.); no images of actual death or killing are shown. Lee's depiction of death in war remains figurative.

The final play featured in this chapter does not shy away from showing literal scenes of death in the First World War. It conjoins reality and fantasy in a less esoteric, but no less artful, manner, and furthers the investigation into the capacity of theatrical representation.

Apparitional death in *The Last Days of Mankind*

Karl Kraus's *The Last Days of Mankind*, written between 1915 and 1917 and first published in revised book form in 1922, is a colossal work. The first edition is over eight hundred pages long. The play has 219 scenes and over five hundred characters. Like *Satan the Waster*, it was written not to be performed but to be read. Only the play's epilogue was performed in Kraus's lifetime (see Perloff, 2014). In the preface Kraus states that the performance of the drama is intended for a theatre on Mars. Theatregoers on this planet would find it unendurable, he states, not just because of its length (he estimates it would take about ten evenings to perform) but also because of its content. 'For it is blood of their blood', he writes, 'and its content derives from the contents of those *unreal unthinkable* years, out of sight and out of mind, inaccessible to memory and preserved only in bloodstained dreams, when operetta figures played out the tragedy of mankind' (2015: 1, my emphasis). Note the language of amazement. Like the commentators briefly quoted in the introduction to this chapter, Kraus suggests the events of the war are extraordinary and inconceivable. The content seems fantastical, and yet, Kraus states: 'The most improbable actions reported here really occurred. Going beyond the realm of Schillerian tragedy, I have portrayed the deeds they [i.e., real-life people] merely performed. The most improbable conversations conducted here were spoken word for word; the most lurid fantasies are quotations' (*ibid.*: 1). Kraus worked as a journalist in Vienna. His docudrama-style play, labelled a tragedy in the work's subtitle, has a five-act structure (extended by a prologue and an epilogue) and a catastrophic conclusion, but other elements of its 'tragic' dramaturgy are unique. This is not the tragedy of a single hero, for example, but of all 'mankind': hence the enormous cast of characters. These characters are basically undeveloped 'types' and stock figures. They frequently serve as mouthpieces for quotations from newspapers, posters, advertisements, letters, and other sources (including overheard conversations in Viennese cafés), which Kraus has appropriated for satirical effect. This recalls the audio-visual 'recordings' of 'real life' conducted by Satan in Lee's play, except Lee fabricated those 'recordings'. Kraus's sources were authentic; many of them have been identified. They provide discursive fodder for the play.

The Last Days of Mankind has recurring themes and motives but no plot as such and little sense of narrative development until the end of the play. This is the part I will focus on here: specifically, the final section of Act 5, where the play's aesthetic shifts from satirical, realist docudrama to something more akin to symbolism or expressionism. This aesthetic shift relates to Kraus's statement in the preface that the 'unreal unthinkable' aspects of the play, although drawn from reality, cannot be consciously apprehended but instead figure in dreams and nightmares. At the end of Act 5 Kraus presents, in fantastical fashion, a panorama of scenes from the war years, many of which involve death and killing. I will consider the dramaturgical, historical, and aesthetic significance of this kaleidoscopic approach to depicting the ravages of war.

In the final scene of the final act of Kraus's play, set near the end of the war, a group of German and Austrian officers carouse at a banquet that is near enough to the front that the sound of artillery can be heard. An Austrian general speechifies at length. He toasts his fellow officers and the brave, enlisted soldiers (who are not present), salutes their collective achievements, and reminds them about the importance of being victorious and achieving glory. Little heed is paid to reports from telephone dispatches concerning the enemy breaking through their lines and mutiny in their own ranks. It is evident that these officers are out of touch, or are in denial about their situation. The horizon is aflame. There is panic. The lights go out. The sound of bombs being dropped from aeroplanes is heard. Then there is silence and something fantastical occurs. '*Those present are asleep, lie in a somnolent stupor or stare blankly at the wall on which the painting* In this Age of Grandeur *hangs, and on which ... apparitions rise up, one after the other*' (539). That is all the explanation Kraus provides, and it leave the proceedings ambiguous, perhaps intentionally. It is difficult to determine precisely the nature and provenance of these 'apparitions' ('*die ... Erscheinungen*' in the original)

(Kraus, 1922: 727). They may derive from the officers' collective subconscious and take form for all to see and hear or they may be supernatural phenomena – ghostly visitations that undercut the jingoistic ribaldry of the banquet and the notional 'age of grandeur' depicted in the mural. They may be a combination of memory, dream, and fantasy – hence the shift into a non-realist mode.

Fifty apparitions appear, sequentially, in total, showing a variety of scenes from the war years, short slices of life – and death. The apparitions include, for example, exhausted and famished Kosovan refugees in transit, almost dead from the cold; war correspondents in the dining car of a train, celebrating their privileged situation and remarking favourably about war; Slovak peasants being brutalised and killed in Russian captivity; the execution of forty-four soldiers in an Austro-Hungarian regiment after drunken insubordination; and two children carrying a child's coffin to a graveyard in Bohemia. The general from the banquet features in one apparition – he is shown giving orders to take the tarpaulin from a wounded man's stretcher and to spread it over his car – but the apparitions are not otherwise directly linked to specific individuals at the banquet; they have much broader scope. Some of the apparitions specify person and place, others do not. Some of them contain speech and convey relatively lengthy scenes; others present a snapshot image with little or no context, as in the following examples:

> Soldiers in their death throes on the barbed-wire entanglements before Przemysl.
> (*The apparition vanishes.*)
>
> Hand-to-hand fighting and mopping up in a trench.
> (*The apparition vanishes.*)
>
> A schoolroom, hit by a bomb dropped from an aeroplane.
> (*The apparition vanishes.*) (Kraus, 2015: 543)

Kraus does not provide any commentary for the apparitions: a scene is outlined with varying degrees of detail and then replaced by another. The lack of commentary lends a dispassionate air to the proceedings. Ghastly scenes of death and killing are presented matter-of-factly, suggesting they are unexceptional and unremarkable, and form part of a much larger canvas.

No explanation is given as to why these scenes have been chosen, or why they appear in this arrangement. They are uniformly bleak, however. Several apparitions feature instances of sadomasochism – random acts of violence, for example:

> *Lull in the fighting on the Drina. A Serb peasant fetches water. A lieutenant on the other bank takes aim. He shoots the peasant dead.*
> (*The apparition vanishes.*) (*ibid.*)

The apparitions feature thoroughly grotesque images and events, depicted with startling brevity:

> *Line of hanged men in Nowy Sacz. Children push and twist the corpses.*
> (*The apparition vanishes.*) ...
>
> *Longuyon set alight with barrels of petroleum, the houses and the churches plundered. The wounded and small children burned alive.*
> (*The apparition vanishes.*) ...
>
> *Winter on the island of Asinara. Prisoners strip the clothes off comrades who have died of cholera. The starving eat the flesh of those who have starved to death.*
> (*The apparition vanishes.*) (544, 545)

Disturbingly, the described apparitions can have a haiku-like beauty, as in the following example: '*Thousands of crosses in a snowfield.* (*The apparition vanishes.*)' (545). The apparitions become more fantastical and expressionistic, and no less heinous, near the end of the sequence. One apparition features soldier-corpses apparently reproaching the officers at the banquet:

> THE SOLDIERS WHO HAVE FROZEN TO DEATH:
>   A night to freeze your breath.
>   Oh, who thought up this death?
>   While you sleep, undisturbed,
>   cold stars stare, unperturbed.
>   We died, without exemption,
>   but you're beyond redemption!
>   (*The apparition vanishes.*)
>
> (546)

A procession of talking gas masks enters the banquet scene. Leonardo da Vinci makes an appearance, saying he will not publish or explain his method for remaining under water, because he fears it would be put to destructive use. Two children who were on board the *Lusitania* when it sunk offer mournful thoughts as they float about in shadowy waters. The natural world is given voice: a dying forest that has been 'shot to pieces, cut down, and sawn up' laments its sorry state and curses its violators: 'Behold me now, after your feud. / I was a wood! I was a wood!' (548). Representatives from the animal world materialise and have their say, including twelve hundred horses who were killed at sea when the ship they were travelling on was attacked and sunk; two actual dogs of war harnessed to a machine gun; and a chorus of ravens who gloat about their lot as they circle above a heap of unburied, half-decayed corpses and spy their pickings. The final apparition is of an unborn son who lights up the banqueting hall with a phosphorescent glow and requests not to be dragged into the earthly realm but to remain unborn. Given the preceding catalogue of horrors, this request is understandable.

One of the curious features of this sequence of apparitions is that the living characters in the scene – the officers at the banquet – ostensibly have no response to the fantastical sights and sounds that appear before them. At least, Kraus does not indicate that that they have any response, aside from groaning in their sleep at one point, but that may be coincidental. Some of the apparitional figures appear to address the officers, or gesture toward them (one soldier, injured by an exploding mine, '*stretches his bloody arm stumps out towards the banqueting hall*') (544). This casts the apparitions in a vengeful, accusatory light, like Banquo's ghost in *Macbeth*, but it is not clear whether any of banqueters are attentive to the apparitions, or what they make of them if they *do* register them. One wonders if we are meant to interpret the officers' apparent non-responsiveness as indifference on their part, as callousness, or lack of empathy: a result of them having become desensitised to widespread suffering, death, and destruction. There may nothing strange about most of these scenes for the officers in question, save the circumstances of their appearance here. These officers, who are enamoured with warfare but seemingly dead to the world and unmindful of the catastrophe to which they have contributed, are a damning indictment of 'mankind'.

Most of the apparitions are based on actual wartime events and real historical figures, in line with Kraus's statement in the preface that 'the most improbable actions reported here really occurred'. Twelve hundred horses may not have spectrally returned to haunt the German officer who sunk the transport ship on which they were travelling, but this attack did occur and the animals did drown (as reported in a *New York Times* article, dated 18 January 1917). At least three of the apparitions are based on photographs taken during the war: an apparition showing the execution of the Italian socialist Cesare Battisti; an apparition depicting a mother and her baby wearing gas masks; and an expressionist vision of Crown Prince Wilhelm with the flamethrowers of the Fifth Army (Lensing, 1982: 496, n. 42). The image of Battisti's execution featured in a propaganda postcard that shows a grinning hangman standing above

Battisti's corpse and satisfied-looking witnesses; Kraus reproduced this image as a frontispiece for the book publication of the text, setting a suitably mordant tone.

Presumably, early readers of Kraus's text would have been more familiar with the events and figures referenced in the apparitions; Kraus's thumbnail sketches could have called the recent history to mind. It is more difficult for a contemporary reader to make these connections, unless one has deep historical knowledge about the period in question. Even with this knowledge, however, Kraus's presentation of these scenes is difficult to process and comprehend. The kaleidoscopic presentation of short scenes from the war years, many of which involve ghastly tableaux of death and killing, threatens to overwhelm with its cumulative force; it almost becomes too much to bear. One imagines that beholding these apparitions, and not just reading about them, would be like watching a series of short snuff films. The rapid-fire appearance and disappearance of these scenes, presented without authorial comment or bridging material, constantly relocating with no obvious directional trajectory, produces a vertiginous effect: one is figuratively set spinning.

Dramaturgically, this is like the *sintesi* of the Italian futurists, who, at the same time Kraus was writing *The Last Days of Mankind*, were experimenting with programmes of extremely short plays that, owing to their brevity, dynamism, synthesis of elements, and lack of explanatory information, were intended to replicate the experience of living in a modern city. The *sintesi* and the series of apparitions in Kraus's play are both examples of modernist fascination with concentrated effect – what John Muse calls the 'dimensions of the moment' – as opposed to nineteenth-century gigantism (e.g., lengthy novels) (2010). However, few dramas are more gigantic than Kraus's play – the series of apparitions constitutes only a small fraction (about one-fiftieth) of the whole text. Furthermore, the expansive reach of just this small section of the play – its referential breadth – is enormous, and exemplifies a modernist impulse (related to nineteenth-century literary gigantism) to create epic artistic works that generate a sense of totality with respect to their contents. James Joyce, for example, is said to have boasted that if Dublin were destroyed it could be entirely rebuilt with reference to *Ulysses*, so detailed, lengthy, and factually fulsome is that novel (Budgen, 1960: 67–8).

The apparitional sequence in Kraus's play gives an impression of the scale of the catastrophe of the First World War – not just the loss of human life but animal death and ecological destruction as well. Few plays about the First World War attempt to encompass this event, or even *gesture* towards encompassing it, nor do they detail its manifold atrocities at much length. Instead, many, if not most, First World War plays typically recreate individual, localised situations on a much smaller and more manageable scale, offering a limited perspective on events (Kosok, 2007: 108). Kraus and Lee, by contrast, respectively offer a Godlike, panoramic view of the catastrophe writ large, yielding an impression of omnipresent 'corpsescapes'.[8] No one could have witnessed all these scenes; at most, they might have had indirect knowledge about them. Kraus invites one to witness an impossible spectacle. He vivifies that which hitherto may only have been intellectually understood, and makes the reality of death-in-war uniquely apparent.

The enormous scale of this play, the broad range of calamitous scenes it presents, works to impress upon the mind the seemingly impossible task of comprehending the mass death incurred by the 'great' war. David Sherman remarks on how the war, which he describes as 'industrially structured, state-sponsored corpse production', marked a 'radical change in the life of the Western war dead'. He writes:

> [The dead] were for the first time both spread across large swaths of Europe and, in an unlikely democratization, granted their private spaces and identities. ... To bring to mind the quantity of dead – nine million soldiers and five million civilians among all European nations – is impossible; but to conceive of this unthinkable quantity together with the discrete, individuated identities it contained is impossible for its quality of paradox: so large, yet so singularized a population of corpses. (2014: 91)

Kraus's apparitional sequence acknowledges the death of individuals (some of whom are named) in specific situations while intimating a mass of unseen others in the darkness of the fade-outs.

Kraus makes scenes from the First World War, and the death incurred therein, seem real and unreal simultaneously. By presenting historical events in an apparitional fashion he blurs the line between reality and fantasy. The sequence of apparitions resembles cinematic montage and creates an illusion of documentary truth (like Satan's film in Lee's play). Leo A. Lensing observes, regarding this section of the play, that 'atrocities which have been reduced to drunken storytelling in the preceding action on the stage [i.e., during the banquet] reassume their horrifying essence by being shown in life-like detail on the monumental screen' (1982: 490). Even so, historical events are also presented by way of fantastical visions of dead, talking horses and trees, and are interposed with apparitions involving talking gas masks and cognisant, unborn children. In the stage directions, Kraus refers to the later apparitions as 'phantasmagoria' ('*Phantoms*' in German), suggesting hallucinations and psychic disturbances, or possibly ghosts (2015: 549; 1922: 741). 'Phantasmagoria' also relates to the tradition of magic-lantern shows, which began in Europe toward the end of the eighteenth century. These were audio-visual performances that 'conjured up gothic images of skeletons, skulls, and spirits ... using optical illusions as well as sound effects and eerie music to frighten the audience', writes Anton Kaes, who adds: 'In an atmosphere of smoke and mirrors along with complete darkness, audiences believed they saw ghosts of the recently deceased' (2009: 124). Kraus's phantasmagorical apparitions invoke this older genre of performance, as well as the newer medium of cinema, to show the Gothic horror of modern warfare – a ghastly mash-up. This is another example of a dramatist fusing past and present to communicate an altered understanding of death in the modern world. Kraus's phantasmal depiction of death suggests reality had shifted: the formerly fantastical had become the newly real. The unimaginable had happened, and humanity might be approaching its twilight. In this fatalistic reckoning, the spectre of total annihilation had become terrifyingly possible. This is dramatised in the play's expressionist, science-fiction-themed epilogue, which imagines the war as a precursor to global apocalypse. Martians, observing recent events, decide to take preventive action in case warlike humanity heads into space, and so they destroy the Earth. As Kraus's play was supposedly written for a theatre on Mars, and thus for a Martian audience, does this count as a tragic dénouement?

Conclusion

The First World War encouraged apocalyptic visions of death on a planetary scale – visions that had previously come into vogue in the *fin de siècle* (see Fuchs, 1999). It is not surprising that such a catastrophic war would encourage fantasies of this kind, and later twentieth-century catastrophes (discussed in Chapter 4) would add new fuel to the fire. The war prompted contemplation of death as something potentially all-encompassing. As discussed in the previous chapter, death was a subject of renewed cultural fascination in the *fin de siècle*. Creators of symbolist plays and performances explored death notionally and atmospherically. The 'Great War' of 1914–18 made death 'all too real', on the one hand, and yet strangely unreal, on the other, due to the types and amount of death it engendered. Thus, there is continuity between the symbolists' abstract and atmospheric evocations of death and the fantastical forms of representation analysed in this chapter. Prompted by the war, modern dramatists deployed dramaturgy that allowed them to capture something of its 'special shock', its disruption of the status quo and of conventional frames of reference.

'The fantastic', remarks Irene Eynat-Confino, 'is a representation of that breach into the unsteady ramparts that surround the ever-changing concept of reality, a breach that enables us to comprehend and accept the illogical, the seemingly impossible, and the out of ordinary as part of human experience' (2008: 112). The plays featured in this chapter exemplify this undertaking with respect to the First World War, which was thought to be paradigm-shifting in relation to conceptions of death (as indicated in Kirkland's treatise *The New Death*). Yet, both Toller's and Lee's plays use conventional iconography (e.g., personification of death as a skeleton) and, in Lee's case, an old dramatic genre (the morality play) and cultural trope (the dance of death). But Toller and Lee put these stylistics 'under pressure'. The skeletal figure of Death-by-War in *The Transfiguration* is derided for being a puppet of a humanly organised war machine. Ballet Master Death in *Satan the Waster* is depicted as being decrepit and outdated; his 'dance of death', though grotesque, is revealed as a theatrical illusion, a pale imitator of an unseen reality. Moreover, *Satan the Waster*, with its centrepiece slasher ballet, more readily connotes an immorality play than a morality play; it is not altogether clear what lessons, if any, one should learn from it. These plays illustrate how the war rattled conventional ways of representing death, revealing their shortcomings.

The plays discussed in this chapter, particularly *The Last Days of Mankind* and *Satan the Waster*, attempt to connote the catastrophe writ large. Given the ambitious effort to encapsulate wartime death, the use of closet drama is understandable. 'Mental theatre' theoretically makes it easier to apprehend the death caused by the war as a totality, perhaps more readily than practical staging. Furthermore, it is notable that both Lee and Kraus turn to filmic (or filmlike) sequences to intimate the unstageable, unseen reality of the war. Their closet drama figuratively swaps theatre for cinema at crucial points. Later twentieth-century dramatists and theatre-makers found other ways of presenting large-scale catastrophe onstage, as will be discussed in Chapter 4.

In *The New Death*, Kirkland suggests that the war fundamentally changed social attitudes to death, making it impossible to deny the reality of death any longer. However, in the aftermath of the war, this pronouncement turned out not to be accurate. The next chapter examines the persistent modern habit of avoiding thinking about death, which even world war did not end.

Notes

1 A word search in this database, which collates personal accounts of the war, highlights this usage: www.firstworldwar.amdigital.co.uk.
2 See also the 'Recovering First World War Theatre' project, led by Helen Brooks: www.gatewaysfww.org.uk/projects/recovering-first-world-war-theatre-0.
3 Compare with the metaphor of an English soldier's dead body as 'richer dust' in the 'rich earth' of a foreign field (doubling as England) in Rupert Brooke's 1915 poem 'The Soldier' (2014: 139).
4 Elsewhere Kirkland makes her antipathy for the Germans plain: 'It is the responsibility of each man and woman and child to-day to see that we Americans shall have as clear and efficient expression for our idealism as the Germans have had for their deviltry' (1918: 99).
5 Richard Armfield's illustrations for the 1915 publication of *The Ballet of the Nations* offer an art noveau or classical Greek-style 'pictorial commentary' on Lee's text, but there is aesthetic disagreement between text and image (see Brockington, 2006).
6 This is not to say that the subject of war is incompatible with ballet as an art-form. Kurt Jooss's ballet *The Green Table* (1932), which features the character of Death, is evidence otherwise.
7 One unexplained element is the fact that the 'recorded speech' is almost all in English (even the 'recording' of the French family).
8 The word 'corpsescape' derives from Booth (1996: 50), where it is used in reference to trench warfare.

3

The absurd drama of modern death denial

Six months after the outbreak of the First World War, Sigmund Freud wrote an essay that endeavoured to shed light on the mental distress it had caused. For Freud, this was connected to the general attitude to death prior to the war – an attitude rooted in denial. 'We showed an unmistakeable tendency to put death on one side, to eliminate it from life. We tried to hush it up [...]. [In] the unconscious every one of us is convinced of his own immortality' (1985 [1915]: 77). The circumstances of war inevitably made it difficult to maintain this mindset, even for non-combatants. Yet, Freud saw an upside. '[War] is bound to sweep away this conventional treatment of death. Death will no longer be denied; we are forced to believe in it. People really die; and no longer one by one, but many, often tens of thousands, in a single day' (ibid.: 79–80). He concludes by suggesting that the 'civilised' attitude toward death, which fosters illusion and self-deception, should be permanently abandoned, asking: 'Would it not be better to give death the place in reality and in our thoughts which is its due, and to give a little more prominence to the unconscious attitude towards death which we have hitherto so carefully suppressed?' (ibid.: 89).

Death denial is a psychological impulse and a cultural attitude that banishes thoughts about death and disavows the reality of personal mortality. Despite Freud's belief that the war would, or should, put an end to death denial, it has seemingly persisted. Scholars have noted the continued existence of death denial, despite world conflicts and repeated incidences of mass death. Jonathan Dollimore remarks: 'This attitude of forgetting [about death] had, apparently, become so habitual by the early twentieth century that the First World War did not make the difference Freud thought it would or should. Nor, according to later writers, did the Second World War; if anything the extent of the denial became even greater' (2001: 120).

Freud posits that literature and theatre offer valuable 'compensation' for what has been lost in life. '*There* we still find people who know how to die', he writes. 'There alone too the condition can be fulfilled which makes it possible for us to reconcile ourselves with death: namely, that behind all the vicissitudes of life we should still be able to preserve a life intact' (1985 [1915]: 79, my emphasis). Theatre and literature allow us to experience death and dying vicariously, Freud suggests, thereby theoretically enriching our outlook and helping us to cope with our mortality. This is plausible, but the learning potential is surely dependent on *the way* death and dying are presented. Also, who are these people who 'know how to die'? This is a cryptic phrase. Who can confidently claim to know *how* to die?

It is not a given that theatre will challenge social convention with respect to attitudes toward death and dying. Death denial can function as an unexamined philosophy and conditioning element in theatre unless it is deliberately foregrounded and challenged (see Chambers, 2010). This chapter looks at four examples that do just that: Dino Buzzati's little-known play *Un caso clinico* (*A Clinical Case*, 1953); *Terminal* (1969–71), a collectively created work by the American experimental company the Open Theater (text by Susan Yankowitz); and two plays by Eugène Ionesco, *Le roi se meurt* (*Exit the King*, 1962) and *Amédée, ou comment s'en débarrasser* (*Amédée, or How to Get Rid of It*, 1953). This is an idiosyncratic grouping that draws together Italian, American, and Romanian-French dramatists and theatre-makers. Buzzati and Ionesco are associated with absurdism, a genre popularised by Martin Esslin in his 1961 study of the 'theatre of the absurd'. This chapter addresses the absurd drama of death denial in everyday life, as manifested in cultural attitudes and social practices relating to mortality, and in the plays and performance pieces discussed herein.

Each of this chapter's case studies highlights the absurdity of death denial in a unique way, exposing the delusional basis of this attitude and its potentially damaging effects on the individual and society. These pieces may thus be understood in the context of the death awareness movement, a 'diverse collection of individuals, groups, and organizations' united by a 'shared ethos in the primacy, inevitability and naturalness of human mortality as well as a shared belief in the potential risk posed to social relationships and psychological well-being if issues of death, dying, and bereavement are not addressed or engaged with in a fully transparent, honest, and mature fashion' (Brennan, 2014: 138). The death awareness movement began in the late 1950s and entered the mainstream (particularly in the US) by the 1970s (*ibid.*, 139). I argue that the plays and performance pieces featured in this chapter, which date from the same period, accord with the tenets of this movement. They offer mordant social commentary by challenging prevailing orthodoxies through the presentation of fantastical, theatrically arresting, and sometimes morbidly funny scenarios.

Debating death denial

In psychoanalytic writing, death denial has not been considered inherently problematic or something that must be corrected. The Ukrainian-American psychoanalyst Gregory Zilboorg stipulates that 'the fear of death is always present in our mental functioning', but he regards it as an 'instinct of self-preservation' that one must generally suppress to cope with the business of living. 'If this fear were as constantly conscious, we should be unable to function normally', he proposes. 'It must be properly repressed to keep us living with any modicum of comfort' (1943: 467). It would do us no good to be constantly fretting about our personal mortality, Zilboorg maintains. We are therefore inclined to operate in a subjunctive psychological mode, behaving 'as if' our lives will continue apace, at least for the foreseeable future, and that our days are not ultimately numbered. Zilboorg elaborates:

> [In] normal times we move about actually without ever believing in our own death, as if we fully believed in our corporeal immortality. We are intent on mastering death. We work out medical problems of longevity; we indulge in planning for the remote future of our family, our country, humanity as a whole; we marshal all the forces which still the voice reminding us that our end must come some day, and we are suffused with the awareness that our lives will go on forever. (*ibid.*: 468)

Zilboorg indicates that a certain amount of self-deception in relation to personal mortality is understandable and not necessarily a bad thing.

Ernest Becker follows suit in his study *The Denial of Death*, first published in 1973. Becker, an American cultural anthropologist, claims that consciousness of death is the primary repression, not sexuality (*pace* Freud), and that '[repression of death] is the repression on which culture is built, a repression unique to the self-conscious animal' (1973: 96). Becker builds on Zilboorg's claims, noting how repression of the fear of death is a learned childhood behaviour that is made to seem natural and proper. '[Repression] is made possible', he remarks, 'by the natural identification of the child with the powers of his parents. If he has been well cared for, identification comes easily and solidly, and his parents' powerful triumph over death automatically becomes his' (*ibid*.: 23). The suggestion that denial as a coping mechanism constitutes a 'triumph over death' seems rather grandiloquent, but Becker is keen to emphasise the vital importance of having a robust psychological defence against the existential threat posed by human frailty and the reality of personal extinction. In a passage that has special bearing on the theatrical examples of this chapter, he muses:

> What would the average man do with a full consciousness of absurdity? He has fashioned his character for the precise purpose of putting it between himself and the facts of life; it is his special *tour-de-force* that allows him to ignore incongruities, to nourish himself on impossibilities, to thrive on blindness. He accomplishes thereby a peculiarly human victory: the ability to be smug about terror. (*ibid*.: 59)

The dramatists and theatre-makers whose work is featured in this chapter address the question that Becker poses. They magnify incongruities, impossibilities, and intentional blindness relating to death, undermining ontological security. In so doing, their work implicitly critiques a widespread culture of death denial.

Theatre artists were not alone in making this criticism. Some anthropologists and historians have been notably critical of death denial, which they regard less as a psychological defence mechanism than as an ideology and set of social practices. In 1955, the English anthropologist Geoffrey Gorer famously likened the contemporary attitude to death to that of pornography: both were aspects of human experience 'treated as inherently shameful or abhorrent, [...] never discussed or referred to openly, and experience of [them] tends to be clandestine and accompanied by feelings of guilt and unworthiness' (1955: 50). Gorer observes that 'whereas copulation has become more and more "mentionable," particularly in the Anglo-Saxon societies, death has become more and more "unmentionable" as a natural process' (*ibid*.). Indeed, in Gorer's view, the natural processes of corruption and decay have become 'disgusting', as the processes of birth and copulation had been considered a century ago; attention given to the natural process of dying is now deemed 'morbid and unhealthy, to be discouraged in all and punished in the young' (*ibid.*: 51). Death denial was regularly conducted as a matter of course, Gorer remarks, and was evident in mortuary practices as well. 'The ugly facts [about death and dying] are relentlessly hidden; the art of the embalmers is an art of complete denial' (*ibid.*). The connection between embalming and death denial is addressed in the Open Theater's *Terminal*.

The French historian Philippe Ariès (whose work is discussed in the Introduction) is probably the best-known proponent of the death denial thesis as it pertains to Western modernity. In the 1970s Ariès made the case for death in the modern West being 'invisible' and 'unreal', driven into secrecy and made taboo by the hospitalisation of the dying, the medicalization of death, and the displacement of the dead to the margins of society. Ariès suggests that the sensibility of the age is one in which, excepting the death of statesmen, death has been 'banished' and made to seem indecent (echoing Gorer). He writes:

> It is no longer acceptable for strangers to come into a room that smells of urine, sweat, and gangrene, and where the sheets are soiled. Access to this room must be forbidden, except to a few intimates capable of overcoming their disgust, or to those indispensable persons who provide certain services. A new image of death is forming: the ugly and hidden death, hidden because it is ugly and dirty. (1981: 569)

Ariès notes that dissimulation has become commonplace in matters involving the dying: people lie to one another and to themselves, refusing to acknowledge the reality of the situation. 'The dying person and those around him continue to play a comedy in which "nothing has changed," "life goes on as usual," and "anything is still possible"' (*ibid.*: 562). He contends that 'the hidden death in the hospital, which began very discreetly in the 1930s and 40s and became widespread after 1950' had become the norm (*ibid.*: 570). Ariès writes about how the hospital facilitates the secretive and solitary way in which dying tends to occur in the modern West; it has become the accepted, and the expected, place where dying takes place – 'the scene of the normal death', as distinct from the home (*ibid.*: 584). Medical professionals manage the dying process, affect its duration, and take it out of the patient's hands, as it were. They make it possible for the dying person to be minimally aware, or even unaware, of the fact that they are dying. Ariès notes that by the middle of the twentieth century this lack of consciousness about death was considered desirable. Evidently, in some cases the dying do not want to know that they are dying; they just want to 'slip away', to use a euphemism. 'It may be desirable to die without being aware of it, but it is also correct to die without anyone else being aware of it either', he remarks drily (*ibid.*: 586–7).

This is a particularly modern quirk, in Ariès's estimation, as is the rejection and elimination of public mourning. 'The tears of the bereaved have become comparable to the excretions of the diseased. Both are distasteful' (*ibid.*: 580). Even more troublingly, the feelings engendered by public mourning 'threaten the order and security necessary to daily activity' and so 'must be repressed' to maintain the status quo, in which matters having to do with death and dying are typically given wide berth and treated in a perfunctory, distanced manner (*ibid.*). Ariès's claims about public mourning may have been valid at the time of his study, but, in recent decades, high-profile deaths have plainly prompted public outpouring of grief. (The death of Diana, Princess of Wales, in 1997 is a clear example in a British context.)

Scholars have critiqued Ariès's history of death in the West, which stretches over a thousand years, questioning his methodology, evidence, and conclusions (see, for example, Whaley, 1981; Porter, 1999; Dollimore, 2001). I will not rehearse these criticisms here. It stands to reason that generalising about attitudes to death in the modern West is problematic and can lead to reductive thinking, inaccuracies, bias, and lack of consideration of national or cultural differences (the West is not monolithic, after all, and personal circumstances, beliefs, and economic situation are obviously crucial factors in shaping attitudes and experiences). Ariès's observations about death denial are probably best considered as providing insight into a *potential* social or personal attitude rather than an all-encompassing worldview. Yet this does not discount death denial as a behavioural and cognitive mode that people may share across national boundaries. Death denial may not be all-encompassing in modernity, but neither is it chimerical or merely a psychological reflex. The fact that dramatists and theatre-makers of various nationalities have taken up this theme indicates its discursive legitimacy and reach. These artists contributed to the discourse about death denial by creating pieces about mortality that encouraged audiences to question personal beliefs and social practices. Their work provides unusual angles on death denial, potentially provoking reconsideration of it.

Death-by-hospital: *A Clinical Case*

Dino Buzzati's play *Un caso clinico* is little known and has received scant scholarly attention. It has not been published in English translation. Based on his 1937 short story 'Sette piani' ('Seven Floors'), it was first staged at the Piccolo Teatro in Milan in 1953. Albert Camus adapted it as *Un cas intéressant* (*An Interesting Case*) for a production at the Théâtre la Bruyère in Paris, directed by Georges Vitaly, in 1955. Martin Esslin produced a radio version of it in 1961 for the BBC's Third Programme.[1] In 1975 it received its English-language stage premiere in a production by the Theatre of Involvement, a Minneapolis-based experimental theatre group that operated from 1967 to 1977, directed by Phillip Zarrilli. This version of the play, and its production, will be the basis of my examination.[2]

A Clinical Case is a Kafkaesque take on common anxieties about the medical profession, and specifically about the hospital as an institution. It dramatises the fear that one can enter a hospital with a minor complaint and end up much worse off – even dead. Consequently, it speaks to Ariès's critical perspective of the modern medicalisation of death and dying, and how patients and doctors participate in, and help to shape, a culture of denial and dissimulation. The play concerns a rich and career-obsessed businessman, Giovanni Corte, who is led to visit a nearby clinic to treat the aural hallucinations he has been experiencing. The facility is configured in a highly stratified manner: patients kept on the top floor have only minor ailments, those on the floor below them are slightly more seriously ill. Each of the lower floors is similarly gradated in terms of patient health; the ground floor is for terminal patients. Corte starts out on the top floor but through a series of ostensibly innocuous events (administrative shuffling and the like), and despite – or perhaps because of – his health, he keeps getting moved down the hospital floors until, disastrously, he reaches the bottom and his fatal spiral is complete. Corte's descent is grimly amusing: one guesses what is going to happen, but the way in which he gradually loses ground is deviously engineered. It is not entirely clear whether Corte's death was inevitable, or, more sinisterly, whether the 'system' fails him and brings about his death. The former scenario suggests a fatalistic, nihilist outlook in which 'man' is a plaything of chaotic forces (an absurdist theme); the latter indicates an indictment of a social attitude, politics, and institutional bureaucracy. Esslin remarks: '[In] the hospital, with its rigid stratification, Buzzati has found a terrifying image of society itself – an impersonal organization that hustles the individual on his way to death, caring for him, providing services, but at the same time distant, rule-ridden, incomprehensible, and cruel' (2001: 278–9).

Both Corte and the medical professionals who treat him engage in avoidance and obfuscation of one kind or another. Corte is initially unwilling to consult with any doctor about his aural hallucinations and is only cajoled into doing so, visiting the clinic as a 'tourist' rather than a prospective patient. After he is admitted he is adamant that he belongs on the top floor, and will be returned to the top floor, even as he progressively gets further and further away from it. At first he approves of the clinic's 'modern methods', its way of grouping patients with similar degrees of relative (ill-)health. He thinks the system will keep him safe, as he tells his secretary: 'It seems that this way [...] there is no longer the danger that a slightly ill person, like me for example, is exposed to a death in the next room. It's not impossible that seeing someone in that condition could bring about a worsening in one's own condition' (Buzzati, 1975: 36). Corte fervently holds on to the belief (or fantasy) that he is only slightly ill, and his doctors enable him in this regard. Dr Claretta, the clinic's assistant director, initially informs him that that he has nothing – or 'almost nothing' – to worry about and that his aural hallucinations are 'a syndrome, if anything, of the most trivial kind' (*ibid.*: 18). He nevertheless recommends a complete examination. Dr Schroeder, the clinic's director, is equally cagey and underplays the seriousness of Corte's case, while quietly impressing on him the need for action.

> CORTE: Then you found something? Serious?
> SCHROEDER: Serious, slight, serious ... expeditious words. If life were equally simple and expeditious! Serious ... serious ... Why force ourselves to definitions that do not bring any practical results? We rather retain that in a very short time everything will return to normal (*in a low voice*) ... after a brief operation. (*ibid.*: 32)

Corte cannot get a straight answer from the doctors about his unnamed condition and continues to get the run-around after he has surgery. Claretta spouts medical gobbledygook:

> This voice could very well come from within you, right? It could be a phenomena of pathological erethism ... explainable in the end ... explainable by the inevitable bearing of the cerebral sector on the pathological case ... if one were to give for example, a syndromatic picture ... (46)

Insidiously, Claretta and the other hospital staff make it seem as if Corte has agency and is the one who is making the decisions about which floor of the hospital he should be on. 'You are the master', Claretta tells him. 'I have only given you an unbiased picture of the situation' (47). Claretta nonetheless continually explains (away) Corte's current floor location, or else makes the case for why it would be better if Corte were on the floor below. It is not until Corte reaches the second floor that a hospital staff member is forthright with him.

> NURSE: The Schroeder method ... hypocrisies ... they don't have the courage to say things as they really are. The Schroeder method ... to arrange these tricks. The director is a genius. He should have been a politician. The things they tell ... [...] Always a new lie, more subtle, more difficult! (55)

By the time Corte has descended to the ground floor he recognises that the system has defeated him: 'With graciousness and grins they destroyed me ... the doctors', he laments. 'A ... a lion ... I was a lion ... and now ... now a little lamb.... This trip is absurd' (*ibid.*).

Corte's trip down the hospital floors *is* absurd and fantastical, as are other elements in the play. The character of Schroeder emerges as an all-powerful, demonic puppet-master figure, operating in the shadows. Claretta tells Corte that Schroeder's 'beneficent force radiates outward' but that '[the] master [i.e. Schroeder] ... reigns, so to speak, between the first and second floors', indicating why it might be advantageous for a patient to be located therein (49). At one point Claretta makes light of Corte's concerns, and jokingly admits that the whole operation is a sham.

> You are aware, right? That it is all a plot? You know that you are in excellent health and don't need any operations ... and you would let Schroeder use his medical instruments on you? This is too much you know! But do you know who Schroeder is? He is a bag of wind. A butcher with a heavy hand! Questionable whether he can even perform appendicitis! But he has a fine barbarian name that people have a hard time pronouncing and so everybody bows to him! (35)

In parodying Corte's fears, Claretta works to negate them, using charm and guile. Claretta and the rest of the hospital staff are presented as caricatures and ciphers, collectively out to 'get' Corte, even though they profess to act in his best interest.

Buzzati depicts the hospital as a nightmare zone, especially on the ground level, where the lights are turned off and the blinds pulled down after a patient's death. It is also suggested that there are supernatural forces at work, connected to the hospital. Corte's aural hallucinations, which prompt the series of events, are of a woman's voice; a mysterious female figure also visits his office. Corte's mother says she can hear this woman too, and implies she is a premonition of Corte's death. 'I had hoped when I heard her come the first time that it was for me' she says. 'Or at least for ... for someone else. Instead it was for him' (16). Corte's mother tells Claretta that the woman in question has entered the house and is in the closet (small storage room). When Claretta opens it he says it is empty, but the stage directions reveal that *'inside is a woman wearing a dark frock, knitting or sewing rapidly'* (17). In the final scene, Corte's mother, who has come to visit her dying son, says that the attending nurse, who is '[*knitting*] *feverishly against the light*', is the same woman who entered the house; the nurse disappears once she sees Corte's visitors (58). It is implied that she is an angel of death or siren figure who has been calling to Corte and leading him to his end, and that the hospital has helped to facilitate his downfall. This fantastical element of the play offers a quasi-mythological sensibility that subverts the logic and rationale of modern medicine, suggesting that the doctors are not as omnipotent as they appear, or would like to believe.

Ariès argues that the 'triumph of medicalization' in the twentieth century is marked by the transformation of death from something that was formerly considered (relatively) instantaneous to a potentially protracted, multiple-stage process, managed and overseen by hospital staff. 'The doctor cannot eliminate death', Ariès notes, 'but he can control its duration, from the few hours it once was, to several days, weeks, months, or even years' (1981: 585). Medical professionals have taken charge of death, Ariès declares, and subsumed it into an all-encompassing organisational-bureaucratic complex.

> For death has been brought under control in order to reconcile an accidental, sometimes inevitable phenomenon with the psychological security of the hospital. ... Death no longer belongs to the dying man, who is first irresponsible, later unconscious, nor to the family, who are convinced of their inadequacy. Death is regulated and organized by bureaucrats whose competence and humanity cannot prevent them from treating death as their 'thing', a thing that must bother them as little as possible in the general interest. (*ibid*.: 587–8)

Ariès is clearly biased against the medical profession, and his blanket statements do not allow for much nuance or complexity, but he articulates a familiar conception of the hospital as a place associated with death and dying, where patients lack agency, are lied to, and made subservient to the dictates of those who treat them.

This conception may not be accurate or universally true, but aspects of it continue to circulate in the popular imaginary. Sandra M. Gilbert, writing about the technologized modern hospital, remarks: '[Whether] one imagines the place as a "vast mechanism" or an "idiot" organism, the contemporary medical center is in fact a kind of surreal city. ... [The] dread evoked by the size of this surreal city may be intensified in the minds of some patients not just by their desperation to survive but also by a concomitant fear that the inhospitable hospital isn't just depersonalizing them but actively destroying them' (2006: 187–8). Buzzati's play invokes this conception, even as it suggests that modern medicine is an instrument of larger cosmic forces that ensnare humankind. Buzzati satirises the figure of Corte, a businessman who thinks he is control of his life and would like to deny that there is anything wrong with his health; the playwright also satirises modern medicine, which is shown to use evasive manoeuvres to string patients along, avoiding honest exchanges. Despite the declared altruism and scientific principles of its staff, the hospital in this play functions as a factory-line for death.

Buzzati's dystopian vision of a medical facility in which patients are seemingly marked for death upon entry and shuttled along to their inevitable extinction, despite official protestations to the contrary, may be thought to connote the spectre of the Holocaust. It would be farfetched to claim that the play is an allegory of the Holocaust, but it does indirectly call it to mind. To put it another way, the Holocaust inflects interpretations of the play. The fascistic character of Dr Schroeder (with his Germanic-sounding name) encourages this line of thought, as does Buzzati's depiction of Corte's dehumanisation under the protocols of scientific method, rationality, and an all-encompassing bureaucratic operation. Buzzati uses satire to dramatise the 'banality of evil' in the context of modern medicine, as exemplified by Schroeder's 'method', which seems inhuman and perverse (see Arendt, 1963). Writing about the Holocaust, Zygmunt Bauman proposes that 'it was the spirit of instrumental rationality, and its modern, bureaucratic form of institutionalization, which had made the Holocaust-style solutions not only possible, but eminently "reasonable" – and increased the probability of their choice' (1989: 18). In Buzzati's play, Corte's transformation into a 'bureaucratic object' against his will connotes the victims of the Holocaust (*ibid.*: 102). Likewise, Buzzati's nightmarish presentation of the hospital as an unacknowledged engine of corpse production links to the Nazi death camps.

Additionally, one could interpret Corte's fateful descent down the hospital floors in light of Martin Heidegger's notion of Being-towards-Death, the 'idea of death as the ontological foundation of totality', which he articulates in *Being and Time* (1927), and which fascism embraced

(Neocleous, 2005: 38). However, Corte's situation does not entirely align with this notion, and relating it to the Holocaust also requires qualification. Todd Samuel Presner writes: 'Although the inmates in the concentration camps existed every second of every day toward death as a permanent possibility, their death does not count as authentic [in the Heideggerian sense] because it conferred no individuality' (2006: 103). Instead, the Holocaust signalled a new, terrible form of 'Being-toward-mass-death', to adapt Heidegger's phrase, whereby 'the potentiality of anonymous mass death is now a potentiality of being' (*ibid.*: 107). This does not directly map on to *A Clinical Case*, which concerns the loss of agency and the implied death of a named individual, not an anonymous mass. The play also does not concern genocide or state-sponsored killing. And yet, after Auschwitz, the play's sly insinuation of modern, scientific, institutionally assisted killing has unsettling historical resonance. The condition – and threat – of anonymous, mass death will be explored in the next chapter.

The production history indicates that Buzzati's play acquired new cultural resonance decades after it was first performed. A press release for the 1975 American production situates it in the context of contemporaneous discourse about death and dying in society, as represented by some key texts on the subject. It includes the following statement:

> Given the recent publication of Elizabeth Kubler-Ross' outstanding and provocative study, *On Death and Dying*, and other widely read books such as Ernest Becker's *The Denial of Death* (Pulitzer Prize Winner of 1974), Buzzati's play seems particularly timely today. As the play traces Corte's confrontation with his own death, we see unfolded the dynamics of every person's denial of their own death.[3]

A production note in the programme reproduces a quotation from Zilboorg's article on the fear of death, cited earlier, concerning the observation that 'in normal times we move about … without ever believing in our own death'. The production clearly aimed to tap into the cultural Zeitgeist surrounding death awareness, a movement that involved exposing personal neuroses as well as institutional ideologies and mendacity. Buzzati's play is set in Italy, but this production made the play resonate for an American audience. In a letter written to a prospective publisher, Zarrilli, who also helped to adapt the text, states how the aim was to create 'a stage version which would be playable for an American audience on the American stage'; he mentions that some cuts were made to the text in order to 'keep the contemporary value of the script alive, for *the deeper issues of the script remain living realities*'.[4]

The absurd drama of modern death denial   109

This was not museum theatre; on the contrary, the production engaged the present-day, albeit through a glass, darkly.

In an interview with me in 2016, Zarrilli offered the following historical contextualisation of the production:

> In that period there was so much ... the government lying ... everything was hidden. Look at Watergate, look at the lies about the Vietnam War, about the whole military-industrial complex, about the civilian deaths in Vietnam, the napalming ... You start looking at the social awakening going on ... Death was everywhere. I felt, as a relatively young person, not very hopeful. I think a part of it [i.e. the production] was ... *wake up!* Look at the world that's around us! How many lies are there? What's hidden? What's revealed? When? By whom? What are the power dynamics of that? Who's holding the power?[5]

Buzzati's depiction of medical deception thus had allegorical resonance with other forms of institutional duplicity, Zarrilli suggests. The play's presentation of a character who is used to being in control of things and thinks he has agency, but discovers he has only had the *illusion* of agency and has in fact been swindled by the system, had special valence for American audiences who were becoming increasingly aware of a range of deceptive practices, including, but not limited to, issues relating to health and mortality (see Figure 3.1).

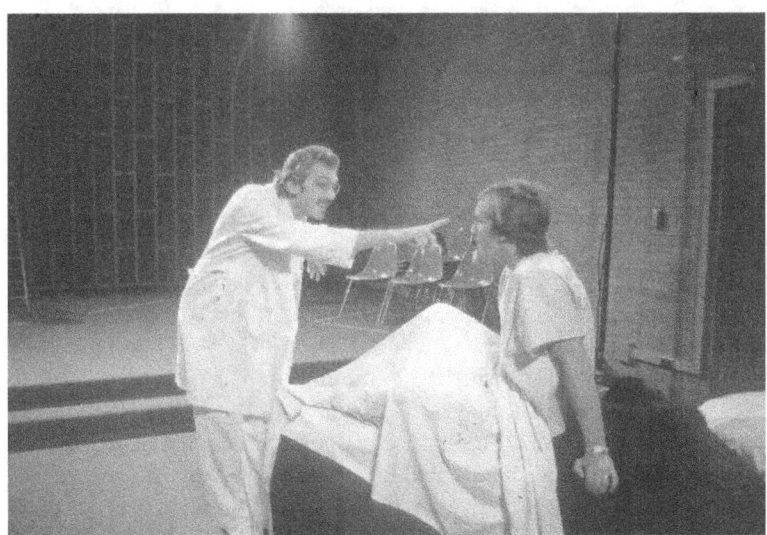

3.1 Medical misadventure in Dino Buzzati's *A Clinical Case*, produced by the Theatre of Involvement in Minneapolis, 1975

Zarrilli's suggestion that 'death was everywhere' at the time is illuminating, though it would seem to contradict the death denial thesis. However, it is possible that one could have had the sense that 'death was everywhere' despite death denial also being in effect. The 1960s brought a great number of violent deaths into American public life by way of assassinations, political protests, and the war in Vietnam. The Cold War had also stoked the possibility of nuclear Armageddon. Television beamed images of violent death in Vietnam into people's homes, although, according to Jennifer C. Malkowski, footage of death in Vietnam was actually quite rare, and was censored by the television networks: 'For all they did show, the networks were nevertheless an obstacle in screening death; still beholden to their advertisers and wary of presenting controversial material, they seemed to volunteer censorship beyond what was sometimes asked of them by the government' (2011: 35–6). This gave rise to the possibility of a skewed, racist perception of death. Robert Fulton and Greg Owen suggest that one of the 'messages' or 'motifs' about death that was conveyed, particularly for those who grew up during the Vietnam War, was that

> when [death] actually occurred, [it] occurred elsewhere and mostly to foreigners, to 'gooks', or to people alien to ourselves in appearance, language, and national ideology. With rare exception during this period of time (the Kennedy assassinations, Lee Harvey Oswald's murder), was the death of an American citizen ever presented on television. Accident and disaster victims always were shown with their bodies covered. Discreet avoidance of the corpse was the more typical practice. ... The death of ordinary citizens ... receded from view, and for a whole generation of young people, if death was seen at all, it was observed at a distance through the opaque glass of a television screen. (1988: 381)

Zarrilli's production of *A Clinical Case* and the Open Theatre's *Terminal* (next to be discussed) offered striking counter-examples to this slanted view of death. This experimental theatre-making offered a corrective to forms of media distantiation and encouraged a more open and honest discussion about mortality.

Zarrilli's production, which was mounted on a shoestring budget, made a virtue of the strange aesthetic blend of Buzzati's play, referred to in the press release as 'a mixture of sober reality and absurd incongruities'. This links to the ostensibly contradictory way in which death was putatively both pervasive and denied at the time. The production aesthetic was notably stylised in several respects. The production featured a preliminary sequence that juxtaposed the mundane reality of Corte's business life with the 'grotesque' world of the hospital personnel via contrasting music and choreography. Some of the parts were double and triple cast (e.g., two women were used to play the phantom woman/nurse figure). The set was 'presentational' and minimalist. White make-up was used for the hospital staff (Schroeder's make-up was especially exaggerated and included black eye make-up). The actors playing the mysterious female figure spoke chorally and were made-up with one half of their faces in white and the other half in black.

Zarrilli's juxtaposition of 'the realistic and the quasi-absurd or grotesque' in this production (which took place at a venue that was also used for religious services) registered Buzzati's intermingling of the ordinary and the extraordinary, the bureaucratic and the mythological, the modern and the premodern, the local and the (notionally) universal.[6] This peculiar aesthetic allowed for the possibility of perceptions about death, and death denial, to be revealed anew and changed, or at least questioned. A reviewer remarked:

> It is never entirely clear in this Kafkaesque work whether the doctors and staff of the clinic are actively bent on reducing their patients from good health to an invalid state to death, or whether their patients are gradually done in simply by incompetence and inflexible, arbitrary rules. [...] Nor is it ever obvious whether the audience is supposed mainly to laugh or worry. (Altman, 1975)

The reviewer might have intended this as a criticism, but there is merit in theatre that cultivates ambiguity and uncertainty about how to respond to difficult subject matter, such as personal mortality and its attendant social conventions. In the 1970s, American experimental theatre-makers sought to present audiences with hard truths about their lives, and their deaths, by troubling existing practices and beliefs and encouraging complex responses.

Terminal and 'the American way of death'

The Open Theater's *Terminal*, co-directed by Joseph Chaikin and Roberta Sklar, with a text prepared by Susan Yankowitz, is a collage of scenes generated through research and devising. It offers a meditation on human mortality as well as an indictment of conventional mortuary practices and stultifying modes of thinking and patterns of behaviour. Like Zarrilli's production of *A Clinical Case*, the Open Theater was in conversation with social critics writing about mortality. However, *Terminal* puts more emphasis on the funeral industry. It thereby exposes a different type of death denial and absurdity.

A 1970 feature article in *The New York Times* provides insight from Chaikin about the piece:

> '"Terminal" is about a conspiracy to make death relevant only to others, never to oneself', says Chaikin, 'a conspiracy to conceal that we will all die. If one doesn't think one will die, it's perfectly plausible to drift, to avoid making decisions, to be caught up in the momentum of making money. When we were creating "Terminal", we realized we were in it now. What we are tomorrow is what we are today'. (quoted in Croyden, 1970: 77)

Sklar offers a similar rationale in a 1971 interview in *TDR*: 'We wanted to meet with the spectator around the same issues that we had met with one another for a year – the assumption that there is a prescribed attitude toward death, that there is a prescribed way of dealing with it, which is *not* dealing with it' (Ryder Ryan and Sklar, 1971: 153). The theme of death-avoidance is not uncommon in twentieth-century American drama. Arthur Miller's *Death of a Salesman* (1949) is a case in point. Jonathan Chambers observes of Miller's play: '[The] very title reveals that death looms large in the play. And yet that death, though ever present, is also consistently denied. Time and again, when the discussion turns to mortality and the prospect of death, it is dismissed as something unspeakable that retards the march of progress and, therefore, is of no concern for the living' (2010: 170).

Sklar has stated that one of the things the company wanted to explore in *Terminal* was the 'subjective aspects of the American way of death' (Ryder Ryan and Sklar, 1971: 154). The phrase 'the American way of death' is the title of a best-selling book by Jessica Mitford, published in 1963, and part of the death awareness movement. Mitford's book offers a pungent critique of American attitudes and practices in relation to death and dying. Mitford, an English writer and journalist, lambastes the American funeral industry, revealing it to be typically extortionist, exploitative, obscene, and rooted in an ideology of death denial. (Mitford's cultural background likely informed her outlook.) She accuses those in charge of this industry of perpetrating 'a huge, macabre and expensive practical joke on the American public' by providing unnecessary and dubious services, including deluxe caskets, tailored burial clothing, embalming, cosmetic work on the deceased, floral displays, and ornate burial grounds (1980 [1963]: 15–16). The 'funeral men', as she calls them, 'have constructed their own grotesque cloud-cuckoo-land where the trappings of Gracious Living are transformed, as in a nightmare, into the trappings of Gracious Dying' (*ibid.*: 16). The funeral has become an exorbitant and gaudy piece of theatre, Mitford suggests, with the funeral director (formerly known as the undertaker) running the show and making a killing in the process. Mitford, in arch fashion, writes:

> If the undertaker is the stage manager of the fabulous production that is the modern American funeral, the stellar role is reserved for the occupant of the open casket. The decor, the stagehands, the supporting cast are all arranged for the most advantageous display of the deceased, without which the rest of the paraphernalia would lose its point – *Hamlet* without the Prince of Denmark. It is to this end that a fantastic array of costly merchandise and services is pyramided to dazzle the mourners and facilitate the plunder of the next of kin. (*ibid.*: 19)

In Mitford's view, the American funeral industry was built upon a web of expensive lies, circumlocutions, and euphemisms, 'dressing up' death to make it seem less frightening, and supposedly easier to bear, for the living. This is a dodge, Mitford suggests, and a racket. The language used by industry practitioners tellingly avoids words that are too frank, including, daftly, the word 'death' itself. Here Mitford paraphrases *Basic Principles of Funeral Service*, an instructional book written by Victor Landig, a funeral director, in 1956:

> [Landig] enjoins the reader to avoid using the word 'death' as much as possible, even sometimes when such avoidance may seem impossible; for example, a death certificate should be referred to as a 'vital statistics form'. One should speak not of the 'job' but rather of the 'call'. We do not 'haul' a dead person, we 'transfer' or 'remove' him – and we do this in a 'service car', not a 'body car'. We 'open and close' his grave rather than dig and fill it, an in it we 'inter' rather than bury him. This is done, not in a graveyard or cemetery but rather in a 'memorial park'. The deceased is beautified, not with makeup, but with 'cosmetics'. Anyway, he didn't die, he 'expired'. (*ibid.*: 78)

This discourse, and its associated practices, allowed for a culture of death denial to thrive and become profitable. The reality of death was circumvented and replaced by a strange unreality in which the dead were made to star in an elaborate and arguably misguided fantasy.

Mitford takes aim at the practices of embalming and 'beautifying' the deceased to make the dead body seem more 'natural' and lifelike.[7] She notes that no law requires embalming, as is assumed to be the case, 'no religious doctrine commends it, nor is it dictated by considerations of health, sanitation, or even of personal daintiness' (*ibid.*: 67). Nonetheless it had become *de rigueur*, although the actual process was not well understood; indeed, there is still ignorance today about what is done to a corpse to make it more 'presentable' for an open-casket display. Mitford gives a pithy overview: 'Alas, poor Yorick! How surprised he would be to see how his counterpart of today is whisked off to a funeral parlor and is in short order sprayed, sliced, pierced, pickled, trussed, trimmed, creamed, waxed, painted, rouged and neatly dressed – transformed from a common corpse into a Beautiful Memory Picture' (*ibid.*: 66–7).

The embalming process is discussed and acted out in a section of *Terminal*. A character called 'the Embalmer' explains the procedure to the audience, while an ensemble member '*illustrates the process in mime and gesture*' using the body of another ensemble member, who lies inert (Yankowitz, 1974: 50). There is no obfuscation here. The facts of embalming are laid bare. The embalmer explains how a tube is inserted into the body to drain the blood, and another tube inserted to replace the blood with embalming fluid. He states how an incision is made in the central abdomen to remove the vital organs, which are replaced by cotton batting, like that used in upholstery, to retain the body's original dimensions. He then reports on the 'cosmetological' procedures:

> Lip slip occurs as fluids drain from the upper lip, causing it to recede, forming a sneer. This is unsightly for those viewing the body, so we stitch the lips together into a more attractive expression. We cut out swollen facial tissue and fill the sunken cheeks by injecting massage creams into them. We then apply conventional makeup, such as rouge and lipstick, to create a natural, lifelike glow. (*ibid.*)

This is an awful lot of work – an awful lot of unpleasant, violent, intrusive work, one might say – to mask the reality of what a recent corpse looks like and make it better resemble the body of a living person. It is something of an absurdity, if not an obscenity (although it can also be a political act, as in the case of Lenin's embalming).

In a version of *Terminal* featured on the programme 'Camera Three' on CBS (an American television network) in 1970 an embalming scene is presented in the manner of a TV news report. The Embalmer adopts the persona of a news reporter and delivers his piece to camera, while behind him team members 'work' on two prostrate bodies. Curiously, and rather disturbingly, one of the supposedly dead bodies shows signs of life and vocalises his distress at the mimed actions that are being done to him. This has the effect of highlighting the intrusiveness of the process and making the physical interventions more viscerally apparent for the viewer, who is thus able to imagine what the process might feel like – even though such a thing could not take place. Ironically, as Mitford notes, one of the arguments made for embalming was that it protected against the possibility of accidentally being buried alive. She glibly remarks: 'once the blood is removed, chances of live burial are indeed remote' (1980 [1963]: 70). *Terminal* undercuts this assurance with its presentation of a live '*victim*' of embalming, who '*screams and writhes*' before growing silent once his mouth is sewn shut (Yankowitz, 1974: 62). Like Buzzati's play, *Terminal* intermixed reality with macabre fantasy to startle audience members and encourage them to rethink what they knew, how they lived their lives, and what they wanted to have happen at the end.

Terminal's aesthetic aided its critique of a culture of death denial. The musical instruments used were basic, taking the form of harmonicas, tambourines, drums, and sticks. The performers were costumed in simple white garments and wore no make-up, jewellery, or shoes (unlike the cosmetic procedures imposed on the deceased, demonstrated in the piece). Per the stage directions, lights were to be hung in plain view of the audience; nothing was to be hidden or disguised, including props, though everything could be repurposed. Blackouts were used to '*delineate distinct thematic areas, but also [to] provide a stylistic counterpart to the cycle of life and death, presence and absence*' (*ibid.*: 41). *Terminal*'s down-to-earth, minimalist aesthetic offset the inauthenticity and gimmickry of the 'American way of death' and revealed its patent absurdity.

Although one would not classify it as absurdist theatre, *Terminal* nevertheless contains elements that are arguably absurd. One scene, entitled 'The Runner Who Never Gets Started', features a runner who '*runs with the top half of his body only*' (*ibid.*: 53). This person is going nowhere fast. In 'The Initiation', a 'new arrival' is approached by ensemble members and either slapped or embraced. '*There is no apparent reason for their choice*', the stage directions state (*ibid.*: 58). Disequilibrium and estrangement are provoked in this scene, which resembles human (de-)programming. Sklar explains:

> 'The Initiation' is something that I think of as a slap-kiss scene. [...] As he becomes accustomed to the slap, he receives an embrace. Once he becomes accustomed to the embrace, he receives a slap, so that this way of emotional relating between people becomes completely arbitrary and one equals the other. Neither of these experiences can be looked forward to by the person. The slap and the kiss are equal. (Ryder Ryan and Sklar, 1971: 152-3)

Relatedly, a process of indoctrination is dramatised in 'The Interview', a Pinteresque scene in which the new arrival is interrogated about whether he liked 'it' (whatever 'it' is) and why he liked it; he is hit until he delivers the correct response. The scene concludes as follows:

> TEAM MEMBER: Why did you like it?
> NEW ARRIVAL: I don't know. (*He is hit.*)
> TEAM MEMBER: Why did you like it?
> NEW ARRIVAL: I liked it because it was different. (*He is hit.*)
> TEAM MEMBER: Why did you like it?
> NEW ARRIVAL: I liked it because I never ... (*He is hit.*)
> TEAM MEMBER: Why did you like it?
> NEW ARRIVAL: I liked it because it was necessary to like it. (Yankowitz, 1974: 60)

The denial that is played out here, and in other parts of *Terminal*, is of independent, critical thinking in lieu of group-think, ideology (or what William Blake calls the 'mind-forg'd manacles'), and habitual disciplining-and-punishing (1992 [1794]: 42). In one section, the spirit of a prisoner about to be executed declares that he is '[free] in the head' and '[full] of imagination', like when he was a child (Yankowitz, 1974: 61). 'My prison's made of steel', he tells his warden; 'yours is in your head' (*ibid.*). In another section, the spirit of a dead soldier marches on the spot, saluting, and repeats variations of a deadly mantra:

> Said yes
> Said yes
> Yessir
> Said yes
> And dead because I said yes
> and dead because you said yes
> and dead because I said yes
> and dead because you said yes
>
> (*ibid.*: 55)

The US was still embroiled in the Vietnam War at the time. Critic John Lahr, writing in *The Village Voice* in 1970, juxtaposes *Terminal* with a riot he witnessed in Cambridge, Massachusetts, where Harvard students took to the streets to protest against the Vietnam War and vent their anger:

> The riot was a living tableau of how deeply the society has been touched by death and how numb it is to life. ... The rioters were prankish, never confronting death. The actors [in *Terminal*] held the experience in front of

their audiences, making them watch their own evasions. ... By recreating the agonizing simplicity of man's final moments and the hypocrisy of his embalming, 'Terminal' sends the audience away with a passion for preserving the gift of life: its gorgeous variety, its possibilities, its essential sweetness. 'Terminal' makes you conscious of death and the limits of time, that you realize the necessity of taking your life into your own hands. (1970: 43)

This review suggests that *Terminal* allowed audience members to reframe current events along with their personal experiences and perceptions by defamiliarising modes of being.

The themes of mental incarceration, force of habit, and spiritual death-in-life are recapitulated in the final scene, entitled 'The Dying Imagine Their Judgment'. A speaker, sitting atop a ladder, drones into a megaphone a series of verdicts upon those around her, who are locked into various patterns of action, such as running in place, forming a human chain that crawls upon the floor, and being carted around in awkward poses. The judge intones in a pitiless monotone:

> You moved from the house to the office, from the office to the house; from sleep to waking and from waking to sleep; you moved from yesterday to today, from today to tomorrow—and you will repeat that movement for eternity. ... You neither faced your death nor participated in your life, but straddled the line between one place and the other, longing for both. The judgment of your life is your life. (Yankowitz, 1974: 64–5)

In the broadcast version of *Terminal*, the judge's speech gradually slurs and loses articulative clarity, becoming a stream of nearly unintelligible phonemes, while beneath her a human chain slithers through her ladder, enacting a '*seemingly endless passage*' that evokes the image of a birth canal (*ibid.*: 65). It is an arresting, disturbing, scene, reminiscent of Hieronymus Bosch's medieval depiction of *The Last Judgement* (see Figure 3.2).

Terminal aims to interconnect life and death, reintegrating the latter into the former rather than denying death and keeping it at bay in thought, word, and deed. As stated in the text: '*The living are also the dying; the dying are potentially the dead. And the dead will become living matter*' (*ibid.*: 43). In the piece, the living 'call up' spirits of the dead and let them possess their bodies and speak through them. The piece therefore posits posthumous spiritual existence, even if the spirits invoked repeat the concerns and outlooks they had when they were still alive (a common feature of spiritualist discourse, as discussed in Chapter 1). Arguably, *Terminal*'s presentation of spirits makes it easier to accept one's own mortality. The piece suggests that death is not the absolute end of one's

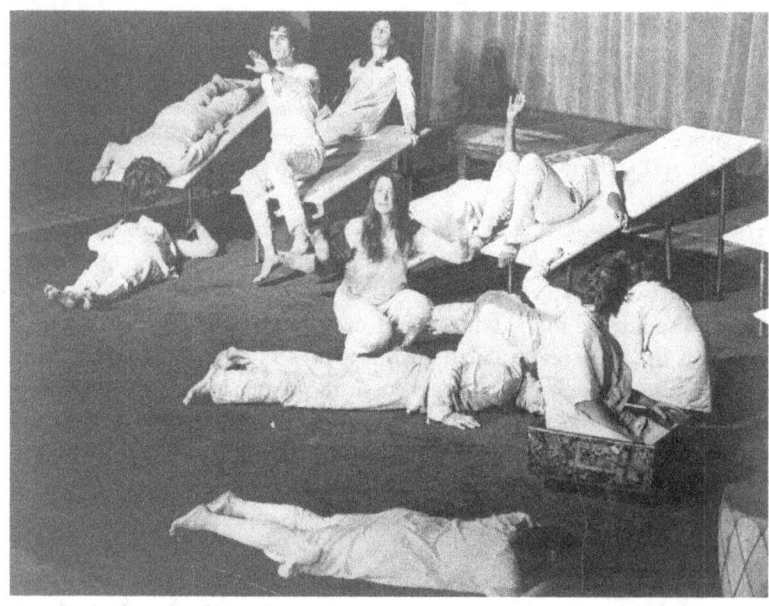

3.2 The dying imagine their final judgement in the Open Theater's *Terminal*, c. 1971

existence. This may be wishful thinking, or a different form of denial, perhaps. Metaphysical implications notwithstanding, the invocation of spirits in *Terminal* has the effect of figuratively bringing the dead into the presence of the living rather than sequestering them or forgetting them entirely (recalling Yeats's *Purgatory*). The performers enact a 'dance on the graves of the dead' as part of the ceremony of spirit invocation and possession. This dance, which is accompanied by repetitive drumbeats and percussive wood-block sounds, conjures a ritualistic atmosphere. It connotes a hybrid and eclectic assortment of diasporic ritual practices, such as shamanism and Vodun.[8] There is a suggestion of primitivism and/or cultural appropriation about this sequence, heightened in the television broadcast by the fact that the ensemble is seemingly all-white, yet the lack of cultural specificity in relation to what is being performed clouds these charges.[9] Even still, the sequence recalls a problematic history of percussive primitivism in the theatrical avant-garde, connected to dada and expressionism in particular (see Curtin, 2013).

The ritualistic dance is part of a recurrent emphasis in this piece on the physicality and corporeal reality of the performers' bodies. Early in the dance, the performers flop over at the waist and stay hanging; they subsequently become erect, open out, and take wide stances and posturing movements, making firm contact with the ground. An earlier section of *Terminal* parallels the biological processes of eating and defecating by simulating these actions; a subsequent section on breathing draws attention to this vital process by demonstrating some of its effects: '*Two actors walk forward, breathing slowly and rhythmically. One actor gasps in counterpoint to their breath. Another actor makes a sucking sound; his hands pulsate, feeling the air*' (Yankowitz, 1974: 46). Throughout the piece the performers make music in the form of '*pure sound and rhythm*', as the stage directions state: '*Some music is simply an extension of the human voice. The actors become instruments ... Some music is an extension of the human body. Hands and feet become instruments for eliciting music from surfaces – floors, walls, beds*' (*ibid.*: 43). Terminal juxtaposed the artifice and chicanery of mortuary practices, along with the implied spiritual bankruptcy of American society, with the 'authenticity' and physical rootedness of the performers, who were connected to each other and by extension to the audience.

Chaikin prioritised 'presence' as a fundamental element of (live) theatre. He writes: 'The attempts to video tape or film the Open Theatre works have all failed to transmit any part of the essential experience, which is the vibrating breathing actor, breathing in the breathing universe. The light of the eyes. The conscious body of the actor moving in the given space. The particular voice creating a living contact with the audience' (quoted in Malpede, 1974: 33). Dorinda Hulton, writing about ensemble exercises developed by the Open Theatre, suggests that a 'sense' of presence can emerge 'that belongs to the whole group and co-exists between them', possibly when a sense of self is absent (2010: 220). Unlike the blinkered, individualistic, nine-to-five work mentalities mentioned in this piece, the Open Theatre performers suggested the possibility of a less self-centred, and more spiritually aware, mode of being. They presented themselves as people who were 'temporarily abled' and cognisant of their mortality.[10]

When Sklar was asked if the actors in *Terminal* had changed their ideas about death after performing the piece, she responded:

> I can't answer for the actors, of course, but I can for myself. It is very difficult in the culture in which we live to find a form to accept death, to accept that I will die, and that every person I know will die. Difficult is an absurd word. It feels impossible. It feels like a completely impenetrable reality. I don't feel that working on a piece about death can counterbalance the weight of my culture. I recognize more clearly now that I've been in a process of change from the moment I was born. It's made me change my relationship to the present. (Ryder Ryan and Sklar, 1971: 153)

The existential challenge of recognising and accepting one's own mortality, and the absurdity that can result from endeavouring to circumvent this process, provides great material for drama. Ionesco, whose work I will now address, latched on to this theme and exaggerated the absurdity factor. In doing so, he contributed to the potential cultivation of more critically astute, mortality-conscious performers and audience members.

Conscious dying: *Exit the King*

Ionesco's *Exit the King* offers a depiction of death denial gradually transformed into begrudging death acceptance. The play features Ionesco's Everyman character, Berenger, as the titular king of an unnamed country. Berenger is several hundred years old and is finally dying, though he is loath to admit this. His kingdom crumbles around him as he becomes increasingly weak and powerless, until he finally expires. The play tracks the fluctuation of his mental attitude as he gradually comes to terms with his impending extinction.

Unlike the previous examples discussed in this chapter, *Exit the King* is not concerned with how death denial is manifested in specific domains (e.g., the hospital) or practices (e.g., embalming). The play is not obviously culturally specific. Instead, it is focused on the fundamental existential challenge – a challenge supposedly unique to humans – of accepting one's own mortality, not just in an abstract sense as inevitable biological destiny deferred into some unknowable point in the future, but in the immediate present. This means dispensing with the psychological mechanisms of avoidance that can help us to get on with the business of living in the normal course of events.

In staging dying and articulating common hopes and fears about this process, the play relates to popular and academic discourse of the time concerning death and dying. Rosette C. Lamont interprets Berenger's grappling with his mortality in the light of Elisabeth Kübler-Ross's famous study *On Death and Dying*, published in 1969 (seven years after the premiere of Ionesco's play), in which the Swiss psychiatrist outlines her theory of the five stages of grief typically experienced by the bereaved (1993: 149–62) (see the Introduction). Lamont observes how Berenger can be thought to travel through these stages as he acts out familiar psychological responses to the reality of his own imminent demise. Ionesco's play thereby notionally dramatises what Kübler-Ross would later theorise.

In the following analysis, I will focus not on the psychological trajectory of denial to acceptance but on the way Ionesco dramatises a dying consciousness, making this multifaceted, potentially chaotic, state of being into a shared theatrical experience, thus raising awareness about death and dying (like Kübler-Ross, Mitford, Becker, *et al.*).

Berenger, having practised death denial for centuries, and initially happy to continue in this vein (he says he will possibly die in a few hundred years, when he has the time, or when he makes up his mind), is forced to accept that his time is up and that he will soon be dead. Consequently, Berenger – and by extension, the audience – is made to experience his dying in an unflinching, protracted manner. Berenger does not simply 'slip away' in a drug-induced fog, even if he does ultimately transform into '*a kind of mist*' (Ionesco, 1994: 95). Queen Marie, Berenger's second wife, opines that it would be better if he were unaware of his own dying. Queen Marguerite, his first wife, does not agree.

> MARIE: No, don't tell him. It's better if he doesn't notice anything.
> MARGUERITE: ... and goes out like a light? That's impossible. (*ibid.*: 12)

In contradistinction to the modern habit of dying unconsciously – dying with little-to-no awareness of the fact (as noted unfavourably by Ariès) – Berenger dies *consciously* and experiences what it means to self-dissipate, while gaining new insight into what it means to be alive.

One of Ionesco's dramatic conceits is that Berenger's failing health is made manifest in the world around him, which is attuned to his general disposition and reacts in kind. There is evidently something rotten in the state of Berenger, and it is Berenger himself. Marguerite remarks: 'His palace is crumbling. His fields lie fallow. His mountains are sinking. The sea has broken the dykes and flooded the country' (*ibid.*: 14). We are led to believe that the king was formerly able to direct the natural world to do his bidding, as in a fairy tale, but now, although he banished the clouds and ordered the sun to come out, this has not happened. Berenger has apparently lost the ability to make things happen by decree; his performative utterances become failed speech acts and ring hollow.

As Berenger nears death the frantic beatings of his heart '*shake the house*' and cause further cracks in the wall to appear (81). Marie suggests her existence is dependent on Berenger: 'I'm nothing if he forgets me' she says, ironically signalling her limited function in the play (*ibid.*). Sure enough, as Berenger begins to move '*like a sleepwalker*' and loses his sense of sight, Marie suddenly disappears '*by some theatrical trick*' (84). Other characters disappear in turn, or make their exit, as Berenger's self-perception, connection with his personal past, and relationship to the world around him becomes increasingly hazy, like that of an infant. 'I no longer know what was there all around me', Berenger says. 'I know I was part of the world, and this world was all around me. I know it was me and what else was there, what else?' (89).

Marguerite remains with Berenger to the end and serves as a psychopomp, or a death doula, helping him out of the world. As the play nears its conclusion, Marguerite figuratively unburdens Berenger from his corporeal connections and earthly ties, cutting the space around him '*as though she had a pair of invisible scissors in her hand*', removing an invisible ball and chain from his feet, taking an imaginary sack from his shoulders, and so forth (*ibid.*). Marguerite oversees Berenger's psychophysical dissolution, guiding him along an imaginative journey that doubles his physical relocation to the throne, where he will finally rest.

> Smell that flower for the last time, then throw it away! Forget its perfume! … Give me your legs! The right one! Now the left! … Give me a finger! Now give me two fingers… three, four … five … all ten fingers! Now let me have your right arm! Your left arm! Your chest, your two shoulders and your stomach!
> *The KING is motionless, still as a statue.*
> There you are, you see! Now you've lost the power of speech, there's no need for your heart to beat, no more need to breathe. (93–5)

Ionesco ends the play with a striking scenographic *coup de théâtre*, instructing that everything, including Berenger, should become insubstantial and slowly disappear. '*This disappearance of the windows, the doors and the walls, the KING and the throne must be very marked, but happen slowly and gradually. The KING sitting on his throne should remain visible for a short time before fading into a kind of mist*' (95).

As Berenger has not prepared for death, his dying is arduous and panicked, but he still manages to achieve newfound insight into his existence and the world around him, as indicated in his exchanges with Juliette, his nurse/servant, late in the play:

> KING: You take the same road twice a day! With the sky above you! You can gaze at it twice a day. And you breathe the air. You never realize you're breathing. You must think about it. Remember! I'm sure it never crosses your mind. It's a miracle! (63)

Berenger imagines that *his* subjectivity is universal, ignoring his gender and other identity markers, such as his elevated social position and ethnicity (which is unspecified). As the dramatic world is effectively constructed around him, the play tacitly works to support a male-authored fantasy of subjective universalism. Although the play reinforces masculinist, heteronormative, monarchical, and ableist forms of privilege, Ionesco still tries to draw attention to common aspects of human experience. Comments Ionesco made in a 1963 *Sunday Times* article echo Berenger's last-minute appreciation of the wonder of being alive:

> [Sometimes] I look at the world as if I'd never seen it before, and when this happens I am simply overwhelmed at the strangeness and the wonder and the marvellousness of it all. ... It's when we behave as if it were the normal unsurprising thing that the petty anxieties of life take over and prevent us from getting back to our original amazement at the fact of being alive. We've got to get back to the point at which we look at a chair and don't know what it is. We've got to look at a wall and not know that it's a wall – and suddenly say 'Why, that's a wall'. (quoted in Anon., 1963b: 22)

Exit the King defamiliarises lived experience by drawing attention to Berenger's conscious dying. The phantasmagorical world of the play can thus be understood as the product of a dying brain that is processing biological breakdown.

Evan Thompson, a philosopher, has written about the phenomenon of conscious dying, a set of meditation practices that derive from Indian and Tibetan yogic traditions that enable practitioners to prepare for death and die with enhanced self-awareness and clarity. He explains:

> Tibetan yogis visualize or rehearse in imagination the entire dissolution process as a way to familiarize themselves with dying and to gain control over the mental states that arise in the course of dying. ... The meditation practice is awakening to the dissolution process and releasing what you take to be your identity into a vast spaciousness and radiance. You release your bodily form, your feelings, your perceptions, your inclination or mental tendencies, and ultimately your consciousness. Through this practice you familiarize yourself with the experience of dying and train yourself to transform it into an experience of enlightenment and liberation. (2014: 279–80)

Thompson gives an account of his participation in the 'Being with Dying' training programme at the Upaya Institute and Zen Center in Santa Fe, New Mexico, led by anthropologist and Zen teacher Joan Halifax (or Roshi Joan). He discusses being guided through a meditation called 'Dissolution of the Body' in which he approximated a dying process:

> I feel heavy, too heavy for the zendo floor to support me, as if I'm going to fall through it into a void. Vertigo takes over and I open my eyes. The room

looks unstable, as if it were about to spin and thrown me into the air, and I want to sit up. ... Your sight is dim, Roshi Joan says. It's difficult to open and close your eyes. Your sensory grip on the world is loosening. As your body slips away, the outside slips away too. You sink deeper and deeper into a blurry mental state. Whatever visions you see are like blue mirages. ... Behind your eyes you see a vision of swirling smoke and a haziness that dissolves all differences. (*ibid.*: 280–1)

Thompson's account illuminates Ionesco's play, which also moves towards a state of dissolution through Berenger's transformation into '*a kind of mist*' after a gradual breakdown of his body and sense of self. Interestingly, *The Tibetan Book of the Dead* was reportedly one of Ionesco's favourite books on the process of dying, so the similarity may not be coincidental (Lamont, 1993: 10). Thompson uses the term 'ritualized phenomenology' to describe the Tibetan Buddhist account of death, saying that the dissolution meditation provides 'a script for enacting certain states of consciousness as one dies' and is 'more performative and prescriptive than descriptive'. He suggests that it 'doesn't so much present a phenomenological description of death as rehearse and enact a phenomenology of death as a ritual performance' (2014: 291). *Exit the King* operates in a similar manner. Marguerite guides Berenger along his final journey just as Halifax guided Thompson in this instance. Moreover, in performance, Berenger can serve as a proxy for the audience, who can vicariously experience a dying process through him, possibly attuning to the actor's psychophysical state – as well as perhaps learning a salutary lesson about the pitfalls of engaging in death denial until the bitter end.

The first British production of this play, which featured Alec Guinness as Berenger, offers insight into its capacity to encourage audiences to contemplate (their) mortality. In 1963 the English Stage Company presented the play in Newcastle's Theatre Royal, the Royal Lyceum Theatre in Edinburgh (as part of the Edinburgh Festival), and at the Royal Court in London, where it had a seven-week run. The critical commentary indicates that several critics were impressed by Ionesco's meditation on death and dying, noting, in some instances, how it affected them personally. In a programme for the BBC's External Services, critic George Melly remarked that 'the bit where suddenly the ferocious Queen says "don't be so sentimental" I was – tears were streaming down my face because it all seemed perfectly relevant and suddenly I thought she's dead right you know'. Ian Rodger, in the same conversation, observed: 'I thought the amazing thing that Ionesco was doing here – if a priest is preparing a man for death – this is a relatively difficult thing to do in itself – but here was Ionesco as I realise, preparing a whole audience to accept death'.[11] A reviewer in the *Newcastle Journal* noted: 'It is a wise and witty comedy that Ionesco has written, but in some respects it is a terrifying one. We can laugh at the feeble agonies of King Berenger as his kingdom disintegrates around him only because we adopt the same blind attitudes and refuse to face the inevitable' (Anon, 1963a). Christopher Small, writing in the *Glasgow Herald*, also picked up on how the play provoked uncomfortable responses because of the way in which it exposes the attitude of death denial:

> [Faced] with death, even with it rammed down our throats, we just can't, won't believe in it. … We laugh at first, a lot, even at the grimmest graveyard observations – it is all so absurd one needn't take it seriously. But we are also uneasy, so that when a joke is handed to us … nobody laughs at all. … [And] so by the end, when all the protests are silent and the victim is at last resigned to what must happen, we are as silent as we might be round an actual death bed. (1963)

Critics attending the performances at the Royal Court also commented on how sounds from outside the theatre affected the audience's experience. The reviewer for the *Eastern Press* noted that 'the occasional rumble of a train in the hades of London's Underground beneath the theatre acts as a suitable auditory backcloth. For this is an inexorable play which will evoke grief in many minds' (Anon, 1963c). The sonic intrusion of the Underground, unexpectedly apropos, literally underscored the resonance of this play, which, 'while set in some historical-looking kingdom […] is a most contemporary play', noted Ronald Mayor in *The Scotsman* (1963). Critics registered that Ionesco's play, which in some ways was out of time (as indicated by Berenger's extended life span), was also timely and spoke to concerns that some people prefer not to countenance.

Ionesco's play is noteworthy not just because it shows Berenger's transition from death denial to death acceptance (this is plain), but because it theatricalises his dying and makes this experience imaginatively available for audience members. The play thus works to counteract or diminish death denial. Like the other dramatists and theatre-makers discussed in this chapter, Ionesco brings personal mortality from the subconscious to the conscious mind, or, to use a theatrical metaphor, he takes it out from the wings and brings it onto the stage for all to see and hear, thereby making the seemingly unmentionable mentionable.

The elephant in the room: *Amédée*

Ionesco's earlier play *Amédée, or How to Get Rid of It* presents death, and arguably death denial, in a comical-grotesque fashion, offering another intriguing variation on this theme. The play obviously features death, but it is not obviously about death denial. However, this is the reading I will offer here. In this play, a middle-aged married couple, Amédée and Madeleine Buccinioni, furtively coexist with a fantastical, ever-expanding corpse that has been lodged in their home for fifteen years, unbeknownst to the outside world. The corpse has been growing progressively larger and now threatens to take over their home. Moreover, it is ostensibly prompting the growth of poisonous mushrooms that are popping up in every room. Amédée and his wife are obsessed and perplexed by the fantastical corpse, but they don't know what to do about it (or 'how to get rid of it'). The corpse impinges on their lives and forces them to adapt to its presence, challenging their existence with its alterity, its otherness.

The larger-than-life corpse, which is the centrepiece of the play, has engaged the attention of critics, who have deliberated over its potential meaning. Linda Davis Kyle suggests the corpse could 'represent Amédée's dead creative energy – both as an artist and a lover' (Amédée is a frustrated playwright) (1976: 284). Willis D. Jacobs suggests 'it is the corpse of their dead love' (meaning Amédée and Madeleine): 'Their love may have been alive and warm once. Now we see literally its cadaver' (1972: 33). Martin Esslin observes that the corpse is a poetic image with multiple potential meanings: '[One] can say that the corpse *might* evoke the growing power of past mistakes or past guilt, perhaps the waning of love or the death of affection – some evil in any case that festers and grows worse with time. The image can stand for any and all of these ideas, and its ability to embrace them all gives it the poetic power it undoubtedly possesses' (1965: 10–11). The corpse in this play clearly has symbolical potential, and it does seem misguided to try to pin it down to any one thing. Like the infamous sound of the breaking string in Anton Chekhov's *The Cherry Orchard* (1904), its open-ended signification is part of its intrigue. However, we should not overlook the fact that, while it may stand for something else, it also 'stands for itself' – in that it is first and foremost a corpse (albeit a most peculiar corpse), and thus a marker of death.

Strangely, this more literal designation has not been the subject of much discussion in the critical literature on the play. Nevertheless,

Amédée, like *Exit the King* and the other pieces discussed in this chapter, illuminates another facet of modern death denial. In this case, death, in the form of a fantastical corpse, is ostensibly preventing (or denying) these characters from leading 'normal' lives – or rather, their inability to extricate themselves from the unruly corpse has given rise to their unhappy circumstances, which constitute a kind of death-in-life. Here, denial relates not to personal mortality (i.e., the death of the self), as in *Exit the King*, or to the social institutions or practices that promote cultural death denial, as in *A Clinical Case* and *Terminal*, but instead to the problems and dilemmas presented by the death of another, especially if this death is kept secret and not fully acknowledged (cf. Ariès's comments about modern repression of mourning, quoted earlier).

The English-language metaphorical idiom 'the elephant in the room', which refers to something that is glaringly obvious but not discussed for some reason, is also associated with death and dying. For example, Terry Kettering's poem 'The Elephant in the Room' (*c.* 1989), which has been reproduced in texts on bereavement, deploys the metaphor to good effect.[12] The poem ends with these lines:

> Oh, please say her name.
> Oh, please, say 'Barbara' again.
> Oh, please, let's talk about the elephant in the room.
> For if we talk about her death,
> Perhaps we can talk about her life?
> Can I say 'Barbara' to you and not have you look away?
> For if I cannot, then you are leaving me
> Alone …
> In a room …
> With an elephant.
> (Wilson and Wilson, 2004: 69–70)

In *Amédée* the proverbial elephant in the room is an actual corpse that has effectively taken over the Buccinionis' home. Amédée and Madeleine are not afraid to speak to *one another* about their 'elephant' (indeed, they spend most of the play conversing on this topic) but they are totally fearful about anyone else finding out. Their inability to 'admit' the presence of the dead body to the wider world has turned them into social recluses who struggle to maintain a status quo with the increasingly unmanageable object or entity. This frazzles their nerves.

The sociologist Eviatar Zerubavel, writing about silence and denial in everyday life, notes that conspiracies of silence can undermine group solidarity 'by impeding the development of honest, trusting relations that presuppose open communication', often making these relations dysfunctional (2006: 85). He notes that metaphorical elephants 'usually grow with time, their figurative size hence reflecting their age. The longer we pretend not to notice them, the larger they loom in our minds. … Given this, how long can people keep pretending not to notice the elephant in the room before it becomes too large (and its presence, therefore, too obvious) to credibly ignore?' (*ibid.*: 59). Ionesco's play engages this question by staging a metaphorical elephant in the form of a dead body that cannot simply be ignored, and whose presence becomes increasingly problematic.

The Buccinionis' world revolves around the corpse – tending to it, trying to 'manage' it, paying attention to it, discussing potential plans of action, and bickering over it. They berate one another for spending too much time with the dead body and becoming entranced by it. The couple have given over their lives to maintaining their deadly secret. They have apparently been shut up in their home, with their blinds lowered and receiving no visitors, since the corpse first took up residence fifteen years ago. Madeleine is forthright about decrying their situation. 'I don't call this living! No, no, it's unbearable', she says. '[It's] not natural, it's inhuman, that's what it is, inhuman, completely inhuman!' (Ionesco, 1965 [1956]: 53).

The Buccinionis' morbid fascination with the uncanny corpse, and their dread that it might be revealed, is understandable given its peculiar properties. Unlike regular corpses, which decompose, this corpse behaves quite differently and has a deathly life of its own. Light apparently shines like beacons from its green eyes. It also makes musical sounds – singing, even though its mouth is sewn shut. Perhaps the most glaring oddity of this corpse, though, is its posthumous growth and ageing. The corpse has grown a great white beard, although the couple estimate its current age at thirty-five. Not only do its nails continue to grow, its whole body does. Amédée diagnoses a case of 'geometrical progression', the 'incurable disease of the dead', though Madeleine suggests it is growing due to vindictiveness and spite (*ibid.*: 52, 43). While the corpse was formerly contained in their bedroom (offstage), it branches out as the play proceeds, making cracking sounds in the process. It refuses to stay out of sight or out of mind. A growth spurt causes its head to smash through the bedroom window, to the couple's alarm; it subsequently encroaches on the Buccinionis' living space, as indicated in a memorable stage direction: '*Amédée and Madeleine, dumb with terror, watch two enormous feet slide slowly through the open door and advance about eighteen inches onto the stage*' (52).

In the first British production of this play, at the Arts Theatre in Cambridge in 1957, directed by Peter Zadek, the problem of the expanding corpse was reportedly solved 'by constructing it with chicken wire so that it could bend and be stored in the wings before being moved more and more into view' (Downes, 1994). In 2017 the Birmingham Repertory Theatre Company staged the play in a production directed by Roxanna Silbert. This production adopted a similar approach to staging the corpse, which took the form of a giant prop body that entered feet-first and then gradually advanced onto the stage. Although the corpse is supposedly a quasi-living thing – growing in death – the way it was staged in this production made it seem as if it was already giant-sized (which it was) and being periodically pushed onto the stage (which, of course, it also was – by some unseen stage-hand). Watching this in the audience, one is more likely to register the corpse as being *pushed into view* rather than *internally expanding*. I suspect this is how the corpse in this play is often staged: a ready-made, oversized puppet-body is incrementally pushed into view. This has symbolic significance over and above the fantastical explanation provided in the play for the corpse's behaviour. In distinction to classical dramaturgy, in which death occurs offstage and the corpse is typically not represented, Ionesco pushes a dead body onto the stage, making it grossly apparent.

By the second act, the corpse has begun to squeeze out Amédée and Madeleine, its feet relentlessly advancing like an occupying force. The gradual domination of the stage by a pair of giant, upturned prop-feet dwarves the actors and makes them resemble Lilliputians (see Figure 3.3). The situation also resembles the surrealist paintings of René Magritte in which a small item such as an apple (in *The Listening Room*, 1952) or a rose (in *The Tomb of the Wrestlers*, 1961) is seemingly blown out of ordinary proportions by being depicted super-sized, occupying nearly all the space in a room, thus distorting perspective and making the familiar strange. At the end of Act 2, the corpse is slid out of a window in full view of the audience. Madeleine acts as a kind of reverse-midwife, assisting Amédée's labour. In the Birmingham Rep production, this sequence had overtones of orgasm crossed with childbirth, as Josie Lawrence (as Madeleine) and Trevor Fox (as Amédée) ejected the body. Once the body was clear, after much heaving and yelling, Lawrence lit a cigarette in a post-coital fashion, fusing *eros* and *thanatos*.

The theatrical presentation of an inanimate object that is supposedly dead and yet shows signs of life through growth and movement, and emits *'green glow'* and *'strange music'*, is an audio-visual and kinetic oddity that defamiliarises the object in question (Ionesco, 1965 [1956]: 79). This corpse is obviously unlike any that one might encounter in

3.3 A scene from a 1957 production of Eugène Ionesco's *Amédée* by Théâtre d'Aujourd'hui at the Alliance Française, Paris. The characters grapple with the giant shoes of their oversized and ever-expanding corpse-lodger

the real world. Its irregularity makes it significant. Ionesco emphasises the alterity of the corpse; he exaggerates its otherness and uncanniness for theatrical effect. This has social resonance when considered in the context of mortuary practices that make the dead seem 'natural' and 'lifelike' for display purposes through artificial means (as demonstrated in *Terminal*), and indeed the wider phenomenon of death denial, which seeks to evade and minimise death as a matter of course. The corpse in *Amédée* is an unruly stage presence that ruptures bourgeois decorum and frustrates efforts to keep it in check (along with its wildly sprouting mushrooms). It effectively refuses to remain invisible (to the audience) and offstage.

In this regard, it is an index of the putative 'wildness' of death in the modern world. This is Ariès's formulation. In the modern age, death has become invisible and wild, Ariès suggests, because it is unfamiliar, terrifying, hidden away, and unrecognised (or misrecognised). He writes: 'The old [premodern] attitude in which death was both familiar and near, evoking no great fear or awe, offers too marked a contrast to ours, where death is so frightful that we dare not utter its name. ... I do not mean that death had once been wild and that it had ceased to be so. I mean, on the contrary, that today it has become wild' (1976: 13–14). Ariès's suggestion that death was formerly 'tame' and later became 'wild' is arguably far too neat. I mention it here because Ionesco's play perversely blurs these categories, making its presentation of death more difficult to classify and decipher. Initially, the corpse is visible only to the characters, and has been hidden away from the outside world for fifteen years. It is gradually revealed to the audience over the course of the play and then to the outside world. It becomes increasingly 'wild' through expansion and associated (mushroom) germination, though it is deeply familiar to Amédée and Madeleine. They are generally not terrified by it; Amédée even professes to be attached to it.

This scenario might be interpreted as a grotesque distortion of the traditional practice of tending to the dead body of a loved one at home before having a funeral – a practice that became less familiar, Ariès notes, as a result of the transfer of the 'scene of the normal death' from the home to the hospital (1981: 584). In *Amédée* the audience is presumably meant to register the presence of the corpse in the Buccinionis' home as an oddity, but Ionesco indicates that the Buccinionis have accommodated themselves to it as best they can. What would appear to be completely abnormal is quite normal for them; they have learned to live with death, even if this has had a negative effect on their lives. Madeleine acknowledges this, and forces Amédée to break their prolonged paralysis and peculiar form of death denial, in which they have kept death secreted away in their home.

The Birmingham Rep production made the Buccinionis' secret part of the show's marketing plan. The poster's tagline was 'What happens when a couple's secret becomes too big to hide?' The show's promotional material gave no clue as to what this secret was – the corpse was not mentioned or shown at all. This was likely intended to stoke interest in the production, making it seem mysterious for audience members unfamiliar with the play. However, it also meant that one could go to this play not knowing about the death aspect – and get an unpleasant surprise, depending on one's sensibilities and attitude toward death and dying. Did the strategy aim to have this effect? One might also posit that Birmingham Rep's marketing campaign contributed – perhaps inadvertently – to the closeting of death that the play implicitly critiques and reveals to be destructive to individual wellbeing, though the very act of mounting the production may make the 'hiddenness' of death a topic of wider discussion.

Amédée is a comedy, not a meditation on personal mortality (like *Exit the King*) or an overt social satire (like *A Clinical Case*), but its humour derives from serious and 'uncomfortable' topics: the relationship between the living and the dead, the 'agency' of the dead, their relative (un)familiarity, and their proper place in society. It may be thought to offer oblique social commentary on these topics, suggesting, for instance, that the dead should not – and perhaps ultimately cannot – be sequestered or denied. The play provides macabre treatment of sentiments that the English canon Henry Scott Holland expressed in a sermon in 1910, following the death of King Edward VII. Part of this sermon, in which Holland ventriloquises a deceased person, regularly features in contemporary funerals. It begins: 'Death is nothing at all. It does not count. *I have only slipped away into the next room.* Nothing has happened. Everything remains exactly as it was' (quoted in Wright, 2011: 20).[13] Ionesco makes this scenario much less comforting and peaceful. He calls attention to death by putting (or rather pushing or dragging) it onstage in the form of an oversized theatrical corpse, thus bodying forth what can often be left hidden or notional. Zerubavel's comments about ending conspiracies of silence – getting rid of the proverbial elephant in the room – support this interpretation of Ionesco's play. He writes:

> [In] order for its presence to be acknowledged the elephant has to be actively noticed. This presupposes pulling it out of the 'background' and turning it into a 'figure' of explicit attention. Calling attention to what is being ignored therefore requires the active reversal of figure and ground. ... Foregrounding the elephant presupposes enhancing its visibility by both turning the proverbial spotlight on it and opening people's eyes so that they become aware of it. (2006: 65)

Ionesco's comedy trumpets the absurdity of death denial and makes confronting the elephant in the room a necessary, but still buoyant, affair.

Conclusion

Denial distorts reality. It allows us to create a version of reality that is more manageable or palatable – something we can live with, even if this involves self-deception and evasion. The theatrical examples discussed in this chapter likewise present distorted realities. They present scenarios that resemble 'the real' in some respects but skew it so that the improbable and fantastical hold sway. They parody the absurd drama of death denial found in modernity. In doing do, they expose distortions of 'the real' in mental attitudes and social practices relating to death and dying. In line with the death awareness movement, these plays and performance pieces address the challenge of recognising and accepting mortality, as well as the warped reality that can result from endeavouring to circumvent this process. This theatre provides audience members with an opportunity to confront anxieties, encounter difficult truths, and alter previously held conceptions. These pieces do not offer much in the way of existential comfort, but it is still possible to learn from how these characters confront (their) mortality. One can subsequently endeavour to circumvent, minimise, or even take lightly the absurdities that death and dying can occasion. However, some forms of modern death, such as the mass death that occurred during the Second World War, make this task difficult, if not impossible, as the next chapter will demonstrate.

Notes

1 The script for this production does not appear to be extant, nor is there a recording of the broadcast.
2 A production history document contained in Phillip Zarrilli's personal archive states that *A Clinical Case* had also been performed in Gemany, China, Argentina, and Sweden prior to the 1975 production. I am very grateful to Phillip Zarrilli for bringing the play to my attention and providing me with materials relating to his production. All relevant documents cited in this chapter, including the unpublished script (translated by Josephine Mangano), are from Zarrilli's personal collection.
3 Press Release for *A Clinical Case*, Theatre of Involvement, dated 7 May 1975.
4 Zarrilli, letter to unidentified publisher, dated 21 June, 1976. My emphasis.
5 Author's interview with Phillip Zarrilli on 27 April 2016 in Berlin.
6 The Theatre of Involvement was part of the 'Midwest Center for Religion and Theatre Arts' in Minneapolis.
7 The lyrics to 'That's Your Funeral', from Lionel Bart's musical *Oliver!* (1960), come to mind: 'We're just here to glamorize you for that endless sleep. / You might just as well look fetching/ When you're six feet deep'. This number is sung by the Sowerberrys – an undertaker couple.
8 I am grateful to Katie Zien for her input on this matter.
9 At one point the company did have at least one African-American company member who was part of the ensemble for *Terminal*. Brenda Dixon is photographed performing the piece in the *New York Times* feature article on Chaikin, cited earlier.
10 Kaite O'Reilly acquainted me with the term 'temporarily abled' as a substitute for 'non-disabled' people. Chaikin, who was seriously ill as a child with rheumatic fever, had ensuing health problems as an adult and was therefore

especially aware of human frailty, particularly his own. Malpede suggests that he lived with death 'intimately' (1974: 174).

11 Transcript of BBC External Services programme segment on *Exit the King*, broadcast on 13 September 1963, and presented by Christopher Saltmarsh. This document is contained in the Royal Court Theatre Archive, contained in the Victoria and Albert Theatre and Performance Archives. All reviews of *Exit the King* quoted hereafter are contained in this archive.

12 Thanks to Cathy Turner for sharing this poem with me.

13 Compare with Arthur Conan Doyle's spiritualist analogy used in *The Land of Mist*, in which he likens being dead to being in the next room, cited in Chapter 1 of this book.

4

Theatres of catastrophe after Auschwitz and Hiroshima

The two place names featured in this chapter's title call to mind atrocities of the Second World War, specifically the Holocaust and the dropping of the atomic bomb in Japan – catastrophic events that are distinguished even within the twentieth century's catalogue of horrors involving mass death.[1] The genocide of up to six million European and Soviet Jews, along with the murder of other groups (e.g., Sinti and Roma, people with disabilities, gay people, and political prisoners), by the Nazis between 1939 and 1945 is a grotesque chapter in human history. Also ghastly was the nuclear devastation of Japanese cities by the US in August 1945, which caused the death of approximately 140,000 people in Hiroshima and 40–70,000 people in Nagasaki, and plagued survivors (*hibakusha*) with radiation sickness and other damaging side-effects (Bryant and Peck, 2009: 711). In relation to aerial bombardment, there was precedent for the bombing of Hiroshima and Nagasaki in the firebombing of major Japanese cities, as well as the bombing of Dresden, Hamburg, London, and other British cities, earlier in the war, though the nature of the destruction wrought upon Hiroshima and Nagasaki was arguably more profound and posited greater world peril. Equally, whilst extermination of ethnic or national groups has occurred throughout history, the industrialised killing conducted in the Nazi death camps was unique, and prompted the coining of the term 'genocide' in 1943 (Frey, 2004: xv).

The Holocaust and the dropping of the atomic bomb are seismic historical events with complex and still-unfolding legacies. Both have given rise to a moral imperative in the form of rallying calls stipulating that such events must not be repeated ('never again'). Both have been met with incomprehension, shame, silence, an impulse to turn away and ignore, and even outright denial, in some quarters, in the case of the Holocaust. German silence about the Holocaust in the decades afterward was paralleled by similar social silence (or silencing) in Japan about the atomic bombings (see, for example, Oe, 1995; Hogan, 1996). Notably, the US has not apologised for the nuclear attacks upon Japan, despite historians' rejections of the argument that the use of atomic warfare was justified to prevent further conflict (see Bosworth, 1993). Grappling with these histories is arduous, unpleasant work; it may seem preferable to avoid thinking about them altogether or to do so as little as possible. ('These sad places, why must you enter them?' muses Howard Barker in an enigmatic collection of aphorisms and pen drawings titled with this question (2014: 16). I have wondered this myself, more generally, while writing this book.) And yet, Auschwitz and Hiroshima, considered as 'synecdoches for Nazi genocide and atomic destruction', cast a shadow over our lives as 'transformative' events that have affected understanding of, among other things, modern death (Milchman and Rosenberg, 2004: 188). After the Second World War, death became a '"lived", subjugated, denatured situation', writes Thérèse Malachy. 'It is no longer an end, a rupture, it is a *state*; it is no longer exorcised by mourning, embellished by memory, cleansed by the tomb. It no longer has anything dignified about it, but is stinking, creeping, dreadful' (1982: 30). The events of the Second World War theoretically led to (negative) perceptions of death-in-life thereafter. This perceptual state, which Malachy calls 'situational death', remains active. The threat of nuclear attack and mutually assured destruction, which underpinned the Cold War, has not gone away. Alarmingly, in 2017, the Doomsday Clock, overseen by the *Bulletin of the Atomic Scientists*, was set to two-and-a-half minutes to midnight – the closest it has been to midnight (i.e., global catastrophe) since 1953, when the US and the Soviet Union began testing hydrogen bombs.[2] (Gulp.)

This chapter examines the shadows cast by the Holocaust, the dropping of the atomic bomb, and the prospect of future nuclear devastation in various 'theatres of catastrophe' from the mid-twentieth century to the early twenty-first century, investigating how plays and performance pieces explore conceptions of death relating to these events and to possible futures stemming from them. The topics in question have broad scope, but focusing on correlations between Auschwitz and Hiroshima, as artists and theorists have done, and relating these correlations to the history of modern death allows for more targeted analysis and makes this enquiry viable and unique.

In addition to plays that *directly* engage the atomic bombing of Hiroshima and/or Nagasaki by citing these events explicitly and exploring their impact on survivors, there is also a set of plays that *evoke* this history, even as they dramatise ostensibly ahistorical or science fiction-type scenarios.[3] These latter plays, which also connote the real-world threat of nuclear war, are the focus of the following three sections of the chapter. I discuss Samuel Beckett's *Fin de partie* (*Endgame*, 1957) and *Happy Days* (1961); Marguerite Duras's *Yes, peut-être* (*Yes, Maybe*, 1968); and Edward Bond's *The Tin Can People* (1984, the second part of his *War Plays* trilogy). The remainder of the chapter analyses two plays that evoke the Holocaust in an abstract fashion: Józef Szajna's *Replika* (*Replica*, produced in various iterations from 1971 to 1988) and Howard Barker's *Found in the Ground* (published in 2001 and produced in 2009).

Some of these plays are not well known, though they are deserving of critical attention. Between them, they respond to various aspects of death and dying exemplified by Auschwitz and Hiroshima. Many of them approach the spectres of the Holocaust and death-by-nuclear attack obliquely, only ever alluding to historical events or evoking them in fantasy. Unsurprisingly, these pieces are not easy going. (Brace yourself!) The demands they make are worthwhile, though, as it is unfortunately necessary to countenance horror and grapple with our inhumanity. In Barker's playlet 'Kiss My Hands' (from *The Possibilities*), a character who is about to be murdered by terrorists philosophises: 'To survive, we must learn everything we had forgotten, and unlearn everything we were taught, and being inhuman, overcome inhumanity' (1987: 16). Is such contradictory action possible? Theatres of catastrophe after the Second World War provide apposite conditions for speculation of this sort by reflecting on human suffering and playing out possible – and hopefully avoidable – futures.

Transformative 'death events'

How did the Holocaust and the dropping of the atomic bomb affect conceptions of death, and what does it mean to bracket these events for critical reflection? Both events have been identified as 'transformative', altering our understanding of humanity, mortality, and Western civilisation, among other weighty topics. They have been jointly figured – perhaps hyperbolically – as epoch-defining: 'Once we divided history into before and after Moses or Buddha or Christ. Now we divide history into before and after Auschwitz and Hiroshima' (Fasching, 2004: 9). Both have been regarded as 'massively traumatic genocidal catastrophes', which have permanently altered the status quo (Ray, 2005: 19). The English literary critic G. Wilson Knight made the following prediction in a book on Hiroshima published just after the attack: 'Remember this: we shall never be at peace again. A war of nerves will continue indefinitely. No organisation conceivable can prevent us knowing what we now know or obliterate the possibility of that knowledge being used on a scale compared to which what we have seen is a pinprick. We have gone one step too far' (1946: 12). What became known in 1945 about the technological capacity for destruction on a previously unimaginable scale, and the willingness to enact this destruction upon civilian populations, could not be un-known. Pandora's box had been opened. Likewise, knowledge about the industrialised, mass extermination of human beings in camps constructed for this purpose could not be un-known, though it could be buried for a while. Moreover, what was revealed, even if later suppressed, about rational, supposedly enlightened 'man' was appalling and did not augur well. In *The Twisted Road to Auschwitz*, historian Karl Schleunes remarks:

> These factories of death are now permanently catalogued in the darkest annals of the human story. Their existence casts a shadow over the hopes for our own future. The realisation that some men will construct a factory in which to kill other men raises the gravest questions about man himself. We have entered an age which we cannot avoid labeling 'After Auschwitz'.
> (1970: vii)

The historical significance of the Holocaust and the dropping of the atomic bomb is not disputed, except by Holocaust deniers. *Linking* the Holocaust and the nuclear holocaust of Hiroshima and Nagasaki is more contentious, as the Holocaust is often considered to be unique, which would make comparing it to other acts of mass murder improper, or even unethical. Furthermore, the original justification for dropping the atomic bomb – that it was a necessary evil, and therefore not a profound moral failing – still holds favour in the US. Historians have challenged this justification, arguing that American decision-makers relied on the bomb for political reasons: namely, 'to preclude Soviet entry into the war against Japan and to give the Truman administration the military leverage it needed to deal successfully with the Soviet Union on postwar issues' (Hogan, 1996: 5).

Scholars who have compared the Holocaust with atomic bombing do not suppose the events in question are uniformly or straightforwardly alike; obviously, they are not. Eric Markusen makes this crystal clear: 'To those who are offended by the placement of the strategic and atomic bombing campaigns in the same analytic context as the Holocaust, I would emphasize that *comparing* two events is not the same as *equating* them or considering them as equivalent' (2004: 27). Nevertheless, he proposes that 'examining the Holocaust and Hiroshima in comparative perspective is a valuable enterprise that can contribute to better understanding of both the nature of modern war and the global problem of genocidal killing' (*ibid.*: 26). Reconfiguring Markusen's observation, I would add that comparing the Holocaust and atomic bombing, and pondering their legacies, can also make evident altered understanding of modern death. Artists and scholars have done this persuasively.

In an essay first published in 1957, the American novelist Norman Mailer explains the phenomenon of the 'hipster' as a response to the 'collective condition' of '[living] with instant death by atomic war, relatively quick death by the State as *l'univers concentrationnaire* [a concentration camp universe], or with a slow death by conformity with every creative and rebellious instinct stifled' (1961: 283). Mailer, surveying this range of unhappy death-options, proposes a 'give up and win'-type philosophy: '[If] the fate of twentieth century man is to live with death from adolescence to premature senescence, why then the only life-giving answer is to accept the terms of death, to live with death as immediate danger, to divorce oneself from society, to exist without roots, to set out on that uncharted journey into the rebellious imperatives of the self' (*ibid.*). Mailer suggests that after Auschwitz and Hiroshima death appeared to be ubiquitous and totalising, capable of coming into effect at any moment, and for the slightest reason. This affected how people made sense of the world and lived their lives. He expounds on this in the opening section of his essay:

> Probably, we will never be able to determine the psychic havoc of the concentration camps and the atom bomb upon the unconscious mind of almost everyone alive in these years. For the first time in civilized history, perhaps for the first time in all of history, we have been forced to live with the suppressed knowledge that the smallest facets of our personality or the most minor projection of our ideas, or indeed the absence of ideas and the absence of personality could mean equally well that we might still be doomed to die as a cipher in some vast statistical operation in which our teeth would be counted, and our hair would be saved, but our death itself

would be unknown, unhonored, and unremarked, a death which could not follow with dignity as a possible consequence to serious actions we had chosen, but rather a death by *deus ex machina* in a gas chamber or a radioactive city. ... [In] the middle of an economic civilization founded upon the confidence that time could indeed be subjected to our will, our psyche was subjected itself to the intolerable anxiety that death being causeless, life was causeless as well, and time deprived of cause and effect had come to a stop. (*ibid.*: 282)

The 'psychic havoc' caused by the Holocaust and the atom bomb merits consideration. After all, mass death is not unique to the Second World War or to the twentieth century, for that matter (see Canning *et al.*, 2004). Additionally, the possibility of sudden death is an age-old fact of life, even if we are accustomed to thinking otherwise in affluent, medically advanced Western societies. However, death denial may have underlined or even enhanced the 'psychic havoc' by giving rise to contradicting viewpoints and disconnect between personal or social belief about mortality and new realities of death and dying. Notionally, death was socially denied and taboo in Western societies in the twentieth century, yet the fact of mass death and the prospect of its reoccurrence were all too real. (This contradictory situation was also posited in the last chapter in relation to US society during the Vietnam War.) Why else might the Holocaust and the atom bomb have caused 'psychic havoc' for a civilian population? Dying as a 'cipher in some vast statistical operation' in which one may be reduced to stray body fragments or eradicated entirely; killed en masse without individual identification or personal recognition; eliminated by a seemingly omnipotent force through technological means – following Mailer, this combination of factors seems qualitatively different and understandably provided cause for concern.

Benjamin Noys, a literary theorist, considers Mailer's essay 'a manifesto of modern death' (2005: 12). Noys picks up on the newfound dislocation, articulated by Mailer, of the 'sense of having a proper time of death'; the perception, after Auschwitz and Hiroshima, that 'death is no longer necessarily an individual matter, but can now be the result of a vast and anonymous operation carried out upon us'; and that in the face of this 'collective mass death' our individual lives – and deaths – might not 'count for anything' (*ibid.*: 13–14). Noys points out that this is 'not simply the anonymous death of the epidemic or war, but a deliberate and organised death, a kind of "rational" or industrialised death at the hands of bureaucratic planners' (*ibid.*: 14). The large-scale corpse-production and reduction of human beings to objects 'to be administered and disposed of by the state', which characterise both the Holocaust and the dropping of the atomic bomb, indicts modernity in general and the Enlightenment in particular, as mentioned in the previous chapter with reference to Zygmunt Bauman's work (Milchman and Rosenberg, 2004: 188). Not only did rationality and the application of the intellect *not* prevent these catastrophic events from occurring, 'techno-bureaucratic rationality' was employed to execute and justify them (Frey, 2004: xvii). This worked to drain death of spiritual meaning.

In her literary study of modern dying and mourning, Sandra M. Gilbert proposes that 'modern death' is increasingly characterised by a view of dying as 'termination' rather than 'expiration', meaning that one dies and that is it: there is no posthumous spiritual existence. One does not 'go on', as it were; one simply ends. Her thesis is that twentieth-century mass death, or 'mass *ex*termination', facilitated the conceptual 'devolution' of 'expiration' into 'termination', and Auschwitz exemplifies this (2006: 136). Gilbert makes a connection between the Nazi death camps and the trenches of the First World War, grimly observing that 'the skeleton in the trench of No Man's Land and the skeleton in the mass grave of the European Holocaust point down to the muck, not up to the sky, and the human smoke belched out by the chimneys of the crematoria dissipates into vacancy' (*ibid.*: 137). The 'death events' of the World Wars may be thought to undermine the prospect of a heavenly afterlife, given their horrific circumstances, and instead betoken 'celestial indifference' (or, indeed, God's non-existence) (*ibid.*: 136). (However, as discussed in Chapter 2, some historical commentators, such as Winifred Kirkland, opined that death in the trenches of the First World War validated spiritualist beliefs, so opinions vary.) Gilbert discusses how technologies and architectures of death link the citylike structure of the trenches with the 'parodic industrial cityscapes' of Auschwitz and the other camps:

> [In the camps] the grotesque lineaments of the front that were entrenched in the First World War were built upward and outward, reified, elaborated. Here unarmed civilians rather than armed combatants were immured. Here a poison gas like the kind that had been an experimental weapon in the earlier 'death event' became a final solution to what was seen as a species of industrial problem. (*ibid.*: 153)

Connecting Auschwitz to earlier (or contemporaneous, for that matter) 'death events' does not make it any less heinous. Rather, it helps us to get a more detailed picture of the history of modern death, reveals the Holocaust to be firmly located within modernity, and discloses the distinctive attributes of the Holocaust as well as its ghoulish development of pre-existing themes.

The same is true of the atomic bombing in Japan, which may be historicised in relation to the aerial bombing of other cities in the Second World War and earlier in the century. However, the deadly precedent set by the atomic bombing inaugurated a nuclear threat that contained the possibility of even-greater catastrophe. The death-as-termination paradigm, hypothetically instantiated by Auschwitz, could theoretically extend to the entire planet if nuclear war occurred. J. Robert Oppenheimer, the so-called 'father of the atomic bomb', recalled witnessing the first detonation of a nuclear weapon and thinking of a (possibly mistranslated) line from the *Bhagavad Gita*: 'Now I am become death, the destroyer of worlds' (quoted in Monk, 2012: 439). Apocalyptic visions predate the twentieth century, and had then been rekindled by the First World War (as seen in Karl Kraus's *The Last Days of Mankind*, discussed in Chapter 2), but nuclear weapons made these visions seem less fantastical. As Robert Jacobs, a cultural historian, remarks, one vision of the future implicit in the nuclear standoff of the Cold War was that 'there might be no future' (2010: 1). Humanity now had the capacity to destroy itself and the entire world, disregarding artificial borders and the collective fiction of the nation state. (Recall Knight's fearful remarks, quoted earlier in this section: '*We have gone one step too far*'.) Jacobs continues:

> If a nuclear war were to break out, the borders so important to humans, between the two sides of the conflict, between combatants and noncombatants, are seen to be illusory. The contamination of radioactive fallout would not stop at the borders that humans draw on maps: the planet as a whole would be affected. And in this sense, the victims of the nuclear war would be all the inhabitants of Earth. The *victim* of a nuclear war would be the Earth itself. (*ibid.*: 190)

Mass death, difficult to grasp in any context, becomes even more imponderable when projected on to a planetary scale. Collective death – *the death of everyone and everything (or most everything)* – threatens to boggle the mind. The vaporised bodies and scorched earth at Hiroshima and Nagasaki laid the foundation for this future fear.

Questions about whether humanity could survive nuclear war and what it would mean to survive in this context were debated by mid- to late twentieth-century writers – and were also taken up by dramatists, as I will presently discuss. Military strategist Herman Kahn, spoofed by Stanley Kubrick as Dr Strangelove in the 1964 film of the same name, argued that Americans *could* survive nuclear war if certain preparatory measures were taken. The term 'megadeath', meaning the death of a million people, especially as the result of nuclear warfare, is associated with Kahn, whose weighty tome *On Thermonuclear War*, published in 1960, endeavours to pragmatise the death of millions in a strangely sober manner for what would appear to be an end-of-the-world scenario (but Kahn suggests otherwise). Whereas Kahn tabulated megadeaths, other American authors, such as Jonathan Schell, in his celebrated antinuclear treatise *The Fate of the Earth*, advanced the premise that nuclear war would mean total extinction, which, he suggests, is worse than death: 'because extinction ends death just as surely as it ends birth and life. Death is only death; extinction is the death of death' (1982: 119). While in Christianity the idea of 'victory' over death is celebrated, this is not the sense of the 'death of death' articulated here. Schell explains: 'when the whole world, in which the dead in a sense live on, is imperilled, [the] effort at remembrance and preservation seems to lose its point, and all lives and deaths are threatened with a common meaninglessness' (*ibid.*: 166). If one's death is not known about because there is no one alive left to know it, then death may have lost its sting, but this is, at best, a Pyrrhic victory.

Several related issues may be foregrounded in writings about mortality after Auschwitz and Hiroshima: namely, deindividuation, lack of agency, incomprehensibility, meaninglessness, death-in-life, and extinction. These issues are threaded into the plays and performance pieces discussed in this chapter. The selected examples typically approach the Holocaust and nuclear devastation in an indirect, fantastical, or metaphorical fashion. In doing so, the enormity of the events in question and the limitation of theatrical representation are acknowledged. Moreover, the complex of ideas concerning death after Auschwitz and Hiroshima, outlined above, is made manifest, though it is not resolved. Rather, one is invited to apprehend the ways in which modern death has been newly put into flux, and enter this precarious state, imaginatively, for oneself.

Evoking nuclear catastrophe: *Endgame* and *Happy Days*

Beckett's plays famously explore existential dilemmas. *Endgame*, for example, is set in what appears to be a total wasteland. Beckett does not specify how the situation presented in this play, in which a quartet of disabled characters eke out an existence that is 'finished, nearly finished' (as Clov comments at the beginning), has come to pass (1958: 1). Nuclear weapons are not mentioned, but are a possible cause for the circumstances. 'Outside of here it's death', the blind Hamm (who cannot stand), twice remarks to Clov (who cannot sit) (9, 70). Clov confirms Hamm's judgement when he trains a telescope on the world outside the bunker-like room in which they (barely) exist, declaring that there is 'zero' to behold and that all is 'corpsed' (29, 30). Clov answers Hamm's pronouncement that '[the] whole place stinks of corpses' with the correction that the 'whole universe' does (46). According to Clov, there is 'no more nature', yet he is bothered by a flea at one point; this, in turn, bothers Hamm, who is surprised by the fact that there are still fleas about (11, 33). This, incidentally, is not incongruous with nuclear devastation. Schell speculates that the aftermath of nuclear war would possibly yield 'a republic of insects and grass' because of their 'higher tolerance to radioactivity' (1982: 65, 63). So, even if human life is (nearly) at an end in Beckett's play, there may still be vestiges of other life-forms. (Hurray?)

Critics are divided about whether *Endgame* should be interpreted in the light of historical events such as the dropping of the atomic bomb in Japan. Elinor Fuchs takes a position concordant with Beckett's own attitude toward his work, stating: '*Endgame* ... is not "about" the Holocaust, Hiroshima, or the silent spring. It is apocalyptic not because of a particular history or prospect it may point to – in fact like the visions of classical apocalypse it points to whatever terminus presses most upon its spectators – but because it is a figure of the end of the world, a version of the narrative at the heart of apocalyptic texts' (1999: 27). Charles A. Carpenter offers a contrasting view, noting that '[intentionally] or not, the situation presented in *Endgame* would have been perceived by many as a post-holocaust shelter situation', given the period in which the play was written and first performed (1999: 136). He gives a persuasive reading of the play in this context, suggesting that the characters' retreat into the shelter 'seems to have followed a nearby catastrophe analogous to, if not modeled on, Hiroshima' (*ibid.*: 139). Theodor Adorno helps to bridge these two perspectives, championing *Endgame* as an example of aesthetic negativity suitable for a post-Second World War context. In his 1958 essay 'Trying to Understand *Endgame*' he makes the case for why Beckett's 'nebulous' approach to history is aesthetically and morally appropriate, referring to the twin concerns of this chapter:

> Any alleged drama of the atomic age would be a mockery of itself, solely because its plot would comfortably falsify the historical horror of anonymity by displacing it onto human characters and actions and by gaping at the 'important people' who are in charge of whether or not the button gets pushed. The violence of the unspeakable is mirrored in the fear of mention-

ing it. Beckett keeps it nebulous. About what is incommensurable with experience as such one can only speak in euphemisms, the way one speaks in Germany of the murder of the Jews. (2003: 263–4)

Adorno's identification of the 'horror of anonymity' and the 'violence of the unspeakable' associated with atomic bombing chimes with the observations cited earlier in this chapter (e.g., by Mailer) about contemplating death after Hiroshima. (Who, precisely, is killed? Who, precisely, are the killers? Mass death events of this sort can make these questions difficult to answer definitively or completely.) *That which is not said* and/or *that which cannot be said* clings to death events such as those exemplified by Hiroshima and Auschwitz, which is why, Adorno writes, '[the] name of the catastrophe is to be spoken only in silence' (*ibid.*: 267). In other words, it is only ever inferred, if that. Following this reasoning, Beckett's hostility to productions of *Endgame* that apparently made inferences in his play too concrete, ignored his directions, and/ or inhibited other interpretative possibilities is understandable, even if it prioritises a 'textocentric' vision of performance (Pavis, 2003: 203). JoAnne Akalaitis's 1984 production at the American Repertory Theatre in Cambridge, Massachusetts, ostensibly set in a North American city after a nuclear holocaust, is a case in point (see Kalb, 1989: 78–87).

As Beckett worked on drafts of his plays, he removed references that might connect a play too explicitly to a real-world context; nevertheless, such contexts still ghost his work. S.E. Gontarski reveals how early drafts of *Happy Days* make 'the suggestion of nuclear devastation' that hovers over the play more apparent (1977: 40). In these drafts, there are reports of rockets having been fired: one 'aberrant rocket' has struck Erin (i.e., *Éirinn*: Ireland), leaving 83 priests surviving (*ibid.*). Gontarski surmises: 'If the section on technological insanity were allowed to stand, the focus of the play would broaden to include a world-wide madness, and the isolated examination of the couple might be lost. And perhaps the madness of modern technological existence and the arbitrariness of survival (a favorite Beckett theme) are too self-evident for Beckett to dramatize so blatantly' (*ibid.*).

Edits made and redrafting completed, the published version of the play still contains several references that connote the effects of nuclear attack and resonate with the atomic bombing in Japan. These include the '*expanse of scorched grass*' leading up to Winnie's mound; Winnie's mention of a 'blaze of hellish light'; her strangely cheerful imagining of 'the happy day to come when flesh melts at so many degrees' and when her body will be 'charred to a black cinder'; and her wondering whether the 'earthball' (the earth) has 'lost its atmosphere' (1963: 9, 11, 6, 29, 39).

Winnie and Willie's nemesis, the 'hellish sun', which exposes them to the 'great heat', might be thought to evoke the atomic devices dropped on Hiroshima and Nagasaki (20, 23). Knight, in his book on Hiroshima, uses the term 'sun-bomb' to refer to the atomic devices, saying: 'The bomb is not to be considered a piece of mechanism; its atom-splitting radio-activity is a small-scale replica of the great Sun's power and heat' (1946: 33). Grotesquely, as recounted by witnesses, the flesh of still-living victims of the Hiroshima bombing melted because of the 300,000-degrees-Centigrade fireball unleashed upon them from above (Hachiya, 1955: 28; Clodfelter, 2017: 526). *The name of the catastrophe is to be spoken only in silence* – yet it is still sounded, if only imaginatively, in Beckett's desolate, arid wastelands.

Devastation, erasure: *Yes, Maybe*

Nuclear catastrophe also underscores Marguerite Duras's short play *Yes, Maybe*, which has some thematic parallels with Beckett's *Endgame*. Duras wrote the screenplay for *Hiroshima Mon Amour* (1959, directed by Alain Resnais), which presents an affair between a French actress and a Japanese architect, coloured by their experiences in the Second World War and by Hiroshima. Duras revisits the theme of nuclear devastation in this play, but sets it in an imaginary world that has apparently been ravaged by nuclear war.

The play, which takes place in a bare, beige landscape in an unidentified country, has three characters: two women, respectively identified as A and B in the text, and a male soldier identified as H. The character of A has dragged H, who is in an exhausted state, from a field of battle, or desert of or for war ('*désert à guerre*') (Duras, 1968: 156).[4] H lies collapsed on the ground and mostly remains unconscious or in a stupor. The play consists of broken, elliptical, recursive dialogue between the two women as they attempt to piece together what they know about their present circumstances, their surroundings, and the recent past. The women have been traumatised by the conflict to the extent that their faculties and sensibilities have been partially erased, making them resemble blank slates. The lack of proper names and identification via single letters (A and B) adds to this effect. The stage directions describe them as being '*innocent, insolent, tender and cheerful, without bitterness, without malice, without kindness, without intelligence, without stupidity, without references, without memory. They are at the same time terri-*

fied' (155–6). The women's speech is atypical; they are possibly aphasic, although they seem to understand each other well enough. They speak in an idiosyncratic, fragmentary type of French, mixed with occasional English words. Personal pronoun usage is askew, and often lacking: the stage directions state that the first-person singular has '*ceased to exist*' and that the '*catastrophe has generalised the use of "we"*' (178, 181).

As in *Endgame*, the precise nature of the catastrophe in this play is not revealed, though nuclear devastation would seem to be the cause. The women are described as each having a gauge on their arms to '*combat the ambient radioactivity*' (155). In conversation, they discuss how the 'desert of war' has been razed, with ashes buried. They speculate that twelve million people have died; later, the figure of 170 million is mentioned (157, 175). They refer to 'the great upset' being 'the fourth fission' – presumably shorthand for an explosion involving nuclear fission (179). B states that in the 'twenty-fourth desert' (a zone of combat?) children would be forcibly aborted because they '[would've] been born blind' – a possible result of radiation (176).

The women's relative lack of knowledge about what has happened and their diminished inability to articulate or explain their situation are indices of the scale of the death and destruction that has occurred, which has worked to expunge both individual and collective memory. At one point, they discuss coming across a stone with inscriptions on it that suggest that history has been erased:

> B: What does it say?
> A: That nothing happened.
> B: Inscriptions to say that nothing has happened?
> A: *Oui*.[5] From such-a-year to such-a-year: *rien* [nothing].
> B, *repeats*: Rien. (*Pause.*) Rien how?
> A, *gestures around her*: Like that, maybe.
> B, *looks around her, not understanding*: Ah. (*Gestures to the desert surrounding them.*) That is *nothing*?
> A, *taken by doubt*: Oui. (171–2)

This exchange perfectly captures the spare, cryptic, circling (and somewhat maddening) nature of the dialogue in this play as these damaged people attempt to reorient themselves in a world that has been annihilated by warfare. The women's evacuated subjectivities reflect, and are mapped onto, the eradicated landscape. Duras writes: '*They behold the desert and speak of it in place of themselves. Their existence surely appears to them, but as an intimidating, almost unseemly, vague notion*' (172). Their existential ambiguity is such that B wonders whether they are, in fact, dead. A says they are alive, but makes this determination '*hesitantly*' (178).

Obliqueness and equivocation suffuse this play, making its title apropos. Nevertheless, its anti-war, anti-military, anti-establishment, anti-patriarchal bent is blatant ('Piss the war! Shit the war!' exclaims B), and is exemplified in the figure of the gruntlike soldier-automaton, whom the women disparage (163). The stage directions state that his torn clothing is *'filled with inscriptions such as "Honour" (on the jacket) and "Fatherland" (on the buttocks) and "God", stars of the American flag, the Gallic cock, the Legion of Honour, or other figures or emblematic words – which will vary according to the country – and which will co-exist with various advertisements'* (155). The mixture of American and French emblems, along with the direction that these can be changed to suit the production context, makes the political critique of the play less fixed, though the fact that it was written at the time of Vietnam War is telling.

The play's evocation of a world and a decimated population profoundly damaged, physically and psychologically, by nuclear explosions is most pertinent for the purpose of this enquiry. Duras's presentation of de-individuated subjectivities (emphasised by the letters for character names), existential uncertainty, and inability to comprehend fully what has happened resonates with the experiences of survivors of the atomic bombings in Japan, who experienced a form of death-in-life. Robert Jay Lifton, writing about the *hibakusha* of Hiroshima, notes: '[There] was a widespread sense that life and death were out of phase with one another, no longer properly distinguishable – which lent an aura of weirdness and unreality to the entire city' (1968: 23). Duras's play also registers the previously mentioned 'common meaninglessness' that Schell hypothesised would afflict survivors of worldwide nuclear destruction, a doomsday scenario compounded, in his estimation, by the potential failure or impossibility of remembrance, as well as the impossibility of comprehending, or surveying, the total significance of the 'death event' for the human race. He asks: 'How are we, who are part of human life, to step back from life and see it whole, in order to assess the meaning of its disappearance?' (1982: 116).[6] Duras's nameless female characters, victims of an implicitly male-authored global catastrophe, cannot extricate themselves from their disastrous circumstances, or make complete sense of them. Moreover, the situation is not theoretical for them; it is personal. They have been indelibly scarred by what has happened and carry this trauma with them. B has seemingly experienced the (forced?) death of her children: an event she has unsuccessfully repressed and that now overwhelms her. B states: 'When they [children] are dead, they must be burned as a stockpile of war, bury the ashes … no … no …' (Duras, 1968: 166). A and B are united in shared distress:

B, *makes a sort of grimace and puts her hand on her chest*: We have suffering here sometimes.
A: *Oui*. Suffering. (*Same gesture as B*) There.
They come so close together that they are as one body. The anguish continues. (178)

Duras traces the consequences of man-made global catastrophe upon the powerless in a complementary fashion to Beckett, except her critique is patently anti-patriarchal and highlights women's lot in times of war. Her play serves as a rebuke of the warring instinct, a sad reflection upon nuclear atrocities already committed, and a warning against future devastation. Form and content are well suited to this purpose. Gabrielle H. Cody observes:

> Like other theater artists of her generation, Duras's counter-aesthetics were a direct response to the relative meaninglessness of mimetic representation (whether political or theatrical) in a post holocaust, post atomic world. ... From Duras's perspective, what happened in Hiroshima or Auschwitz is unlocatable for the survivor of history as well as the spectator of history, that is, irretrievable through mimetic means. Such experience is not materially or psychically commensurable. (2000: 16–17)

Rather than attempt to represent the horror of the atomic bombing in Japan through realistic re-enactment, Duras conjures some of its experiential effects – its emotional legacy – by presenting occupants of an imaginary world scarred by nuclear war. This is hinted at in Beckett's work, or rather it is available as an interpretative possibility. This dramatic strategy is implemented more overtly, and is further fleshed out, in the next example

The Tin Can People and the trauma of survival

In *The Tin Can People*, Edward Bond adopts a similar approach to Duras in dramatising catastrophe. The play presents an imagined world in which nuclear war has taken place, evoking, in the process, the history of the atomic bombing in Japan. Bond does this more explicitly than Duras, using the events of 1945 as a basis for exploring the psychological effects of nuclear attack. Although the catastrophe described in this play is fictional, it is ghosted by real-world events. In his commentary on the *War Plays*, Bond writes: 'We can ask what is fiction? The borderline between writer and character, actor and role, audience and story, is not as impenetrable as the boundary which joins them. If I write of a holocaust, the dead of Hiroshima, Auschwitz, and Dresden use me' (1998: 342). Bond's personal notebooks, which document his creative process in writing his plays, contain the following reflection concerning *The Tin Can People* that provides further insight into his use of fact in fiction:

> The trauma cant [sic] be discounted. The lives of Japanese who lived on after being in the first two A bombings were changed by it: many reported forty years later that they could not escape from despair and suffering at the pain they'd seen.
>
> These victims were in an atom world surrounded by a normal world: there was an abiding contrast between their interior image of desolation and terror and the everyday commercial, biological, even jocular life outside the two death cities. With my people its [sic] as if the whole of the world had peeled away leaving the white apple flesh. (Bond and Stuart, 1995: 174)

Bond's 'people' are the characters in his play – a group of generally unnamed survivors of what appears to have been a massive nuclear war. The survivors find themselves in a peculiar and unexpected state of being. Bond ironically calls it 'paradise in hell', as, liberated from the threat of nuclear attack (the worst has already happened) and able to live in relative luxury on the goods left behind (e.g., storehouses of tinned food), they are relatively content – and yet they quickly descend into anarchy and reveal themselves to be psychologically unstable. This is initiated by the arrival of a stranger into their midst – the first other survivor they have encountered in seventeen years since the catastrophe. They blame the newcomer for a sudden rash of deaths among their group; fearing he has brought a disease, they ostracise him and collectively go 'mad' and riot.

The play is principally a parable-like examination of how negative aspects of human nature may be revealed in dire circumstances, especially in a privileged economic situation. As Bond explains in a letter: 'oddly enough they're in what should be a paradise, but they don't have to practically produce their lives, so like all "elites" they become irrational and destructive when faced with the non-economic problems of life' (Bond and Stuart, 1995: 96). The collective trauma they have experienced is not discounted; on the contrary, it is a leitmotif that increasingly grows more persistent. Chorus members and characters describe scenes they have witnessed that continue to haunt them. The horrid imagery that is evoked is reminiscent of the testimony of *hibakusha* and witnesses to the atomic bombings in Japan. The opening speech by the First Chorus paints a grisly scene of mass injury and disfigurement post-nuclear attack:

> People fled in all directions from one hell into another
> I thought the explosions had thrown strange sea creatures onto the bridge whose ancestors had long ago retreated under the ocean
> (You see how confused I was)
> These fish-shaped fin-footed creatures stood on one spot and swayed
> Green seaweed hung from their walrus heads
> If in hell there are zoos they would have been shown in them
> Then I saw that they were people whose skin hung down in knotted strips
> I told them to die
> They couldnt be helped and as everything was at an end it was pointless to suffer
> Many fell from the bridge onto the backs of others in the river – it was already full of these strange creatures
> The skin of one person clothed the bones of another
> It was one animal with a hundred thousand legs and arms and one body covered with mouths that shouted its pain (1998: 51)

Bond's poetic language does not disguise the hideous effects of nuclear conflagration on human flesh; rather, it burns its awfulness into the mind's eye, like the verbal eyewitness accounts of the atomic bombing in Japan. Compare the First Chorus's speech with this testimony made by a Hiroshima resident:

> The appearance of people was ... well, they all had skin blackened by burns ... They had no hair because their hair was burned, and at a glance you couldn't tell whether you were looking at them from in front or in back ... their skin – not only on their hands, but on their faces and bodies too – hung down ... wherever I walked I met these people... They didn't look like people of this world. (quoted in Lifton, 1968: 27)

The bellies of the survivors depicted in Bond's play may be full, but their minds are damaged by what they have witnessed (like the characters of A and B in Duras's play). As the character of Third Woman in Bond's play remarks, 'How can you talk about the destruction of the world and be normal?' (1998: 57). Third Woman asks to be interrupted when relating traumatic memories because she says she is unable to stop herself from speaking. Her dreadful remembrance, which includes seeing maggots crawling from the dead onto the living, babies suckling dead mothers and mothers trying to give milk to dead babies, ratchets up the horror as she describes encountering a bomb site containing a mass disintegration of human bodies:

> I saw something I shouldnt have seen – because no human being should ever be in the world where it happened because they could never be at home there. ... [Dotted] across [the ground] were dark shapes – long black brown bundles – melted – gluey – I didnt know what they were – brown – streaked with red and yellow – and I thought they were giant's turds – the simplest explanation was that a giant had walked over the square and shat – and as there were bones in the turds I saw they were bodies
> So I said die die die ... I told everything I saw to die (59)

This speech turns the stomach, and if it did not have a historical parallel (i.e., the famous images of shadow-imprints of incinerated people cast onto physical structures after the Hiroshima and Nagasaki bombings), one might think it distasteful or simply macabre. But Bond uses it as part of a wider matrix that endeavours to account for the ways in which a massive 'death event' of this type can affect self-perception, perception of the world (including humanity), and ideas about mortality. Third Woman's statement about not being able to be 'at home' in the world following the scenes she has witnessed indicates psycho-geographical rupture and profound existential discomfort – a complete shifting of the ground beneath one's feet. The aftershock of nuclear catastrophe continues to rumble throughout the play.

One can detect it in the impersonal way the characters are identified in the text – First Man, Second Woman, etc. (cf. Duras's naming strategy in *Yes, Maybe*); the characters rarely mention one another by name. The catastrophe has seemingly stripped their identities (cf. the presentation of the war dead as unnamed, seemingly identical soldier-skeletons in Ernst Toller's First World War drama *The Transfiguration*, discussed in Chapter 2), just as the explosions created a grotesque amalgam of fused bodies and messy, barely distinguishable, human remains. In his commentary on the *War Plays*, Bond remarks of the characters: 'They have lost their names because they have lost themselves. Names are a sign of our humanity. In a nuclear age we still have to create our humanity. I would have felt I was christening bits of limbs I had dragged from rubble' (*ibid.*: 361). Bond's impersonally designated characters reflect the disregard for individuation that is part of the paradigm of industrialised mass-death epitomised by Hiroshima and Auschwitz. Loss of personhood inevitably gives rise to ontological doubt and confusion.

This is connected to the issue of remembering – or not remembering – the dead, which is discussed in the play. Although the biological remains of bomb victims dot the earth, the characters disagree about whether they should strive to keep the dead alive in memory, as this exchange, concerning a recently deceased survivor, shows:

SECOND MAN: Talk to us about him
People used to talk about their dead
It was one of the things that made them human
SECOND WOMAN: What's the use?
Tomorrow we could all be dead from radiation
Not even one of us left to bury the rest

(54)

Second Woman's imagining of a total extinction of the human population evokes Schell's idea (previously cited) of the 'death of death' that nuclear war could prompt, as the imaginative or spiritual connection between the living and dead, and the duty of the former to the latter, would no longer be relevant and could not be sustained (because there would be no mourners left). As Second Man remarks, talking about the dead is a distinguishing feature of being human. Losing this capacity, or considering it to be futile, raises the possibility of identity crisis, as bonds between self and other, and between the living and the dead, unravel. Second Man's remark suggests that *not* talking about the dead would make the survivors inhuman; the implication is that perhaps they already are other-than-human in some way. Schell's speculation about how survivors of a global nuclear catastrophe might fare is reflected in Bond's drama. Schell writes:

> To [the survivors], the futility of all the activities of the common world – of marriage, of politics, of the arts, of learning, and, for that matter, of war – would be driven home inexorably. They would experience in their own lives the breakdown of the ties that bind individual human beings together into a community and a species, and they would feel the current of our common life grow cold within them. And as their number was steadily reduced by death they would witness the final victory of death over life. One wonders whether in these circumstances people would want to go on living at all – or whether they might not choose to end their own lives. (1982: 169)

This nihilistic scenario threatens to come into total, lasting effect in Bond's play as the survivors, affected by the rising number of sudden, inexplicable deaths of members of their group, become violent and go 'mad'. Traumatised by mass death, they are easily triggered and prone to making 'extreme' statements and actions. Additionally, like the characters of A and B in Duras's *Yes, Maybe,* and the *hibakusha* of Hiroshima and Nagasaki, Bond's survivors raise the possibility that they are more dead than alive.

Second Woman states that 'we've been dead since [the bombs] fell' and that '[our] pulses are watches ticking on dead people's wrists' – a cryptic utterance that appears to emphasise the peculiar condition of being an (un)knowing living corpse (a trope also used in First World War drama, discussed in Chapter 2) (Bond, 1998: 55). First Man, who is the newcomer to the group, and has been on his own for seventeen years, consolidates this perception by greeting the others with an observation that is telling about his state of mind and what he has seen during his time alone: 'I know you're people because you're corpse-shaped' (60). In this vein, Fourth Woman, frightened by the spate of sudden deaths that has afflicted the group, and remembering witnessing her mother's death in the bombing, seizes on the idea of pretending to be dead as a stratagem to stay alive – as though death were an entity that was stalking them (recalling Maeterlinck's *The Intruder*, discussed in Chapter 1). Earlier, she ruminates that having nothing to do with death might be the key to surviving, but now she flips on this idea. Yet rather than 'play dead' by falling to the ground and lying still, as one might expect, Fourth Woman '*slowly walks about pretending to be dead*' – an ostensibly nonsensical action, unless she is rehearsing being a zombie (i.e., the walking dead). Bond mentions Fourth Woman's particular strand of 'madness' in a letter to the director Alain Françon, written in 1994: 'The irony is that she needs to demonstrate death – she cant [sic] just lie down and imitate it that way. The "threat" might think she's asleep. So she must contrive movement to show she cant move: really this sort of problem is at the base of all art, to demonstrate one thing by its opposite and so isolate its "essence" ... from its mere factual and limiting embodiment' (1995: 122). Fourth Woman must convey the idea of death by evoking it in live performance – an animating paradox at the heart of this study. 'We must practise how to be dead' Fourth Woman states, and she proceeds to practice this non-intuitive action for the rest of the scene as other characters argue and fight with one another (Bond, 1998: 91).

Having a character walk about pretending to be dead is rather unusual, and points to psychological instability (cf. the character of Irene in Henrik Ibsen's 1899 play *When We Dead Awaken*, who purports to be dead, even if she is only spiritually dead). This could be a striking visual image and stage presence in performance, though it is difficult to picture. How does one pretend to be dead while ambulating? Of course, if one is in profound shock, one does not have to pretend. A witness of the aftermath of the Hiroshima bombing describes the *hibakusha* as 'walking ghosts', saying '[they] had a special way of walking – very slowly' (quoted in Lifton, 1968: 27). The prompt book for the RSC's 1985 production of this play at The Pit in London indicates that Fourth Woman, played by Ann Mitchell, had a piece of cloth, referred to as a 'security blanket', in this scene. A blocking note mentions Fourth Woman veiling herself and then wandering about upstage away from the other characters.[7] In practising being dead on her feet, she occupied her own territory, it would seem, before quitting the scene. One wonders whether she drew the audience's attention in her deathly strolling, and what they made of this arresting move on her part – and on Bond's.

Bond has stated that Fourth Woman's effort to evade death by pretending to be dead has symbolic significance. In the letter to Françon, he says that '[what] she is doing ... points to the great perversion of our social life: because she does individually what was actually done collectively in order to create the bombs: if *she* had a bomb she would nurse it as a baby' (1995: 122). The meaning of this statement is not immediately clear, though it recalls the full title of Kubrick's film *Dr. Strangelove, or How I Learned to Stop Worrying and Love the Bomb*. Bond seems to be saying that, by accepting her situation and accommodating herself to it, Fourth Woman is metaphorically complicit with a corrupt and dangerous state of affairs – a.k.a. the 'thanopolitics of modernity', a phrase used by the Italian philosopher Giorgio Agamben (Noys, 2005: 19). In this context, thanopolitics is linked to accepting, or even working to enable, the existence and proliferation of nuclear weapons as part of an unavoidable, unchangeable status quo (i.e., mutually assured destruction).

Bond, unsurprisingly, has opposed nuclear weapons, saying: '[they] cause the fear that eats into our morality, trivialises our emotions and narrows our mind. One day out of sheer stupidity, vanity and petulance we will wander into the final confrontation and lash out with the final terror. We will destroy the world out of apathy' (1998: 285). In a letter written in 1990, he suggests the *War Plays* can be considered a critique of insufficient social resistance to nuclear weapons, saying: 'I see in the *War Plays* not merely a report from a possible nuclear war – but the mind of a society which could let itself fall into nuclear war. I do not believe for a second that we have put into the struggle for peace one ten-thousandth of the effort we have put into making weapons. Such a society is in great danger' (1995: 110). He reiterates this point in his published commentary on the *War Plays*, indicating how ethics and aesthetics are bound up with fiction and history: 'Fiction is a specific reality that combines real and possible events. If anything determined us it would be the paradox, in which we take responsibility for the world. That sounds grandiose till we think of Hiroshima and Auschwitz and then it seems the minimum condition for being human' (1998: 281). A simple distillation of his statement: act or catastrophe will ensue (though it is not always clear what one can do, save protesting and campaigning. Carol Ann Duffy's *Everyman*, discussed in Chapter 5, touches on this conundrum). Later in Bond's commentary, when discussing how the *War Plays* repeat and vary 'a few simple events', he remarks: 'This helps the audience to reach an abstract understanding grounded in material, particular reality – the events are not true but the metaphors become true' (*ibid.*: 338). Encouraging an audience to reach an 'abstract understanding' of subject matter (including ideas about mortality) by grounding it in 'material, particular reality' (i.e., historical events) is how all the examples discussed in this chapter theoretically work.

Whether this works in practice is another matter. Bond's *War Plays* trilogy had a famously troubled RSC production (Bond exited as director during the rehearsal period). Bond has since privately savaged the RSC production. In a letter written in 1986, he calls it 'a vulgar and incompetent travesty' (1995: 97). In other letters, he elaborates on his critical opinion, saying that the RSC actors were 'unable to use the language of the times', unfavourably comparing the RSC production with the premiere production of *The Tin Can People* by the Birmingham-based company Bread and Circuses Theatre in 1984: 'in Birmingham the play was related to the players' (and audiences') practical living problems – in the RSC it was as if "Art" still had something to do with an "other world"' (*ibid.*: 94). Although the play has a fantastical premise, Bond stressed its historical specificity and contemporary relevance, stating: 'I dont [sic] wish the play to be seen as mythic. It is practical and belongs to the technological age' (*ibid.*: 102–3).

Interestingly, RSC production records suggest an overall attempt to ground the production in historical fact and realistic detail. The rehearsal notes mention a visiting speaker giving a talk 'about the medical effects of nuclear war'; it was noted (on 24 April 1985) that 'slides of burns etc' will be useful for make-up design. Bond's desire to show gory detail in this regard is evident in this rehearsal note from 13 May: 'The Second Man may possibly need loose tufts of hair which can be pulled out during the "kicking" scene. Edward [Bond] has suggested this have pieces of scalp attached to expose the second man's brains'. (The spirit of Grand Guignol lives on!) There is a rehearsal note (on 30 April) asking 'could we get some books on madness (neurosis, hysteria) for Josette [Simon, who played Second Woman] from the Barbican library', and another (on 2 May) involving arranging for Ian McDiarmid (who played First Man) to have a first-aid lesson in how to do artificial respiration. The production records indicate that the cast and crew did their homework about researching the historical events underlying the fictional catastrophe presented in the play. One note (dated 14 May) asks: 'Could we have a VHS video recorder in rehearsal to play last night's Hiroshima tape'.

The critical response to the production was generally mixed, with critics complaining about the length and dourness of the trilogy, and likening it to an endurance exercise. The issue of the production's overall aesthetic or tone, which so aggrieved Bond, was also noted as a problematic element. The critic for the *Daily Telegraph* observed that the production 'never makes up its mind whether to go for realism (and we are spared few radiation horrors) or for a heightened, tragic, poetic manner' (Miscellaneous, 1985: 720). The critic points to Bond's writing as contributing to this issue, saying: 'Mr. Bond's way of composing dialogue, which brims with improbable metaphors, though often striking, seldom succeeds in drawing us into a scene without defying verisimilitude' (*ibid.*). Still, other critics found much to praise about the production and registered its contemporary relevance. The critic from the *Listener* stated: 'what matters most is that Bond confronts, squarely, the issue of the age. And in imagining both the moment of conflagration and the subsequent activities of surviving communities, he achieves theatrical poetry of astounding power' (*ibid.*: 718). The critic for *Time Out* reached a similar conclusion, applauding the production for its visceral and intellectual intensity: 'Bond's view of a world in overextended extremis reaches into the mind-guts. His challenge to the audience of these plays is to accept the results of nuclear warfare as a terrible given, and go on from there – to learn from the dead about living. Forty years after Hiroshima and Nagasaki is not too late for this production to be reminding us of our capacity for self-extinction' (*ibid.*: 717).

Endgame, *Yes, Maybe* and *The Tin Can People* dramatise the aftermath of fictitious catastrophes and are ghosted, to a greater or lesser extent, by the atomic bombing in Japan. They all explore conditions of life after mass death – what it means to survive a catastrophic event such as nuclear devastation, and how this throws existence (one's own and that of the whole world) into question. In doing so, they expose precarious subjectivities and altered conceptions of mortality. Bond's desire to have an audience reach an 'abstract understanding grounded in material, particular reality' – a difficult nut to crack, and a possible contributor to the mixed reception of the RSC production – has been taken up by other theatre artists as well, and used to reflect upon and respond to the aftermath of the Holocaust. What does it mean to have survived this catastrophe and to live in the world after it? The final two examples tackle these thorny questions.

Abstracting catastrophe: *Replica*

Józef Szajna's *Replica* is formally different from the other examples featured in this chapter. It is not dramatic theatre but a 'spatial composition' involving human actors and props (cf. Wassily Kandinsky's early twentieth-century concept of a 'stage composition' involving abstract play of light, sound, and movement). Szajna, a Catholic Pole who worked against the Nazi occupation, was a Holocaust survivor who spent four years at Auschwitz and Buchenwald. He was part of an 'alternative' or avant-garde theatre scene in Poland in the 1960s to 1980s that included Jerzy Grotowski and Tadeusz Kantor. In 1962 he designed and co-created, with Grotowski, a famous and well-regarded production of Stanisław Wyspiański's epic drama *Akropolis* (first published in 1904), changing the setting from Wawel Cathedral in Kraków to the extermination camp at Auschwitz. Wyspiański's text mythologises Polish history; Grotowski and Szajna's production repurposed this history in light of the Holocaust. Szajna's designs for *Akropolis* were informed by his experience as a former occupant of the camps. Eschewing literal representation, Szajna sought to evoke the camps symbolically, commenting:

> I moved into metaphor. I wanted to find a 'context' binding today with yesterday, and people together, inside and outside the wire. ... I suggested to Grotowski that there must be total action, a welter of activity. ... Hence the wheelbarrows, which destroy the human being; hence the exhausted hands and tired, naked legs; hence the reduction of man to uniformity, which in the camp was embodied in those stripes. ... It was a production full of camp allusions, associations, reminiscences. But it wasn't documentary cinema, it was a metaphorical performance. Everything in it was minutely redrawn and transposed. (quoted in Howard and Łubiensk, 1989: 249, 251)

Szajna developed and refined his approach to evoking the Holocaust through stage imagery in the subsequent performance pieces he created. Kathleen M. Cioffi observes: 'Working with Grotowski ... clearly had an effect on Józef Szajna; many of the images he had created in *Akropolis* re-appeared in production after production' (1996: 103).

Replica, performed in Poland and around the world, is one such production. More accurately, it is a series of sequential productions beginning in 1971 with *Replika I*, a 'plastic-spatial' composition that did not involve actors, followed by *Replika II* in 1972, which *did* use actors, *Replika III* in 1973, which made further changes to the composition, and so on.[8] *Replika VII*, dating from 1986, looks to be the last in the series, though a television version broadcast in 1988 may also lay claim to this title.⁹ *Replica* also exists in textual form, courtesy of a scenario authored by Szajna. This text was sometimes reproduced in the programme (as in the programme for *Replika IV* at the Studio Theatre, Łódź, Poland, in 1973); the scenario has subsequently been translated into English. My analysis of *Replica* principally uses the English-language translation of the scenario and a recording of the 1988 television production. The broadcast version is effectively a filmed performance that substitutes the camera for live spectators, integrating it into the 'spatial composition' via direct address and use of close-ups.

The scenario comprises a brief account of the setting, followed by short narrative descriptions of ten individually titled sections. The opening image is of a mound resembling a 'huge refuse-dump' containing 'the scraps of civilization', all covered with peat and earth (Szajna, 1987: 149). The mound is initially motionless but then emits smoke and begins to stir. Body parts come into view; human beings extricate themselves. They are 'simple and coarse, dressed in gray sacks, barefooted, with their hair cropped' (*ibid.*). They excavate puppets from the mound, making appeals to the audience for assistance. A 'representative of automatism' – a superman – is roused and bends the recently exhumed humans to his will (150). They erect a monument to him and participate in '[something] bordering on a pagan ritual' (151). The superman-figure attacks them with 'a hissing fire extinguisher, resembling a machine gun', and then expires (*ibid.*). The last section refers to the actors spreading out 'a long roll of old photographs', using them as a 'shroud to cover the mound' (152). The photographs are trampled down by boots that fall out of sacks. The piece ends after a 'colorful tune-producing top' (a child's toy) is put into motion (*ibid.*).

As this synopsis indicates, this is not a plot-heavy piece. The plot provides a basic frame upon which to 'hang' a series of images, and these images – rendered dynamic in performance by the incorporation of live actors – are what drives the piece. It is difficult to make complete sense of *Replica* just by reading the scenario; the actions are not all intelligible, making the text seem partially obscure. Moreover, the text may be considered a rough sketch of what *might* happen in performance, rather than a prescriptive score. There are discrepancies between the English-language scenario, which dates from the mid-1970s, and the television broadcast from the late 1980s. The sequence of events is different in places and there is more simultaneity of action in the recording than is indicated in the text. This is understandable, given that these are different iterations of the piece. Nevertheless, the actors' performances in the broadcast version have an improvisational quality that suggests that Szajna (unlike Beckett, for example) did not have a 'textocentric' view of performance. Although the setting of *Replica* is reminiscent of Beckett's short play *Breath* (1969), which also features a stage littered with rubbish, Szajna seems to have taken a 'looser' approach to crafting performance. Agnieszka Jelewska-Michas reports that Szajna gave his actors considerable licence: 'To him ... the actor was not an element that had to submit completely to the will of the artist in the way Craig or Kantor demanded that their actors should. He left the actor with quite a wide range of freedom and relied on his creativity. The actor's presence on stage in Szajna's performances reminded the audience of the human element immanent in all art' (2006: 84). Like Beckett, though, Szajna was allusive, and his work is interestingly open to interpretation.

The programme is instrumental in helping one to interpret the piece. The programme for a performance that took place at the Brooklyn Academy of Music (BAM) in New York City in 1976 contains the following précis: '*A wordless odyssey through the holocaust, Replika depicts the indomitable spirit of man, tempered by the inhumanity directed against him by himself*.'[10] The progamme thus informs us that the piece is about the Holocaust. If one did not have this contextual information, including knowing about Szajna's status as a Holocaust survivor, one would probably still register that the piece is a response to the Holocaust (the word 'replika' in Polish can mean both 'duplicate' and 'answer' or 'rejoinder'), but this is not guaranteed. The Holocaust is evoked imagistically, but it is not directly mentioned. I have had students ask whether this piece is really 'about' the Holocaust, or if one must project this meaning onto it. It's a fair question. Szajna has, to a certain extent, abstracted the Holocaust and used it to create a performance piece that is suggestive of it, but is not limited to it.

Indeed, in a note on the text published in 1987, Szajna indicates that the piece has broader relevance, saying: 'The name *Replika* does not simply mean repetition of a historical event. Perhaps it is more like a history lesson. From the Holocaust to the mass suicide of madmen by nuclear explosions is only a step away. Through *Replika* I warn our times and indict power and violence' (148). Szajna thus connects the Holocaust to the threat of nuclear apocalypse, suggesting that his piece engages both historical and future-potential catastrophes. The programme for the 1976 performance at BAM contains a comment made by the Polish writer Andrzej Wydrzynski that provides an earlier articulation of this connection:

> *Replika*, this unusual theatrical poem, does not exclusively relate to the debasement of man in the concentration camps. The work has much wider

scope, touching upon universal tragedy. It also applies to Hiroshima and man's place in a world threatened with total annihilation. It presents a metaphoric world which we live in and is an apocalyptic warning. *Replika*, according to Szajna, is 'about the agony of our world and about our great optimism'.[11]

Additionally, in an interview published in 1989, Szajna, discussing the longevity of *Replica*, mentioned that 'the Japanese hope to show it – not just in Tokyo but at the sites of the camps and in Hiroshima' (quoted in Howard and Łubiensk, 1989: 254). To my knowledge, *Replica* was not performed in Hiroshima or elsewhere in Japan, but the fact that this was apparently proposed is significant for this chapter's juxtaposition of catastrophic events.

The scenario of *Replica* is replete with images and actions that connote the Holocaust, but that might also conjure the aftermath of a different catastrophe, such as nuclear attack. The opening image of a refuse-mound containing 'the scraps of civilization', including human beings buried within it, is one such example. It recalls photographs of piled corpses in Nazi extermination camps, but the hodgepodge composition of the mound, which contains mannequins, wheels and shoes, old stovepipes, torn newspaper and sacks, ropes, canvas, and plastic – also suggests a more generic catastrophe. The mound begins to emit smoke, which might lead one to think of Nazi crematoria. The human beings in the mound are apparently starved, as camp inmates were. The scenario describes a hand slowly emerging from the mound, 'clawing' for a chunk of bread: 'Seizing it, the hand swiftly disappears, trembling with fear of losing it' (Szajna, 1987: 149). The self-exhumed people, barefoot and dressed in grey sacks with their hair cropped, are visually suggestive of camp inmates. Szajna describes them as being 'frightened and blinded by the daylight, slowly accustoming themselves to the space' (*ibid.*: 149–50). They excavate puppets from the mound and try to 'bring them back from life' by manipulating and speaking to them (150). These people are seemingly traumatised and virtually speechless, managing only to utter occasional single words. Szajna calls them 'relics of the dead, living reminders of those who managed to survive' (*ibid.*). They resemble Holocaust survivors who were rendered mute by their experience, at least initially, though, in their harrowed state, they also recall the stupefied and traumatised dispositions of the *hibakusha* and witnesses to the atomic bombings. The superman figure, a 'usurper of power whose terrifying screams silence the others into obedience' is, of course, reminiscent of Hitler, and his figuration as a 'representative of automatism' links to the industrialised killing at the

4.1 The superman – the representative of automatism and the usurper of power – in Józef Szajna's *Replika* (1988)

Nazi extermination camps (*ibid.*). Still, as a mechanistic bogeyman, he has broader potential signification, and might also represent a technological threat. In performance, he was costumed with a long, metallic-looking pipe for an arm and a glowing light on his chest (see Figure 4.1), and was introduced with an ominous music cue featuring a ticking sound, composed by Bogusław Schaeffer. His capricious enactment of power seems designed to exhaust those under his proverbial heel, and to break their spirit, like how camp inmates were harassed and sometimes forced to execute absurd, physically strenuous chores. 'New prisoners particularly were forced to perform nonsensical tasks, such as carrying heavy rocks from one place to another, and after a while back to the place where they had picked them up. On other days they were forced to dig holes in the ground with their bare hands, although tools were available' (Bettelheim, 1979: 77). Szajna's text describes a comparable situation: '[The usurper] is power here. To the exhausted he throws motorcycle wheels. The people catch these wheels. They groan while carrying them. They run around the common grave, the mound. … Off-guard, they have involuntarily become the penal colony of common serfdom' (Szajna, 1987: 151).

The broadcast version of *Replica* indicates that Holocaust imagery was possibly more prevalent, and therefore more apparent, in performance than in the textual scenario. This version of *Replica* begins with a man picking up stones from the earth and chucking them into a wheelbarrow before running around the mound, wheelbarrow in hand. He unearths a photograph of someone wearing what looks to be the striped uniform of a camp inmate. The man winces at this discovery and stores the photograph on his person. Numbers written on a large, upright, tombstone-like rock evoke the serial numbers tattooed on to prisoners' arms at Auschwitz. An expanse of shoes individually placed on the ground is suggestive, in miniature, of photographs of large piles of shoes of victims who perished in the camps. An arm emerging from the mound caressing the hair of a mannequin's head recalls the grotesque mound of hair cut from camp inmates (which has subsequently been put on display at the museum section of Auschwitz). Prosthetic limbs extracted from the mound evoke the artificial legs and crutches used by people brought to the camps for extermination (also displayed at Auschwitz).[12] The superman's attack on his minions using a gas canister, which he sprays at them, has obvious resonance, although here, in an ironic reversal, the gas attack leads to the superman's own death. Finally, the carpet-like roll of photographs that the actors bring out at end of the piece is a mosaic of photographs of camp inmates wearing striped prisoner attire. The actors having left, Szajna comes on to the set dressed in contemporary clothes, carrying a picture frame and a spinning top. He places the frame over part of the photographic roll, makes a few adjustments to the set, puts the top into motion on the frame, and exits. A major-triad chord is quietly sustained on (what sounds like) a pipe organ, effecting a note of optimism after the bleak and disturbing scenes that have gone before.

Replica offers many signs and symbols, the meanings of which are sometimes ambiguous, obscure, or potentially polyvalent, depending one's cultural and historical knowledge. Arguably, it connotes a type of 'modern death' exemplified by Auschwitz (and Hiroshima) – namely, collective, anonymous, industrialised mass death that rubbishes humanity, literally and figuratively. The humans in this piece have been junked, put on the same level as inanimate objects, thereby suggesting an entirely non-spiritual view of death as termination rather than expiration (per Gilbert's thesis, outlined earlier). The individuality, and perhaps even the humanity, of these people has been lost. Initially they are presented as a collective biological entity. The scenario states: 'One can see that the entire mound pulsates and undulates in rhythm of a chewing organism' (149). The image of an amorphous, biological blob may also be thought to invoke, obliquely, fears of radiation-damaged humanity. Kenaburo Oe adumbrates this fear: 'What happened in Hiroshima ... may be the first harbinger of the world's real end, in which the human race as we know it will be succeeded by beings with blood and cells so ruined that they cannot be called human. The most terrifying monster lurking in the darkness of Hiroshima is precisely the possibility that man might become no longer human' (1995: 182).

The humans that emerge from the mound are not radiation-damaged, but they are seemingly in a state of collapse, and show signs of psychological and physical instability. In the broadcast version, the actors occasionally freeze where they stand; words seem to stick in their throats. They make guttural, gurgling sounds, groaning and crying out. They are unsteady on their feet. One of them tries to walk on all fours using a pair of artificial legs. One uses the wrong side of a comb to brush her bandaged scalp. Another puts a small mirror in her mouth and rattles it against her teeth. Later, she looks at herself in the mirror and appears appalled and shaken by her reflection. As with other characters discussed in this chapter who are survivors of catastrophe, these figures are ostensibly in a strange, paradoxical, deathly state of being. Szajna states in the text that 'the puppets imitate life' and that '[death] will be played by an actor' (in the original: 'Kukły imitują tu życie, śmierć zagra żywy człowiek') (1987: 149). (The Polish word 'kukły', here translated as 'puppets', can also mean 'effigies', 'dolls', or 'dummies'.) On the face of it, this is topsy-turvy and non-intuitive; after all, puppets require animation by human actors and more obviously connote death than a living performer. Indeed, this seems to be Szajna's meaning. The text states that '[the] actors try to bring the puppets back to life', treating them 'as their partners in the play' (ibid.). The actors treat the puppets as though they were formerly living people – victims who did not survive the catastrophe. The line about death being played by an actor may refer to the superman/usurper figure, symbolising a powerful, deathly force – perhaps he caused the initial death and destruction. Szajna's mixture (or mix-up) of animate performers and inanimate objects (replicas or simulacra of humans) suggests slippage between life and death, and the apprehension of death-in-life.

Kantor used marionettes for similar ends in his work (e.g., *The Dead Class*, 1975); he may have been influenced by Szajna in this regard (Cioffi, 1996: 103). Kantor writes about the deathly potential of mannequins in his 1975 manifesto 'The Theatre of Death', referencing Craig's concept of the *Über-Marionette* as well as the writing of Heinrich von Kleist on this topic. Kantor announces: 'I do not believe that a MANNEQUIN (or a WAX FIGURE) could replace a LIVE ACTOR, as Kleist and Craig wanted. This would be too simple and too naïve. ... The MANNEQUIN in my theatre will be a MEDIUM through which passes a strong feeling of DEATH and the condition of the Dead. A model for the Live ACTOR' (quoted in Kobialka, 2009: 235–6). Magda Romanska explains Kantor's use of marionettes in his work:

> For Kantor, the model for an actor should be the marionette, a form which is both dead and alive. Straddling life and death, the marionette simultaneously negates and asserts life. Becoming semi-puppets, the actors in Kantor's Theatre of Death multiply the meanings of their presence; they illustrate both the condition of death through the apparent absence of life (like a marionette), and the condition of life through their apparent presence (as human beings). Hovering ambiguously between life and death, they become alternately either the body devoid of essence, or the essence separated from the body. The identity of the actors is simultaneously destroyed and brought forward through this destruction. (2012: 265)

Szajna's use of puppets, mannequins, and dolls in *Replica* aligns with this usage. Both Szajna and Kantor used human simulacra in theatre to cast a deathly aura over living performers, suggesting an interchange or substitution between the living and the dead (or the non-living, in the case of puppets). Szajna's actors *enlivened* their object-partners, who, in turn, *deadened* the living performers – a fair exchange for artistic purposes?[13] Szajna's depiction of a post-catastrophic state in *Replica*, in which the animate and the inanimate are interrelated, evokes an impression of death-in-life – a morbid sensibility that cannot simply be shaken off, as it were, but that hangs over one's perception. This gloomy worldview came to the fore after Auschwitz and Hiroshima, and not just among survivors, as Mailer's essay (cited earlier) shows.

Replica's plot, such as it is, factors into this too. The 'awakening' of the superman/usurper figure (who may represent death) and his subsequent terrorising of the people who exhumed themselves from the mound may be taken to symbolise the condition of being continually 'under threat' from death and destruction, of having to live with the prospect of omnipresent death-by-power. These characters have presumably already endured some sort of major death-event, and are only beginning to claw their way back to life, when they are figuratively held hostage by the appearance (or reappearance) of a human-mechanical menace. This accords with Benjamin Noys's conception of modern death after Auschwitz and Hiroshima. Here, he synthesises ideas from Mailer and Agamben (e.g., the 'thanopolitics of modernity'):

> The situation of being left exposed to death can explain what Norman Mailer suggested: that life today is lived under the constant threat of death, from beginning to end and that the 'end' loses its sense of finality and meaning. What is peculiar about the modern culture of death is that the dividing

line between life and death is particularly unstable. We live in a 'zone of indistinction' between life and death, as Agamben puts it. (2005: 19)

Replica makes this zone apparent in theatrical performance, inviting spectators to witness and imaginatively enter it. However, Szajna does not present a uniformly nihilistic scenario. Although the awakening of the superman suggests that despot figures will always rise and threaten death, they need not have lasting authority. Szajna states: 'Power can never be right: the rights of man must always overpower power' (1987: 148). Hence, the superman figure in this text is defeated or expires (it is unclear how this happens), and the 'colourful, tune-producing' top that is sent spinning at the end of the piece suggests jollity and energetic optimism – but entropy, too, and the condition of teetering-on-the-brink. Elinor Fuchs calls the spinning top in this piece 'an emblem of humanity's crazy optimism in the face of catastrophe, but also of global catastrophe itself as the toy careens out of control and topples' (1987: xviii).

Replica offers a parable about the Holocaust and a warning to humanity. Szajna dedicated the piece 'to all those murdered by fascism' and 'to all those governing today as a pledge of honour ... that such horror will never happen again' (1987: 148). He creatively redeploys Holocaust imagery, encouraging audiences to learn from history and find parallels in other situations. 'We build theatrical reality ourselves', Szajna stated in an interview. 'I think the poetics of the theatre resembles the poetics of a dream: every element or fragment of it is a reflection of reality; it is true and concrete, yet it is ordered differently, thus obtaining new meanings' (quoted in Howard and Łubiensk, 1989: 245). Szajna's didactical, dreamlike abstraction of the Holocaust in *Replica* is a noble, moral endeavour, boosted – and perhaps validated – by his status as a Holocaust survivor.

The final play discussed in this chapter also abstracts the Holocaust for theatrical purposes, but, in contrast, does not aim to offer the audience a history lesson or edify them. More unsettlingly, this example invokes the idea of history as a nightmare from which we cannot awake, or readily fathom.[14]

Found in the Ground: a nightmare of history

Found in the Ground is an unusual and formally distinctive play, even in the context of Howard Barker's work. Barker has called it a 'play of landscape rather than identity' because it is less invested in character exploration and narrative intricacy than in patterning images, gestures, speech, and sound (Bosanquet and Caird, 2009). 'It is entirely impressionistic', he remarks, 'with a cascading number of scenes, all related but not always consecutive. So it operates differently from all other plays of mine, by breaking down the narrative that has always been at the centre of theatre in my and nearly all dramatic text' (*ibid.*). Elsewhere, he describes it as 'a balletic, imagistic, anti-linear series of dreams and chorus' (Brown, 2011: 184). A reviewer of The Wrestling School's 2009 production at the Riverside Studios in London noted that it was more like an installation piece than a 'traditional play' (Chew, 2009). Barker directed this production; he also designed the set, costumes, and sound, using various aliases.

Found in the Ground is also one of the weirder products of Barker's imagination in terms of its content, which is saying something. The chief character of the piece is Lord Toonelhuis, a former Nuremberg judge, now a nonagenarian, who is invalided, dying, and is having his book collection burnt. He periodically calls for the earthen remains of Nazi officers he sentenced to death to be served to him for his consumption. His attendants present him with earthen piles, not commenting on the oddness of this activity. He wants to eat Hitler ('the great meal / **The ultimate dish**'), but as Hitler was never formally judged, this wish cannot be granted (Barker, 2001: 337, emphasis in original). Nevertheless, Hitler does appear, as an infant in the arms of Toonelhuis's daughter, Burgteata – a woman who is erotically fixated with the dying and 'sleeps' with them. Hitler also appears as an adult, alongside his infant-self; adult Hitler discourses on artistic matters. At one point, Burgteata simultaneously suckles Toonelhuis and the infant Hitler – only one of the many confounding, disconcerting images in the play. Other characters make cryptic appearances, including the fantastical Knox, a 'spirit of a war criminal' who meditates on past actions, and a headless woman named Macedonia, who perambulates, naked, embodying and declaiming the victims of the Holocaust ('I am all the Ann Franks ... / All the Ann Franks me') and urinating on the ground (*ibid.*: 310). Welcome to Barker's surrealistic nightmare of history, in which *eros* and *thanatos* are problematically crossed and interlaced with philosophical speculation, individual and collective memory, private fantasy, psychological obsession, and bodily functions. One could approach this play from many perspectives, given its compositional density and assorted provocations and quirks. (Alternatively, one could back away from it and engage with something less odd and unpleasant, but then one would miss out on its interesting strangeness.)

I will focus on the way in which Barker abstracts the Holocaust, on what this suggests for our understanding of this history, and on the effects of the play in performance.

Found in the Ground draws on the Second World War and the Holocaust as part of its thematic content; it is ghosted by this history, connoting it in subtle, oblique, and direct ways, like *Replica*. Some of this is done scenographically. The play is seemingly set in the retirement home in which Toonelhuis is resident, yet the world of the play is capacious and abstract – a psychic landscape more than a fixed physical place. In this regard, it accords with Barker's vocabulary for the 'art of theatre' (a designation for his own theatre), which, he suggests, matches the attributes of death: 'Infinite ... / Nowhere / Incalculable / Illogical / Arbitrary' (2005: 92). The stage directions include sonic references that enhance the play's ambiguity and potential significations. A 'repetitive sound of an industrial process', first referenced in the exordium (a pre-show section that is scenographically constituted) recurs periodically: this could relate to work being done in the retirement home (there is a workman present), but it also might connote the Nazi military-industrial murder complex (2001: 287). Does this sound have a single origin? Who or what is making it? Which character or characters are hearing it? One cannot say for sure. The dramatic sound world is ambiguously constituted. The first scene begins with '*the sound of infinite distance*' – a wholly abstract reference (*ibid.*). When Toonelhuis kneads a mess of earth mixed with water – the apparent remains of a Nazi war criminal he judged named Hoss – a '*long cry of despair travels over the landscape*' and the '*industrial process starts up*' (288). Who or what is uttering this long cry of despair? Might it be uttered by Holocaust victims? 'Hoss' presumably refers to Rudolf Höss, founder and commandant of Auschwitz, who, by his own admission, created 'the largest installation for the annihilation of human beings of all time' (quoted in Levy, 2005: 324). Höss was tried at Nuremberg and sentenced to death. Toonelhuis, who apparently has discriminating taste-buds, remarks that the mud his nurses have served him 'was more Funck than Hoss' (Barker, 2001: 290). 'Funck' may refer to Walther Funk, *Reich* minister for Economic Affairs from 1939 to 1945, tried at Nuremberg and accused, among other things, of crimes against humanity. It is unclear whether the inaccurate spellings of the Nazis' names are intentional distortions or mistakes on Barker's part. ('Anne Frank' is similarly misspelled as 'Ann Frank' in the published text and the rehearsal script.)

Other scenographic elements of the play that evoke the history surrounding the Holocaust include the pile of smouldering books – the result of Toonelhuis's (unexplained) order that his library should be burned. This recalls public book-burning of material deemed to be 'un-German', including books by Jewish authors, in university towns across Germany on the evening of 10 May 1933. Yet Toonelhuis is not a Nazi, and he has commanded his books to be burned indiscriminately, though he has directed his librarian, Denmark (a Hamlet-like figure), to 'concentrate on the Humanities' (ouch) (*ibid*.: 311). Toonelhuis's trio of mechanical dogs, who '*erupt from their kennels and travel downstage on wheels*', barking, evoke the image of three-headed Cerberus, the hound of Hades, but they are also a reminder of dogs used to attack inmates in concentration camps (277). Scenic images of death are presented in filmic form near the end of the play (recall Satan's film about the First World War, presented in Lee's play *Satan the Waster*, discussed in Chapter 2). While Barker does not stipulate that the imagery relates to the Holocaust, the fact that the film is projected onto a screen positioned in front of Macedonia (a character who represents Holocaust victims), would make this apposite. '*A screen falls in front of the headless woman. It ... seems to rest on her shoulders. Instantly film of extermination and execution is projected onto the screen. The Workman rushes over the stage depositing a chair on which Hitler, curious and stimulated, sits. He stares like a man addicted to television. The industrial sound erupts*' (357). In the Wrestling School production, black-and-white wartime photographs of ruined cities were projected, both during the exordium and in this scene.

The character of Knox (a homonym of the Latin word '*nox*', meaning 'night') similarly evokes the Second World War and the Holocaust, though he may not be a criminal from this war, or only from this war. His war criminality is potentially more unfixed and transhistorical.[15] Yet, a lot of Knox's discourse resonates with the state-sponsored, bureaucratic, rationalised, and industrialised mass killing of the Holocaust. Knox mentions the 'rational pleasures' that 'accompanied, conditioned, and stimulated' his murders (294). He discusses rounding people up to be killed: 'I found them in their houses / I found them in the street / And these were / I vaguely knew it at the time / The finest individuals in the land' (307). He notes how 'with mass murder / strictly speaking / nothing is personal', how '[these] fellow human beings meant nothing to me', and how '[the] victims were individually / Nay / Collectively / Irrelevant' (315, 316, 326). A historical parallel: dehumanisation of prisoners by guards in the camps facilitated the mass extermination (see Waller, 2007). Knox links himself to the events of the Holocaust when he self-identifies as 'the utterer of Auschwitz / I the mundane bureaucrat' (Barker, 2001: 343–4). This spirit of the night – possibly of humanity's darkest night – hovers over the play like a spectre, attempting to rationalise monstrous actions, like the Nazi war criminals over whose trials Toonelhuis presided at Nuremberg.

Knox's alternate is Macedonia, who is disconnected from the main narrative and functions almost as a walking, talking part of the scenography. Her refrain about being 'all the Ann Franks' is accompanied by a list of names of professions of people filling the ditches and pits. It is an eclectic list, including composers, violinists, physicists, crop irrigation engineers, gym teachers, florists, office cleaners, an abortionist, a kidnapper, a prostitute, and the **'child molesting wife of a sadist'** (*ibid*.: 335, emphasis in original). Presumably, people who committed immoral and criminal acts were included among Holocaust victims, although this is an odd supposition, and one that is presumably meant to be shocking and/or disquieting. Linking Anne Frank with kidnappers and child molesters is jarring. A 'sanctified' version of Frank has come to represent Holocaust victims through the publication of an edited version of her diary and various adaptations of it for theatre and film. Frank has been turned into 'a symbol for human tolerance and the inner goodness of man' as part of a constructed public image that abstracts her from historical reality (Wertheim, 2009: 158). With Macedonia, Barker both invokes and subverts Frank's iconicity in this regard. Like Walt Whitman in his poem 'Song of Myself' (1855), Macedonia contains multitudes.

Macedonia is obviously a provocative, contentious character, given what she represents and how she is presented. The fact that she is headless could be taken to signify her status as a representative of the dead (after all, if you're without your head, you're probably dead, or possibly dreaming).[16] Being headless, she has no identifying facial features, which theoretically makes her a suitable signifier for the many faces of the victims she represents, who can notionally be projected onto her, much like the film of extermination and execution is projected onto a screen in front of her. Her nakedness might be thought to correlate with the unclothed, piled corpses found in concentration camps, yet it also potentially figures her as an object of sexual desire or fascination. Barker's frequently problematic gender politics are in evidence here. Other female characters in this play, such as Burgteata and the nurses, principally serve as objects of desire for men, and their sexuality is paramount, so it is difficult not to interpret Macedonia in this light. Still, she is not lusted after by other characters in the play, perhaps because she exists outside their framework (other characters do not interact with her, and may not even see her). Lara Kipp contends that Macedonia is not straightforwardly sexualised. She writes:

[High-heeled] and graceful, Macedonia is not without a certain erotic appeal; however, coupled with the images of war-torn civilisation and, more importantly, by virtue of the fact that she is headless ... (portrayed through an ingenious hat design in Barker's production), which effectively de-individuates her, any possible effect of sexual arousal is complicated by her positioning as part of the catastrophic and anonymous wasteland of the projections: she becomes an unidentifiable victim of war crimes, the faceless stand-in for millions of violated bodies, displayed for the visual stimulation of others. (2017)

Macedonia's alignment with scenes of catastrophic death certainly complicates her 'erotic appeal', but it does not erase its potential, which is one of the things that makes this play challenging and possibly objectionable. Presenting a character who ostensibly embodies and 'speaks for' Holocaust victims in a manner that suggests sexual objectification is ethically suspect, to say the least. This is not obviously a respectful remembrance. Rather, one may find it immoral and/or fetishistic – though, as is often the case, Barker's aesthetics and dramaturgy are interestingly complicated and merit further analysis.

In the Wrestling School production, Macedonia, played by Vanessa-Faye Stanley, was naked from the waist up (excluding her angled hat, which in the darkness obscured her head); she wore a flesh-coloured short skirt (see Figure 4.2). Her physical movement was slow and

4.2 Macedonia (Vanessa-Faye Stanley) and Hitler (Alan Cox) in The Wrestling School's 2009 production of Howard Barker's *Found in the Ground*

stylised, drawing on elements of Butoh, and was curiously captivating. Her beautiful movements created cognitive dissonance in the context of her signification. One does not readily associate beauty with dead Holocaust victims. Associations of this sort are, however, made in Barker's theatre. In Barker's play *Und* (1999), a Jewish aristocrat named Und awaits the arrival of her guest, a Nazi officer who is possibly her lover. Und reports that the Nazi officer sees beauty in the dead: 'The dead acquired a certain beauty / notwithstanding their agonized expressions / twisted limbs eviscerations a certain beauty so / he said' (2012: 14). Barker, in his theoretical writing, has established mismatched apprehensions of beauty and ugliness as one of the building blocks of his self-styled 'theatre of catastrophe': 'It was beautiful', he writes, 'but not in any way I already understood the beautiful. This particular beauty came in the guise of the ugly' (1997: 127). Macedonia exemplifies this strange and unsettling contradiction. Furthermore, as an ambulatory signifier of – and mouthpiece for – the dead, she may be compared to the character of Fourth Woman in Bond's *The Tin Can People*, who pretends to be a 'dead woman walking' as a stratagem for avoiding death. Macedonia, by contrast, is not seeking to avoid death. She is not ostensibly seeking anything at all, though she does make death figuratively present through the spectacle of her existence, and by invoking the dead in her speech.

Toonelhuis also makes death figuratively present through his bizarre meal requests. His habit of consuming, in earthen form, Nazis he has sentenced to death does not make literal sense. After all, people do not transform into earth when they die, although, if buried, decomposition of a corpse into soil will eventually occur. Barker is presumably drawing on this association; he also presents a dead body in earthen form in *Und* (2012: 46). Earth is likewise an important component of Szajna's *Replica*. In that piece, the performers, having exhumed themselves from the mound, take clumps of earth in their hands and shower it over their heads in a cleansing gesture. However, Szajna uses earth in a quasi-spiritual way. In an interview, Szajna stated: '[*Replica*] takes place on soil, in soil, people grow out of it, are born a second time: it's like an event which has already taken place and is coming round again, as life itself is reborn spasmodically' (quoted in Howard and Łubiensk, 1989: 255). In *Found in the Ground*, Toonelhuis derives peculiar satisfaction from kneading Nazis in earthen form. A stage direction refers to him working the mess '*with a sort of ecstasy*' (Barker, 2001: 289). This is perplexing: is Toonelhuis revelling in the fact that they are dead, or in having physical contact with them in this weird, transmuted form? Perhaps both.

Toonelhuis's muddy cannibalism is sickening. It recalls imagery from the poetry of Paul Celan, a Holocaust survivor for whose work

Barker has expressed admiration.[17] A poem by Celan, dating from 1959, conjures a scene of prisoners in Nazi death camps. It begins with the lines 'THERE WAS EARTH INSIDE THEM, and / they dug' (1996: 157). 'Psalm' (1963), another poem by Celan that evokes the Holocaust, begins with the following stanza: 'No one moulds us again out of earth and clay, / no one conjures our dust. / No one' (*ibid.*: 179). Toonelhuis is supposedly kneading and ingesting Nazis-as-earth, not camp inmates, but the link is still suggestive. Moreover, in performance, the earthen piles mixed with water visually resembled excrement, paralleling the thematic and symbolic importance of urination in the play. Macedonia periodically urinates onto the ground. Additionally, Toonelhuis recalls a time when, having sentenced five people to be executed, he sought air and went for a walk in a forest east of Mecklenberg, where he encountered a young girl 'pissing' and was entranced by 'the music of her urine' (Barker, 2001: 300). The sound haunts him, pleasurably, despite, or perhaps because of, its associations, and it features as one of the leitmotifs of the play. A non-sexual, non-poetic, entirely awful historical reality relating to the play's conjuration of bodily waste concerns the way in which camp inmates were degraded by being forced to soil themselves. Reska Weiss, a Holocaust survivor, reported about a death march: 'Urine and excreta poured down the prisoners' legs, and by nightfall the excrement, which had frozen to our limbs, gave off its stench. We were really no longer human beings in the accepted sense. Not even animals, but putrefying corpses moving on two legs' (quoted in Niewyk, 2003: 114). What is one to make of Macedonia's urination and Toonelhuis's fascination with urination and his ingestion of excrement-like mud in this context? Does it pertain? Is some type of transposition in operation?

Toonelhuis's ingestion of dead Nazis may be interpreted as a metaphor for the act of 'taking in' or absorbing traumatic history – elements that society would much rather eject from the system, or the body politic. Toonelhuis perversely savours that which is commonly abjured and treated as abject. His various compulsions and obsessions, along with those of other characters in the play, create the impression of a kind of psychic echo-chamber in which traumatic memory and history are made to resound, albeit in a distorted manner. Material is perpetually chewed over, as it were, but remains undigested and indigestible. Knox and Toonelhuis have an exchange that speaks to their compulsive behaviour:

> KNOX: I can't stop
> I can't stop

TOONELHUIS: Nobody can
KNOX: I can't because
TOONELHUIS: Nobody can
KNOX: I'd like to
TOONELHUIS: They all would
  All of them
  Would like to
  But they can't
KNOX: I can't
TOONELHUIS: You can't certainly

(Barker, 2001: 289)

The characters are caught in a kind of loop, neurotically picking over and revisiting the things that obsess them. This has social significance, particularly in relation to the Holocaust. In a note titled 'Eating the Dead' in the production programme, Barker indicates that the play manifests '[the] requirement to digest all that is terrible in human experience ... a need which the plethora of historical documents, memoirs, theses and analyses cannot satisfy, nor the reiteration of dogmatic attitudes'.[18] Elsewhere, Barker notes how death can be socially denied, but not indefinitely, stating: 'Death enters, retreats and re-enters society as it enters and re-enters the individual life, sometimes marginal in its effects, sometimes a deluge. It can be denied for only so long, since in its long silences it becomes a subject of *longing*' (2005: 99–100). *Found in the Ground* may be thought to transmute and obliquely connote the way in which the Holocaust haunts the West's 'cultural unconscious' (Gilbert, 2006: 136). A line from W.G. Sebald's collection of short stories *Die Ausgewanderten* (*The Emigrants*, 1992), which cryptically blends fact and fiction in relating how a set of characters have repressed their experiences in the Second World War, only to suffer psychological crises later in life, resonates here: 'And so they are ever returning to us, the dead' (2003: 23). Despite its abundant peculiarities, Barker's play validates this sentiment, challenging us to face the (faceless) dead, and to wrestle with a history of death that cannot – and should not – be set aside and bracketed off. Like it or not, we must still grapple with this history and its legacy.

This does not make for a straightforwardly enjoyable experience, either as a reader or as an audience member. I must confess, I quite dislike this play. I find it intriguing, but also maddening, unpleasant, and occasionally excruciating. It's a long, dense, knotty text that offers no relief, and is almost unrelentingly horrible. The Wrestling School's production clocked in at just under two hours and was performed without an intermission, as is Barker's wont. His production tapped into the harsh, brutal qualities of the play, showcasing them scenographically and in the actors' performances. The sound design amplified heightened moments in the staging and connoted the impressionistic, hallucinatory mode in which the play is written. The repetitive, clanking sound of a pile-driver (a mechanical device used in construction to drive piles (poles) into soil) heard over a drone in the exordium initiated an oppressive, quasi-hypnotic sound world. The sound design combined naturalistic elements, such as the intermittent barking and whimpering of Toonelhuis's dogs, with recurrent snatches of modernist and contemporary music by composers such as Karlheinz Stockhausen, György Ligeti, and Thomas Köner. The effect was to create 'a constant wave of sounds/moods', as mentioned in rehearsal notes; many of these sounds were strident or otherworldly.[19] Toonelhuis's hallucinatory reality thus became a theatrical experience, as the 'echo chamber' of his thoughts and obsessions was replicated in performance over the loudspeakers and through the actors' voices: earworms, found in the ground, but capable of burrowing into one's own consciousness.

Barker scholars have written about how his theatre can work to overwhelm one's perception through its intensity via the combination of the text, the actors' performances, and the scenography (like Antonin Artaud's 'theatre of cruelty'). Kipp, writing about Barker's production of *Found in the Ground*, observes:

> By utilising scenography conceptually (in attesting beyond that which is manifested to things invisible, inaudible or simply impossible to actualise) as well as the tangible spatio-temporal realisation in production (with its affective impact on the audience's senses), Barker extends his thematic considerations of violence into the physical presentation of the stage worlds. This serves not only to render them perceptible but crucially offers the resulting sensual assault as something beyond reason to invite, excite and overwhelm the audience's imaginations. (2017)

Similarly, in an essay on poetry and intensification in Barker's 'theatre of plethora', Karoline Gritzner theorises how Barker's work approaches the formal condition of formlessness, stating:

> When we confront it, when we participate in it, we feel our intellect waver, our senses overflowing, because we can only respond to the 'too much' by listening to our instincts. I abandon myself to the work and what it does to me. The question is no longer what it means but what it does. Participating in it is also a mode of doing; it is an action, which leaves me breathless, exhausted and exhilarated, lost for words but also restless and exhilarated. (2012: 344)

I cannot claim to have had an ecstatic experience with this production, although – full disclosure – I have not experienced it live, but only in recorded form.[20]

The critical response to Barker's production of *Found in the Ground* was, overall, not so rapturous; as with much of The Wrestling School's work, British critics were ambivalent about it. Lyn Gardner, in the *Guardian*, commented that the production '[felt] both monumental and unassailable, like a vast piece of theatrical granite' (2009). Honour Bayes, writing for *The Public Reviews*, concluded: 'love it or hate it, it is undeniable that this piece will leave an indelible stain on both one's body and mind' (2009). Fittingly, this last comment strikes a chord with statements Barker has made about his artistic aspirations and his ideas about art. Barker has discussed the 'art of theatre' metaphorically *wounding* the person who encounters it, enacting a psychic cost and rupturing equanimity. In an interview with Mark Brown, Barker outlines why he rejects catharsis as an aesthetic theory and professes not to comprehend it: 'I can't see the point of creating a work of art which enables a public to discharge some anxiety in order to leave the theatre in a healthier condition than when it came in. I don't ask that of the public or of the actors. If good art wounds you, I want that wound to be experienced continuously, not resolved' (Brown, 2011: 195). He reiterates this point in the programme for *Found in the Ground*, saying: 'The Art of Theatre re-opens the wound and whilst never daring to speak of healing (a preposterous claim) reminds us how beauty resides only in the tenderest places, a pain we are adult enough to tolerate … even to recognise as the essence of life …'. *Found in the Ground* certainly does not offer anything remotely resembling healing; on the contrary, it presses a finger on various sore spots and reminds us of their existence.

Other examples of theatre discussed in this chapter that confront historical and/or imagined future catastrophe, such as Duras's *Yes, Maybe*, Bond's *The Tin Can People*, and Szajna's *Replica*, are also tremendously bleak, but they still offer some morsels of comfort, and may be thought to have a moral agenda or a didactic bent. These pieces hold out the possibility of humanity beginning again from the ashes of ruin, and perhaps learning from past mistakes. *Found in the Ground*, in line with Barker's amoral, non-didactic theatre, does not do this, but instead 'wounds' the audience by making them experience a twisted, perverse nightmare of history that is arguably a fitting correlate to the events it strangely refracts. Although objectionable in certain respects (e.g., its representation of women and Holocaust victims), the play testifies, obliquely, to the importance of registering the ongoing trauma of historical catastrophe and recognising that we live in its wake.

Sarah Goldingay has written about how Barker's work offers a 'poetic lens through which to examine our relationship to pain in the twenty-first century' (2012: 335). Her remarks have bearing on how the Holocaust is remembered (or not). She proposes that Barker's theatre of catastrophe 'might ... be seen as an analgesic of sorts. This is not because it numbs the pain ... but because it honours the existence of pain and in so doing offers the means for the audience to reconsider it and relocate it in our own particular realm of experience' (*ibid.*: 356). In *Found in the Ground*, pain relates to 'man's inhumanity to man', to the millions of murdered Holocaust victims, the survivors of the catastrophe, and to the situation of those of us who have not been directly affected by it, except in ways that are not always immediately evident (e.g., in our conceptions of death and dying). Barker writes: 'Profound emotional experiences even where they fill the audience with despair (perceived 'negativity') serve to increase resistance to social coercion ... The pessimistic work ... strengthens the observer by obliging him to include death in his categories of thought' (2005: 13–14). Barker's theatre thus both potentially *wounds* and *strengthens* its audience through its pessimism – another contradictory feature, and something to mull over.

Through its phantasmagorical presentation of death, *Found in the Ground* poses the question (posed by Adorno and others) of what it means to live 'after Auschwitz', to recognise inherent barbarity and capacity for evil, and to reckon with the impact – and taint – of this catastrophe as an ongoing, irresolvable dilemma. In entering Toonelhuis's warped universe, we (re-)acquaint ourselves with historical catastrophe and the dangerous impulses that motivated it – impulses that, disturbingly, continue to crop up.

A final complication: *Found in the Ground* presents a catastrophic scenario, but Barker does not consider the play an example of his 'theatre of catastrophe' because it is not a tragedy (Bosanquet and Caird, 2009). In Barker's estimation, tragic characters 'go beyond' life as it is known and seek out death – typically their own – to transgress, ecstatically, and 'steal power', and perhaps knowledge, too, from this 'unknowable' domain. The death that underlies *Found in the Ground* is of a different, and much less grandiose, order. Barker writes: 'The art of the apocalypse, the art of death unwilled, of death inflicted and not embraced, of coercion, of life robbed not yielded, of death as only one iota of universal slaughter, is a victim's art, one of pity therefore, or of indignation that this *need not have been*. In tragedy, there are no victims, only sacrifices ...' (2005: 100–1). The play treats catastrophic events but it is not, according to Barker, an example of his 'theatre of catastrophe'.

Conclusion

As this chapter has demonstrated, theatre from the mid-twentieth century onward that explores the significance and after-effects of the Holocaust and the dropping of the atomic bomb does not engage the concept of catastrophe uniformly. Why should it? The historical events in question are clearly distinctive, and the possibility of further nuclear devastation remains a *hypothetical* disaster. Nonetheless, there are significant correspondences between these examples relating to their presentation of ideas about mortality, and the fact that dramatic/theatrical representations of catastrophe – both historical and imaginary – flourished after the Second World War is hardly coincidental. Despite the obvious differences between the Nazi death camps and death by nuclear bombing, they both factored into a formulation of modern death as techno-bureaucratically executed mass death, resulting in perceptions of death-in-life and existential meaninglessness. The benefit of analysing 'the matrix constituted by Auschwitz and Hiroshima together' and relating this to examples of modern drama and theatre is that these conceptions of mortality become newly and uniquely apparent (Milchman and Rosenberg, 2004: 188). The examples of plays and performance pieces discussed herein are bleak in terms of their content and relatively oblique in terms of their connection to history and their signification. They offer examples of theatrical art as a 'problem of understanding' – a problem that may prove exasperating and remain unsolvable, but that challenges us to meet its demands, despite potential unwillingness and discomfort (Barker, 1997: 91).

Death and dying yield innumerable problems of understanding, both on the 'macro' level, as discussed in this chapter, and on the individual or 'micro' level, as discussed in the next. The drama of dying in the early twenty-first century is shadowed by the catastrophes of the twentieth – and yet, à la Beckett, *we go on* ...

Notes

1. I follow Donald Niewyk and Francis Nicosia in using the term 'Holocaust' (capitalised) to refer to Nazi genocide – 'the systematic, state-sponsored murder of entire groups determined by heredity. This applied to Jews, Gypsies, and the handicapped' (2000: 52). Niewyk and Nicosia discuss the problematic issues relating to using and defining this term.

2 Since 2007, climate change has also been taken into consideration when setting the time of the Doomsday Clock.
3 For a collection of Japanese plays about the bombings, see Goodman (1994).
4 I am grateful for the assistance of Audrey Keyes and Dominique Lampron Thibault in helping me to translate this text. Quotations from Duras's play are translations made by one or more of us, and endeavour to preserve the distinctive (i.e., ungrammatical) elements of the original.
5 To preserve the macaronic nature of Duras's text in translation, words are presented in French that are in English in the original.
6 Schell is referring here to the difficulty of reckoning with the future non-existence of unborn generations, but his point is also applicable to the contemplation of massive death of the world's existing human population.
7 The prompt book and production records for this play (subsequently cited) are available at the Shakespeare Birthplace Trust in Stratford-upon-Avon.
8 The first form that *Replica* took, as detailed in the programme for the 1975 performance at the Brooklyn Academy of Music, was in Szajna's piece *Reminiscences*, exhibited in Kraków in 1969.
9 This version of *Replica* was first broadcast by the Polish television channel TVP2 on 23 March 1988. It has subsequently been rebroadcast by the Polish television channel TVP Kultura, from whom I acquired a recording.
10 This programme is held at the Brooklyn Academy of Music (BAM) Hamm Archives.
11 I quote from the programme held at the BAM Hamm Archives. The comment is unattributed in the BAM programme but *is* attributed in the Polish-language programme for the 1974 production.
12 Photographs of the exhibits at the memorial-museum at Auschwitz-Birkenau may be viewed here: http://auschwitz.org/en/gallery/exhibits/evidence-of-crimes,1.html.
13 Rebecca Schneider, writing about theatre and history, asks of performance: 'For why is it only the dead that appear to come alive? Do not the living also cross a kind of threshold away from the strictly immediate present moment?' (2014: 44–5).
14 I reference a famous line from James Joyce's *Ulysses* (1922): 'History, Stephen said, is a nightmare from which I am trying to awake' (1986: 22).
15 Adding to this uncertainty, he is referred to as a boy in the stage directions, but in the Wrestling School production, a woman (Julia Tarnoky) performed the role.
16 An exception: if one's head is separated from one's body and cryogenically frozen, one might still be partially 'alive' in some respects. For a philosophical discussion of personal identity and mortality vis-à-vis hypothetical brain transplantation, see Kagan, 2012: 98–131.
17 See, for example, Barker, 2007: 70.
18 A programme for The Wrestling School's production of *Found in the Ground* is contained in the Howard Barker Digital Archive at the University of Exeter.

19 I quote from Paul Bull's personal production file, made available to me courtesy of Rachel Sutton. Bull was credited for 'sound realisation' for this production.
20 I did, however, attend a stage reading of the play at a Wrestling School workshop in London in 2005. The format did not facilitate the kind of ecstatic audience response described by Gritzner.

5

The drama of dying in the early twenty-first century

Death and dying are hot topics in the early twenty-first century, though they have not lost their power to chill. As discussed in Chapter 3, the 'death awareness movement', which began in the mid-twentieth century, raised consciousness and advocated for transparency about issues relating to mortality. The hospice movement, led by Cecily Saunders in England in the 1960s, likewise advanced a patient-centred approach to care for the terminally ill. In the latter decades of the twentieth century, the multidisciplinary field of death studies took shape in the academy, amassing a considerable body of literature and normalising scholarly enquiry into death and dying. In *The Hour of Our Death*, Philippe Ariès humorously observes the renewed contemporary social interest in the topic, writing: 'Shown the door by society, death is coming back in through the window, and it is returning just as quickly as it disappeared' (1981: 560). Forty years later, Ariès's observation is still resonant, although, conceivably, both processes are concurrently in effect: death is still 'shown the door' even as it 'comes back in through the window', and so forth, in a loop. It is not as though there is a uniform social attitude toward mortality in the West in the early twenty-first century or at any other time. Moreover, even though death and dying appear to be more widely discussed than they were in previous decades, this does not make them less contentious. Euphemistic ways of speaking about death endure. Grappling with mortality remains challenging, and the impulse to avoid this subject whenever possible, or at least not to dwell on it, has not gone away.

This is understandable. Death and dying invariably involve a plethora of thorny issues. With increased secularisation in many industrialised Western societies, religious assurances about the existence of an afterlife have faded, lending credence to the rationalist credo that one's earthly existence is total. And yet, belief in posthumous spiritual existence persists. Most pressing are concerns about end-of-life: specifically, the form it will take, its duration, and the degree of agency one will have. It is common for dying people – as well as the not-yet-terminal – to wish to take as much charge over their dying as they can, and die as they have lived, individualistically. However, this is not always possible or permitted: hence, the right-to-die movement. Due to the interventions of modern medicine, which continually work to extend life, dying in the early twenty-first century can be a protracted process, and may be burdensome both for the dying person and for care-givers. Achieving a 'good death' is certainly not guaranteed or always readily accomplished. It can involve significant emotional and financial costs and may be logistically complicated. Moreover, the idea of what constitutes a 'good death' is not universally shared. Indeed, it is potentially problematic and may be context-specific, varying widely in multicultural societies (Walter, 2003: 218). Even defining death is not always straightforward. As scientific understanding of different types of death (e.g., clinical, brain, cellular) develops, new realities of human existence emerge, raising questions for which there are no easy answers.

This chapter surveys attitudes toward death and dying in the early twenty-first century and investigates how a selection of British and Irish dramatists and theatre-makers have explored end-of-life scenarios and provided insight into this domain. My case studies are Carol Ann Duffy's *Everyman* (2015); *Woman and Scarecrow* (2006) by Marina Carr; Caryl Churchill's *Here We Go* (2015); and Kaite O'Reilly's *Cosy* (2016). This selection is not meant to represent the West in general or to provide complete coverage of the ways in which twenty-first-century dramatists and theatre-makers have treated this subject. Nevertheless, these pieces are not so culturally specific that they relate only to Britain and Ireland. Rather, they collectively engage a range of widely-pertinent issues concerning death and dying, dramatising elements of 'what happens now' as well as posing this as a question for individuals and society.

Taboo or not taboo

The idea that death is taboo in Western societies persists, despite evidence to the contrary. This is curious. One might suppose there is no longer cause to make this claim or proffer it as a truism. It is not apparent that it necessarily *is* true, given the substantial amount of media discourse and public (or semi-public) engagement on issues relating to death and dying. This includes, for example, numerous journalistic reports on end-of-life; opinion pieces on 'dying well'; television programmes devoted to the subject (such as *Billy Connolly's Big Send Off*, first broadcast in the UK on ITV in 2014); electronic mourning of celebrities on social media and other types of online memorialisation (see Walter *et al.*, 2011); a wide variety of representations of death and dying in popular culture, helping to constitute a cultic 'celebration' and fetishising of death (Khapaeva, 2017); and national coalitions devoted to raising awareness (e.g., the UK-based organisation Dying Matters, founded in 2009). The international success of the 'death café' phenomenon, launched in 2004, in which a 'pop-up' event is locally organised to allow a small number of people to get together and chat about death in a relaxed and friendly environment (with tea and cake!), indicates that discussing death among strangers in public is not an unbreakable social taboo (see Miles and Corr, 2015). However, the existence of organisations such as Dying Matters and initiatives such as death café suggests that consciousness-raising is still necessary, or is thought to be necessary, and that there are people – and not just the recently bereaved – who want, and perhaps need, to talk about death (more) openly. Evidently, even with widespread social commentary and pervasive – albeit sometimes tokenistic or sensational – popular-cultural engagement, including vicarious death, dying, and killing in video games, death still casts a pall, necessitating continued enlightenment.[1]

Research conducted by the National Centre for Social Research in 2012 on British social attitudes to dying supports this hypothesis. Although 70 per cent of the 2,145 adults in Britain who were interviewed for the survey stated that they felt comfortable talking about death, 43 per cent of respondents had not discussed their wishes for their own end-of-life because death seemed far off; this was also the case for 23 per cent of respondents aged seventy-five and above (Shucksmith *et al.*, 2013: 1). It would seem as though there is a strong distinction, and perhaps a disconnect, between being comfortable about death in the abstract and making decisions and arrangements about one's own extinction. Disturbingly, the main reason offered by respondents aged seventy-five and over as to why they had not discussed end-of-life issues was that 'other people do not want to talk to me about my death' (*ibid.*: 12). The authors conclude that 'there is a need to normalise death and build the conversation about better ways of dying' (*ibid.*: 17).

A national survey of Irish attitudes to death, dying, and bereavement, conducted by the Irish Hospice Association in 2014, yielded similar findings. The survey of 891 Irish adults living in the Republic of Ireland found that only 'a third of the Irish adult population believe that discussion around death and dying is sufficient in Irish society, with almost six in ten adults saying that the level of discourse is not enough', an increase of six percentage points in ten years from 51 per cent to 57 per cent (Weafer, 2014: 5). 23 per cent of respondents said they were 'completely comfortable' with discussing death or dying. 18 per cent professed to be 'very comfortable'. 44 per cent said they were 'relatively comfortable' (*ibid.*). Nevertheless, 65 per cent of respondents (and 57 per cent of respondents aged 65 and above) said that they had taken no action regarding personal preferences for care at the end of life. 73 per cent said they had taken no action about an 'advance care directive' and 76 per cent had taken no action regarding power of attorney (9). The author concludes:

> Most Irish people do not have arrangements in place for what they would like to happen if they became terminally ill or died. The most popular actions included making known their views about organ donation, burial or cremation, making a will, and carrying a list of key people in case of emergency. [...] It may be that actions focussed on making things easier for others / for those left behind are prioritised over actions focussing on actual personal dying and end of life, traditionally a more difficult concept to engage with. (5, 9)

Although death is a questionable or challenged taboo in Britain and the Republic of Ireland (and possibly in other Western nations too), people claim to be notionally comfortable about it but, tellingly, circumvent it to a greater or lesser extent in relation to their own future dying.

In a sociological examination of the death taboo in modernity, Raymond L.M. Lee suggests that 'if there was ever a death taboo, something has happened in recent decades to attenuate or even nullify it' (2008: 746). To justify this claim, Lee cites the proliferation of scholarly research on human mortality, the spread of the hospice movement, cinematic depictions of dying and the afterlife, 'lively' interest in near-death experiences and after-death communications, and New Age redefinition of death as spiritual transcendence (*ibid.*). These phenomena prompt

Lee to ask if 'we are now witnessing the twilight of the death taboo and the efflorescence of alternative conceptions of death challenging the silence of the grave' (*ibid.*). There are, as Lee notes, alternative (i.e., non-denial-based) 'narratives' about death in operation in the early twenty-first century (though they hark back to discourses that were popular in the *fin de siècle*, e.g., spiritualism – see Chapter 1). However, it seems misguided to contend that these narratives mean that the death taboo has 'lost its impact' (*ibid.*: 757). Perhaps it has 'for the segment of society open to New Age and esoteric ideas concerning life beyond death', but, for many people, death can still provoke psychological unrest and emotional and financial concern (*ibid.*). Can one afford to have 'a good death'? Will one's dependants be financially secure? Death may not be wholly taboo, but it remains a potentially fraught topic, which means that contemplation of it and personal planning are frequently (and sometimes perpetually) deferred, or are not given extensive thought.

Dying isn't necessarily any easier than living, and dying unprepared can compound the difficulty. The well-known remark attributed to Woody Allen – 'I am not afraid of death; I just don't want to be there when it happens' – is funny because it is true, or at least it is true for many people who profess to fear dying more than death itself. After all, death is a seemingly unknowable state of (non-?)being, especially if one does not hold religious belief. Death may be nothing at all, so why should one fear it? Dying, on the other hand, is recognisably experiential. It is undoubtedly *something*, even if it is not fully knowable, in a phenomenological sense, except to the one who is dying. However, as noted in Chapter 3, dying individuals do not always want to know that they are dying (as in the case of Berenger in Ionesco's *Exit the King*). Pain-relief drugs can facilitate this un-knowing. Moreover, prior to their dying, these individuals may choose not to contemplate their own mortality, extensively or at all. Riffing on the Woody Allen line, they don't want to be 'there' (i.e., in the state of dying) *before* 'it happens' either, even imaginatively. As Tony Walter remarks, not wanting to know one is dying and choosing not to express feelings of grief are part of the 'wide diversity in how human beings encounter death'; these approaches 'may work' for individuals and 'must be respected' (1994: 186). Not being aware of dying might constitute a 'good death' for these people. Nevertheless, always referring to death obliquely and euphemistically, and endeavouring to ignore its reality, if possible, means that one will probably be less ready for difficult, end-of-life choices that often must be faced (Shucksmith *et al.*, 2013: 13). Five hundred years ago, dying unprepared would have been a disastrous occurrence for a god-fearing individual worried about the fate of their eternal soul.[2] In the early twenty-first century, in rapidly secularising societies, dying unprepared can still provoke existential crisis and personal drama.

Rather than suppose that a widespread shift has occurred in the twenty-first century (one that perhaps began in the mid-to-late twentieth century) from denial to acceptance, it seems more prudent to postulate the simultaneous co-existence of a range of attitudes toward death and dying in Western societies. This is less clear-cut, but likely more accurate. On this point, Benjamin Noys suggests that the idea of death as taboo is inadequate and misses the bigger picture: 'The idea that death is taboo in modern culture or the idea that we are now witnessing the end of the death taboo fail both to deal with the complex ways in which death is invisible and highly visible in modern culture' (2005: 3). Noys juxtaposes the decline in death rates in the affluent cultures of the West (making death 'invisible') with everyday media exposure to death (which makes it 'visible'). He also factors in the existential situation of living with the abstract threat of nuclear destruction, ecological catastrophe, and the emergence of untreatable epidemic diseases. (See also: terrorist attacks.) These situations, or potential situations, have varying forms of (in)visibility and recognition or non-recognition in our day-to-day life. 'In modern culture death is not simply invisible or taboo but bound up with new structures that expose us to death. ... To analyse death in terms of exposure is also to move beyond the clichés of death as taboo or the end of the death taboo and into the *contradictory and uncertain space* of death in modern culture' (*ibid.*, my emphasis).

In this murky light, it is virtually impossible to live without some consideration of the shadow of death, though its seeming omnipresence – or perhaps its diversity – might lead one to treat it as a type of background hum: the 'white noise' of living in the modern world. Just as one can, in certain circumstances, choose to ignore ambient sound and not consciously hear it, so too can one accustom oneself to having partial or limited engagement with the information about death and dying to which we are frequently exposed, and regulate one's attention and intake. This might be considered a necessary coping mechanism. Who has not, on occasion, read a news headline about some awful event and opted not to read further at that moment? ('Not now ... I don't want to read about that now ... That won't do me any good ...') But what is the ethical cost of abstaining, of 'turning away'? (Duffy's *Everyman* picks up on this.)

Walter is also leery of the notion that death denial is in general operation in the 'modern era', though he acknowledges that it is not a black-and-white issue. In *The Revival of Death*, he notes the irony that despite continued announcements that death is taboo and that 'our society' (presumably British society) denies death, it is more and more discussed, adding that in 'some circles, not least the quality media, death and our feelings about death are no longer taboo but the new radical chic' (1994: 1, 2). Nonetheless, Walter highlights a discrepancy between private experience and public discourse: 'When individuals who are dying or bereaved complain that "death is a taboo subject", this does not mean that there are no publicly available languages for talking about death but that these languages do not make sense of the experiences and feelings of the individual and his or her friends, family, and neighbours. They therefore do not know what to say or how to say it' (1994: 23-4). Notwithstanding standard condolences, verbal communication with and among the recently bereaved can be difficult and seem inadequate, which bespeaks the profound sense of loss and personal trauma that death can occasion. This should not be used to lend credence to the 'death denial' thesis, Walter proposes, as it is a general human predicament and not one that is necessarily historically specific. He elaborates on this theme in a later piece of scholarship:

> [In] Britain today, clearly some aspects of death are highly visible, not least in the mass media, while at the same time some bereaved individuals feel shunned and people tend to die out of sight in hospitals and institutions. It's a mixed picture. And it is a mixed picture between individuals, which often causes difficulties in families – long after a death, she still wants to talk, he goes on silent fishing trips; she thinks he doesn't care, he thinks she should be over it by now. (2008a: 9)

Acknowledging the 'mixed picture' of death in the early twenty-first century, along with the 'contradictory and uncertain space' in which it operates, invites consideration of multiple narratives and viewpoints rather than an overarching grand narrative; hence, the selection of case studies in this chapter, which is intended to reflect this, in part.

While attitudes to death are unlikely to be identical in any society at any time, it would seem as though a 'culture of individualism' has encouraged a broader range of attitudes to death and ways of dying than had previously existed (Walter, 1994: 2). It is fitting, then, that Frank Sinatra's song 'My Way' topped the chart of popular funeral music, compiled by the UK-based Co-op Funeralcare, in 2016.[3] Walter remarks: 'Individualism's requirement that I live my own way is increasingly being extended to a requirement that I die and mourn my own way' (*ibid.*). Elsewhere, he notes, in relation to the development of personal spirituality (e.g., idiosyncratically borrowing from various faith traditions): 'The ultimate authority is not one's community, nor the sacred text of one's chosen religion, but "what works for me"' (Walter,

2003: 219). Individuals will not necessarily know *how* they want to die or grieve, however, especially if there is an array of available options; they may be directed in this regard by medical professionals and members of the funeral industry (Walter, 1994: 3). Theoretically, loss of shared meanings in relation to death and dying may result in a paradox of choice, a type of paralysis that disables one's ability to make decisions about end-of-life, or to do so confidently. Brian Heaphy, writing about Anthony Giddens's (1991) study of the self and society in the 'late modern age', summarises some of the effects of the breakdown of shared meanings:

> The post-traditional order is increasingly characterized by contingency and radical doubt. There are few, if any, given authorities, and multiple (and often conflicting) sources of expertise mean that all claims to truth are open to revision. Individuals are therefore faced with a multiplicity of competing 'truths' on any given issue, and there is no one framework that explains the meaning of things, or tells people how they should live. (2007: 98)

Heaphy connects this to mortality, paraphrasing Phillip A. Mellor and Chris Shilling's (1993) work on self-identity and the 'sequestration' of death in 'late' modernity:

> [The] decline of the sacred, increasing individualization and the growing significance of the body to self-identity imply that death is more problematic in late modernity than ever before. This implies that the risk of death is profoundly threatening for a sense of personal security in late modernity. Death and dying are nowadays individual problems and there are few collective resources that can be drawn upon to make sense of them. (2007: 161)

The 'Dying Matters' organisation and the death café initiative mentioned earlier work to counteract the grim spectre of 'atomized and lonely modern individuals who are left without meaning and are thrown back on their own resources when faced with their own mortality' – a distressing picture indeed (Heaphy, 2007: 149). Time to join AA (Anomie Anonymous), perhaps?

As an art-form that traditionally seeks to exploit communal experience, theatre can – and arguably does – serve as another vital collective resource for facing mortality, potentially helping audiences to cope a little better with ontological insecurities, and possibly providing them with valuable information about death and dying as well (e.g., regarding assisted suicide in *Cosy*, or CPR in Unlimited Theatre's *Am I Dead Yet?*). This depends on the piece in question, of course, and on an audience member's personal disposition; theatre that is thematically about death can also be discomfiting and unnerving, as has been shown throughout this book. This chapter's case studies illustrate how modern theatre can serve as a memento mori for audiences, a rehearsal space for dying, and an imaginative exploration of what may come 'after' in human experience. The proverbial mirror these pieces hold up to nature is cracked and splintered, in keeping with the 'mixed picture' of death in the West in the early twenty-first century and the 'contradictory and uncertain' space in which it operates. The stylistic and formal variance of these pieces matches this conceptualisation too, yielding an overall impression of a complex and contingent situation with no simple solutions.

Everyman's existential crisis

Carol Ann Duffy's adaptation of the medieval Christian (and specifically Catholic) morality play *Everyman*, produced at the National Theatre (NT) in London in 2015, offers a striking example of how a dramatic text and theatrical production can incorporate both transhistorical and historically specific attitudes toward human mortality. One might assume that the 'original', English *Everyman*, which dates from either the late fifteenth or the early sixteenth century, could function only as a period piece in twenty-first-century Britain, given the strikingly different sociocultural contexts and belief structures (or lack thereof), yet the NT production was praised for its contemporary relevance. This updated *Everyman*, directed by Rufus Norris, was still able to resonate with audiences (at the National Theatre and in cinemas as part of the NT Live programme), even though divine judgement is presumably not a concern for non-religious people living in the UK. Indeed, even devout Christians do not necessarily believe in hell any more. As mentioned in Chapter 2, the notion of hell has been on the decline in Britain since the First World War (Walter, 1994: 15). If these spiritual concerns are no longer (as) pressing for audience members (who may also be agnostic or of other faiths), does this undercut the drama of *Everyman* and render it less affecting? This is debatable. Nevertheless, as Walter remarks in a short video included as part of the digital programme for the NT production, what has *not* changed between the early sixteenth century and the early twenty-first century is that death still typically poses great difficulties, both for the dying person and for their friends and family, who can be great companions when all is well, but may be unwilling or unable to lend much assistance when one is dying. In this respect, the dilemma presented in *Everyman* is recognisable as it is still played out in people's lives. Everyman's existential crisis is brought about by being unprepared for death. This continues to have valence, even in what is for many people a godless world. It parallels the continued reluctance to make decisions about, and arrangements for, end-of-life, as articulated in national surveys.

Duffy transports *Everyman* to the twenty-first century but largely retains the narrative of the medieval text. God, disapproving of humanity, commands Death to find (an) everyman and bring him to a reckoning. Death 'taps' the character of Everyman, who, panicked at this prospect, tries to get help from collective entities represented in character form (e.g., Fellowship, Goods, Knowledge) and from his kindred; ultimately, he discovers he is on his own and must take leave of his Senses and Wits (e.g., Sight, Passion, Conscience) before he dies. Early in the play, Everyman is celebrating his fortieth birthday when, in a drug-induced high, he falls off a balcony. The subsequent action ostensibly takes place '*in his head during his fall to his death*' (Duffy, 2015: 11). Presenting *Everyman* as an 'interior, mental drama' (a familiar technique in modern drama – cf. Ionesco's *Exit the King*, discussed in Chapter 3) may make its abstract characters and narrative construction more identifiable, or less stylistically strange or passé, for a contemporary audience (Innes, 1981: 120). The idea that your life can flash before your eyes when you die is commonplace. Duffy uses this trope to frame most of the play's action as the mental drama of someone in free fall, swiftly moving toward death.

God, in Duffy's drama, is a female cleaner (see Figure 5.1). The play begins in a low-key fashion with God cleaning the stage. The depiction of God as a manual worker doing a low-status job might be taken to signify the lowly, or at least diminished, status of the Christian God in contemporary British society. Alternatively, one could interpret it as a reminder of God's supposed omnipresence, with a feminist twist, as in: *she* works in mysterious ways and can appear in unexpected forms. Interestingly, Duffy pairs the characters of God and Good Deeds; they are to be played by the same actor. What are we to make of this doubling? One might surmise that *God is in the good deeds that you do* rather than (just?) a discrete, supernatural entity (see also the Christian concept of the Holy Spirit). This is possibly a more palatable idea for audience members who may be sceptical or dismissive of the idea of divinity, or who may have a different notion of divinity. At Everyman's birthday party, one of his friends raps that they are all godlike in their current state of alcohol- and cocaine-fuelled abandon:

5.1 Chiwetel Ejiofor as Everyman and Kate Duchêne as God in the National Theatre's 2015 production of Carol Ann Duffy's *Everyman*

> FELLOWSHIP: Masters of the Universe, you're –
> listen to me listen to me – you're God.
> What's God like God like God like God like –
> you're God-like, listen to the truth.
>
> (Duffy, 2015: 4)

Fellowship reverses the Christian doctrine of God becoming man, positing a collective and possibly transitory delusion of grandeur. Yet, Everyman is ambivalent about putting faith in God, even after he is approached by God's representative (or 'God's heavy', as he calls himself), Death (*ibid.*: 8). 'I don't even know if I believe', Everyman tells Fellowship, implicitly referring to belief in God (14). In flight from Death he explicitly articulates his doubting sensibility, rehearsing a common line of thought that questions how a benevolent God could let 'bad' things happen:

> What God? What God?
> Show yourself!
> I don't know you!
> You've never answered my prayers.
> What about dementia and cancer?
> What about my mum and dad?
> Cure them.

> Who are you?
> The creator ... of the mosquito?
> One child dead every thirty seconds
> from an insect bite?
> Bravo for that, you sick fuck!
> If you do exist, you're a wanker.
> Answer!
>
> (28–9)

In this play God *does* exist and so could answer Everyman's questions, but she does not, although she does converse with him before he dies (at least in his head).

Everyman makes this invocation to God after having visited his family. He hopes to get them to speak for him during his reckoning, but is unsuccessful and is rebuked. In Duffy's version, Everyman's parents are not in good health, as indicated in the quotation above. His mother has a portable oxygen machine and uses a colostomy bag. His father appears to have dementia. He does not recognise Everyman or understand that it is his birthday. He mostly recites quotations from texts he has learned by heart. One of them is a quotation from Thomas Paine's pamphlet *Common Sense*, published in 1776: 'It is the good fortune of many, / To live distant from the scene of sorrow' (21). Paine's lines, though plucked out of context, resonate with this domestic scene (and perhaps Everyman's father realises this on some level). Everyman's sister chides Everyman for his infrequent visits, reminding him that *she* has been their parents' primary carer for years, to the detriment of her own self-development and life experience:

> What about my 'Reckoning'?
> All the things I haven't done yet?
> I've had to be the strong one here
> because you can't cope
> with them getting old and senile and ill.
>
> (27)

Everyman says he has paid off the mortgage on their parents' home, but otherwise does not offer much of a defence to his sister's criticism, acknowledging that he has 'been an arsehole' (*ibid.*).

In this scene Duffy sketches, in miniature, a recognisable and disconcerting picture of living into old age in the twenty-first century, along with the demands this can place on family members who take on the role of primary carer. Dying slowly of a chronic, degenerative, but not immediately terminal, condition is one of the hallmarks of life in developed countries. One may or may not consider this to be favourable, depending on the circumstances and on one's perspective. Surveying this situation, Guy Brown remarks:

> [The] vast majority of people in the developed world (and increasingly in the developing world) die from degenerative diseases, such as cancer and heart disease. These diseases are caused by age, and dying from them is slow and becoming slower, so that the processes of death and aging are merging into one. Death is currently preceded by an average of 10 years of chronic ill health, and this figure is rising. ... Few people survive until death without significant physical and/or mental disabilities, extending over decades. Death is no longer an event, it has become a long, drawn-out process. (2008: 6)

Several hundred years ago, when *Everyman* was first composed, one might expect to die over a short period – a few days, perhaps. In the twenty-first century, this process is often protracted and less readily defined.

Everyman's decision to minimise contact with his ailing parents is understandable, though it obviously does not reflect well on him. As God observes about humanity at the outset of the play, 'Everyman liveth only for his pleasure' (Duffy, 2015: 5). Duffy uses the character of Everyman to critique modern consumer culture, the acquisition of wealth-for-wealth's sake, and widespread disregard – both of less-fortunate people and of the planet. The poster image for the NT production shows Chiwetel Ejiofor, as Everyman, absorbed with his mobile phone, oblivious to God's giant finger pointing down at him. In a clever piece of marketing, the image of the giant hand with a downwardly pointing finger was installed onto the side of the National Theatre building during the production run, allowing members of the public to stand in for Everyman, and to be pointed at by 'God'. Talk about tempting fate![4] In posing as Everyman, were members of the public knowingly or unknowingly indicting themselves (i.e., as being similarly caught up in their own affairs, oblivious to the world around them)?

In keeping with the didactic tradition of the morality play, Everyman comes to realise his imperfections and limitations. '[Call] it obscene, / but I've always loved my stuff', he tells the character of Goods, presented in the NT production as a posse of excessively gilded, shiny, plasticky people (*ibid.*: 31). Everyman is, by his own admission, 'a deeply sentimental, shallow guy' who has taken and used resources unmindfully and selfishly, not wanting to think about the consequences of his lifestyle, or, indeed, the finite nature of his own existence (45). He has embraced the philosophy of *carpe diem*, of living-in-the-now, and letting the future take whatever course it will. When Death embroils Everyman in a storm of rubbish, he is made to confront his wasteful habits and avoidance of seemingly insurmountable problems that are not uniquely his own, or caused by him alone:

> EVERYMAN: I kept my head down. Looked away.
> There's always be another day.
> The waste.
> I thought the Earth was mine to spend,
> a coin in space.
> I hated the News. The News.
> Didn't want to hear it –
> floods, fires, melting, burning, droughts, extinctions…
> too much!
> What could I do? Me?
> My parents used to watch the News
> and then the Weather.
> I saw the Weather turn into the fucking News.
> I put my hands over my ears,
> like a spoiled child. I admit it!
> I confess!
>
> (44)

Everyman's lack of engagement with the grand challenges of combating environmental destruction and climate change ('Forgive me if I didn't save the fucking planet / single-handed'), and his blocking-out of information about other calamitous world events, is *one* way of being-in-the-world, of living with the reality of being continually exposed to information about death and destruction, previously referenced (43). However, it registers as being misguided, as it is bound up with Everyman's unmindfulness concerning his own mortality, which is presented in kind. Duffy turns the traditional directive to look-to-one's-own-death into a parallel parable about looking to the future of the planet, prompting Kirsten Shepherd-Barr, in an essay contained in the programme for the NT production, to describe Duffy's *Everyman* as a play for the Anthropocene age.

Everyman eventually exchanges the directive of *carpe diem* for that of *temet nosce* – 'know thyself'. This involves letting go of the vestiges of his religious faith, to which he initially clings. As his reckoning nears, in desperation he recites a prayer, the Act of Contrition, which he sang in school as a child. In the NT production, Ejiofor knelt in a crucifix position, removed his belt, and whipped himself on the back while reciting the lines. (This action is not specified in the play-text.) In the medieval version, Everyman, eager to avoid purgatory, successfully does penance and empowers his 'good deeds' by physically punishing himself. Duffy's Everyman, in contrast, breaks off his attempt at doing penance. For him, the language of repentance is inauthentic and meaningless: 'No, no, no! Dead language. / It means nothing. / It isn't me' (50). In performance, Ejiofor lashed himself a few times, then threw his belt away. Duffy's Everyman finds solace in coming to terms with who he has been: a flawed human being with a mixture of 'good' and 'bad' qualities, a 'ragbag of a man' (as he calls himself), who realises in retrospect that he could have led a better life and better appreciated its wonders (54). As he nears death, he cherishes the earthly, embodied experiences he has had. He offers a paean for his life:

> Thank you, thank you
> for the sweet, sour, ugly, beautiful, the cool, the crap,
> for discord and harmony, rough, smooth,
> for the fragrant or foul, the fucking lot of it.
> My whole life all I've ever wanted
> was to be alive; awaken
> to the light and air of here. Now.
>
> (52)

Although he discounts religion (as, notably, does God, who says religion is a 'man-made thing' that will 'pass'), Everyman retains the possibility that he has a soul and wonders where it will go (65). 'To Nothingness? ... To God?' (63).

In the NT production, after Ejiofor had delivered his last line (in which Everyman calls Death a 'cunt'), a dummy, representing Everyman's body, quickly dropped into a pit behind him, marking the moment of Everyman's death (*ibid.*). (The puppet-drop is not in the play-text.) Ejiofor continued to sit on a bench, staring vacantly, before getting up and exiting with Kate Duchêne, who played God/Good Deeds, after her final speech. (This *is* in the play-text.) In God's speech, delivered after Everyman has supposedly died but before the character/actor leaves the stage, God appears to validate Everyman's posthumous existence, saying: 'I see his soul, its flickering little flame. / I am well pleased' (*ibid.*).[5] Is this all still somehow part of Everyman's imagination – an indicator of conscious awareness even after death? It would seem Everyman has 'done enough' to guarantee his soul's survival. Secular self-reckoning has apparently been substituted for divine reckoning, or perhaps it complements it.

On this point, an online commenter ('valerieinthegallery') on the *Guardian* website responded to a review of the production, in which the reviewer suggested that Everyman's lack of fear of divine judgement in Duffy's adaptation is a script difficulty. The commenter stated: 'Interesting that being secular means "taking away the fear of judgement." As a secularist, I take responsibility for my own judgement – at the moment of death, will I feel content that I have done my best, in good faith? Can I live with myself? Far harsher than awaiting the judgement of Another, who will forgive me anyway, if I repent' (Clapp, 2015). The NT production of Duffy's *Everyman* (and/or a discussion of it) apparently resonated with secular audience members, despite the deistic framework. This may be because Duffy uses the characters of God and Death to facilitate Everyman's journey of self-discovery. Alternatively, one might posit that Everyman has conjured these figures for his own purposes: he draws on them as stock characters to judge himself before he dies.

Although Everyman was not 'prepared' to die before making his fatal descent, the mental and spiritual journey of self-discovery he undertakes during his few seconds of free fall allows him to come to terms with the swift and clumsy ending of his life, resolving it and making it beautiful. This is an appealing turn. It speaks to the desire to obtain psychological 'closure' about one's life – to wrap things up, for oneself if not for others – and to better understand oneself *through* the act of dying.[6] The attempt to wrest meaning from death by making one's own dying *meaningful for oneself* is notionally empowering, even if the derived meaning is self-fabricated and fantastical. This does not necessarily make it less apt or true. Contemporary dramatists and theatre-makers explore self-discovery through dying, creatively redeploying archetypes and folkloric elements to realise this objective.

Raging against dying: *Woman and Scarecrow*

Marina Carr's play *Woman and Scarecrow*, first performed at the Royal Court Theatre in London in 2006, further exemplifies a modern drama of dying in which the central protagonist, the eponymous Woman, unwilling and unprepared to die, rages on her deathbed 'against the dying of the light', to quote from Dylan Thomas's famous poem (2003: 148), and gradually comes to a newfound understanding of herself and the life she has lived. It parallels Duffy's *Everyman* in this regard and recalls other Irish deathbed dramas (e.g., Tom Murphy's 1980 play *Bailegangaire* and Sebastian Barry's 1998 play *Our Lady of Sligo*). Likewise, it tracks with Carr's general thematic interest in death, which figures in many of her plays and is frequently coupled with self-discovery. Melissa Sihra remarks: 'In Carr's plays from 1994–1998, it is through the act of death that the protagonists commence new processes of selfhood and, perhaps, fulfilment. [...] In Carr's theatre, death is not the end, but rather, a way to excavate the life that has been lived, and to process experience, as the passage continues' (2008: 28, 34). In conversation with Sihra, Carr has stated:

> The fact that we are dying probably is the only significant thing for all of us. And *how* we live, and *how* we die. I think that is so important – *how* one dies. I love biography because I love reading about how people die. I think it says everything about how they have lived – it is extraordinary. I love the idea of the tragedy of man and woman. It *is* the only significant thing about us – that we are going to die, and that we all get it so wrong. (quoted in Chambers, 2001: 56)

We all get it so wrong. But, as has previously been mooted (e.g., in relation to Freud's comments about people knowing 'how to die', discussed in Chapter 3), is there a 'right' way to die, an optimal *ars moriendi* (art of dying)? The question will return when discussing *Cosy*.

As the discussion of Duffy's *Everyman* illustrates, Carr is not unique in making dying a type of learning activity for characters – and, by extension, for readers and audience members. Nor is this solely a literary device; it has wider social expression. Walter observes that 'the notion that dying provides a last opportunity for the person to become truly authentic, to acknowledge his or her real inner self' is a particularly modern, post-Freudian conception of personhood in which there is 'a distinction between "inner self" and "outer expression"' (1994: 44). In this play, Carr foregrounds the search for personal 'authenticity' by splitting a dying character into two parts, Woman and Scarecrow. The latter is an alter-ego figure that only Woman can see and hear (cf. the personified Senses and Wits in *Everyman*).[7] The friction between these two figures, along with the difficulty and painfulness of dying bitterly and regretfully, generates dramatic conflict and pathos.

Woman and Scarecrow is set in a bedroom in 'the present', somewhere in the Irish Republic. Woman is dying of an unspecified condition. Woman has had eight children with her unfaithful husband, referred to as Him in the text, and thinks she is three months pregnant. Her children do not appear in the play, but the character of Him does, along with Auntie Ah – the woman who raised Woman after the death of her mother, and with whom Woman has a combative, aggrieved relationship. The bulk of the play takes the form of dialogue between Woman and Scarecrow as they review the events of Woman's life and try to determine how and why it proceeded the way that it did. Lurking in the wardrobe is a nameless, male, winged creature that makes its presence felt intermittently and with increasing force; this 'thing' is understood to be an embodiment of death. At the end of the play, Scarecrow merges with The Thing in the Wardrobe (as it is referred to in the stage directions) and initiates and presides over Woman's final breaths.

This rich and fascinating play offers many ambiguities and unresolved questions. What exactly *is* Scarecrow? What is the nature of her relationship to Woman? What is the significance of Scarecrow's ultimate merging with The Thing in the Wardrobe? Carr blurs the line between the real and the fantastical, as is her wont as a dramatist (see Leeney and McMullan, 2003). The most logical reading of the play is that it is a mental drama, like Duffy's *Everyman*. Woman, who has returned home from hospital to die, is in (and out of?) an altered state of consciousness – a dream state, perhaps, and maybe even a waking dream – and therefore mentally evokes Scarecrow and The Thing in the Wardrobe as indices of her *agon* over her dying. The text provides some justification for this reading. At one point, Woman tells Scarecrow that she would write down something Scarecrow has just said 'if I wasn't unconscious' (Carr, 2006: 18). The fantastical characters may thus be understood as psychological projections – mechanisms by which Woman can conduct a self-reckoning before she dies (like Duffy's Everyman). This does not prohibit a supernatural, spiritual, or poetic interpretation, which might posit Scarecrow as Woman's soul, heart, or conscience, for instance. The matter is open-ended.

The fantastical characters have various symbolic and cultural associations, and it is readily understandable why Woman might conjure them in these circumstances. Crows are commonly associated with death. The function of a scarecrow is obviously to keep crows and other birds away. In keeping with her designation, Scarecrow does battle with The Thing in the Wardrobe to delay Woman's death. The 'Thing' is notably avian. Scarecrow refers to '[hearing] him sucking his oily black wings' (*ibid*.: 12). The 'Thing' is mostly heard but not seen (the opposite of what children should be, in the well-known axiom), though he does extend a wing and a clawed foot out of the wardrobe at the end of the first act – an intimation of his inevitable approach. The 'Thing' invokes childish fears of unseen entities hiding somewhere in the bedroom dark (e.g., under the bed). Also in play is the trope of 'the wardrobe as a fairy-tale-like site for death, pulling us strongly into a threshold beyond the realistic dimension', as in C.S. Lewis's Narnia books (Sihra, 2008: 32). The figure of Scarecrow recalls the 'Keres' (female death-spirits, or daemons, in Greek mythology – the daughters of Nyx, the Greek goddess of the night), and the banshee (*bean sí*) of Irish mythology – a female spirit who heralds the death of a family member. Scarecrow also partially resembles a guardian angel. The idea of a guardian angel is ancient, and, curiously, in vogue in contemporary mourning (see Walter, 2016). Scarecrow is not simply any *one* of these figures. In magpie fashion, Carr appears to have collected and interwoven an assortment of cultural tropes – or, to think of it another way, her text has multiple, perceptible cultural resonances. Referential collage is similarly evident in Woman's wide-ranging points of interest and observations, which encompass an idiosyncratic hodgepodge of elements from culture and society, and from her own life.

One might suppose, given the character's name, that Woman herself is archetypal – an Everywoman figure. Her biography is certainly not atypical, especially in the context of women in Catholic Ireland in the twentieth century (i.e., a difficult upbringing, lots of children, an everyday struggle-to-cope). Yet, it is not clear that Woman is meant to represent all women, or all Irish women – any more than the character of Him is meant to represent all men or all cheating husbands. The play does not operate on an allegorical level in the manner of the medieval *Everyman*. Carr's Woman is not a simple abstraction, but is, in fact, highly individuated (cf. Sophie Treadwell's 1928 play *Machinal*). She has been shaped by her society, but is not merely a generalised gender personification. Miriam Haughton states: 'while Carr clearly signals an economy of power in relation to the subjugated role of women in patriarchal societies … she does not construct Woman as a victim. … Carr places much accountability for Woman's bitterness at her own door, or in this case deathbed' (2013: 76). Woman is her own person, even if this personhood is composed of more than one part, or has more than one articulation (i.e., Scarecrow).

The Thing in the Wardrobe might also be considered a part of Woman – a part she has suppressed, or possibly repressed, relating to apprehension of her own mortality. The fact that it is unnamed, referred to only as a 'thing', is a potential indicator of the fear she has for it. (Per common wisdom, the ability to name a source of anxiety may make it less worrisome, and not naming it more worrisome.) As discussed elsewhere in this study, death has frequently been figured as a bugaboo in the West in the twentieth century, as something that should not be mentioned and might best be sequestered. Carr deploys this trope. Death, in the form of a malevolent creature, is literally closeted in this play; the symbolism is striking. Now, on her deathbed, Woman cannot ignore the reality of her own extinction – something that is all too readily banished from conscious thought.

Scarecrow suggests that Woman is dying because she has 'decided to die' (*ibid*.: 14–15). Woman disputes this, saying: 'I'm sick. The body has caved in ... My body has betrayed me or I have betrayed it or the betrayal was mutual. Who cares! I'm fatal. Terminal. Hopeless' (15). Scarecrow later tells her she is dying because Scarecrow has 'given up', effectively deciding (for her) that Woman must die (51). Given that we are led to understand that Scarecrow is a part of Woman and interlinked with her (e.g., when Woman, in a snit, refuses to breathe for a few moments, this affects Scarecrow too), this suggests that Woman has perhaps subconsciously willed her own death. This would accord with Freud's idea of the 'death drive', the psychological pull toward self-destruction: 'an instinctual reaching towards that state in which there is the complete absence of excitation, a state of zero tension characteristic of the inorganic or the inanimate' (Dollimore, 2001: 186).

Even if Woman has not literally initiated her own death, she is particular about her funeral wishes, which she wants to be specific to her as an individual: a death practice that has enjoyed renewed popularity since the late twentieth century (see Walter, 1994).[8] Although Woman is dismissive about religion, saying 'God is for the living' (and is therefore of no use to the dying), she still wants to have a Catholic funeral mass (Carr, 2006: 42). This suggests Woman might be a lapsed Catholic, of which there are increasingly many in twenty-first-century Ireland. Woman may also be part of the 'faithless flock', an 'à-la-carte Catholic': in other words, someone who picks and chooses what they believe, and may mainly participate in church rituals for certain major life (and death) events only. Woman provides written instructions for how her unborn child (if indeed she is pregnant) should be buried in a separate coffin on top of hers; how she would like four black horses with black plumes, and to have one of her favourite Demis Roussos songs played as she is carried up the aisle by her sons; which priest should say the mass; what her funeral clothes should be; how she should be made up and laid out; and so forth.

Woman's thoughts turn to what might happen to her after she dies. She seems to think that she *will* have some sort of posthumous existence. In her darker moments, she contemplates the terror of being consciously buried: 'I see tombs in shadow, mossy, weather-scarred tombs and all the dead squashed in and me with them wondering if there is starlight above. I'm being buried alive. I am my own ghost' (40). In a feisty exchange with Him (i.e., her husband, not God), she sardonically imagines herself landing in eternity and praising her beloved crocodile-skin boots to God: 'I'll describe them to Him [i.e., God, not her husband] till He aches to have a human foot the size of mine that He can encase in crocodile-skin boots' (57). (The textual references to Him can get a bit confusing – God and Woman's husband threaten to merge.) Later in the same conversation, Woman offers what appears to be a genuine metaphysical musing:

> Try to keep me alive for them [i.e., her children], for lately I have begun to suspect if there is such a thing as eternity it resides in the hearts and minds of those who have loved us, for time, memory, eternity are merely constructs of this fallen world and it is here among the fallen we will be remembered and forgotten. (63)

This reflects the common notion that having children can provide a type of immortality. It also connotes a model of selfhood that is not individualistic and not strictly circumscribed by a single person or entity. Guy Brown elaborates on this idea, which has valence in a globalised, technologically interconnected world:

> If we entertain the notion that beyond death various components of ourselves, spiritual, genetic or cultural, will survive in non-individual form, then our concept of the monolithic self may fracture and dissolve into a web of interacting components, the genes and memes that we share with our family and culture. The classical atomic theory of self (where the self was single, separate, unified, digital and unchanging) needs to be replaced by a wave theory (where the self is multiple, overlapping, distributed, analogue and changeable). If the self is not digital (all or nothing), this implies that we can lose parts of the self ... but it also suggests that parts of the self may survive the death of the individual. (2008: 11)

Carr's play may be thought to illustrate the idea of a multiple, distributed, wave-self via the interlinked characters of Woman, Scarecrow, and The Thing in the Wardrobe, who are eventually brought together as part of a symbolic (or psychological) process of self-reckoning through dying.

The symbolic significance of Scarecrow transforming into The Thing in the Wardrobe at the end of the play to extinguish Woman's life is that death may (or should?) be thought of as being *internal* to us rather than an 'external' entity we might evade (although medical science is newly challenging the 'impossibility' of evading death, as I will discuss in the last chapter of this book). Brown encapsulates what it means to 'draw death into life', aligning it with ageing: 'Death is no longer out there waiting at the end of the tunnel; it is inside all of us all the time. And death will grow inside us until it bursts apart' (2008: 137). The idea that death is interior to life – that we 'carry death within us' – is not new; it recurs throughout Western philosophy and psychoanalytic theory (e.g., Nietzsche, Schopenhauer, Freud) (for a discussion of this, see Dollimore, 2001). It is also true on a cellular level, and is necessary for continued survival. Haider Warraich reminds us: 'At any breathing moment in our lives, we have cells being bequeathed life and cells that are signalled to die. So even as we live, parts of us are dying' (2017: 14). Apoptosis, meaning organically programmed cell-death, is triggered when cells accumulate disrepair and need to be replaced. Significantly, as Warraich observes, it is when certain cells (e.g., cancer cells) do *not* die and instead strive for cellular 'immortality' that biological problems ensue, which can lead to a person's death (2017: 15, 23).

In Carr's play, Woman has kept death in the proverbial closet for much of her life, banishing it while she got caught up in the routine of living (but not thriving). On her deathbed, she reflects, in a mordant fashion, on not having previously been more mindful of her mortality (a common refrain):

> WOMAN: We should all live beside graveyards, otherwise we're likely to forget.
> AUNTIE AH: Forget what?
> WOMAN: That the whole point of living is preparing to die. Why did no one ever teach me that? (Carr, 2006: 43)

Recall Carr's statement about dying, quoted earlier: 'we all get it so wrong'. Carr's darkly humorous play serves as a memento mori for readers and audience members. Róisín O'Gorman concludes a review of the 2006 Royal Court Theatre production of the play with the following remarks: 'As the audience emerged into the hot bustle of a London summer, going into the Underground seemed less appealing than ever. So we walked in the open air, searching for the possibilities in whatever time is left us' (2007: 103). In the twenty-first century, theatre can provide a vital opportunity for existential pondering (as it has for centuries), if one is so inclined. The next example illustrates this well.

Facing (non-)existence: *Here We Go*

Caryl Churchill's short dramatic triptych *Here We Go*, first performed in the Lyttelton Theatre (at the National Theatre) in London in 2015 in a production directed by Dominic Cooke, offers a powerful meditation on metaphysical and existential matters, informed by realities of death and dying in the early twenty-first century. The play explores many difficult-to-answer questions, such as: what would it be like to exist posthumously? What differentiates 'existing' from 'living'? And how might existing (for the sake of it) come to resemble non-existence, and foreshadow death? Churchill invokes these ponderous questions subtly and imaginatively.

The play comprises three scenes. The first scene shares the play's title and presents a post-funeral gathering of those attending (mourners). The second, titled 'After', takes the form of a monologue delivered by a character who has seemingly died and is apparently in some sort of afterlife. The third scene, titled 'Getting There', presents '[*a*] *very old or ill person and a carer*' as they cycle through a routine of dressing and undressing (Churchill, 2015: 29). The stage directions state that the character in 'After' need not be the character whose funeral is presented in the first scene; this is also true of the '*very old or ill person*' presented in 'Getting There'. So, the three scenes may or may not relate to a specific individual (i.e., the man whose funeral it is in the first scene); they may or may not illustrate a single narrative presented in a non-linear fashion. Churchill allows for multiple interpretative possibilities. Likewise, she provides flexibility regarding the age and sex of all the actors as well as the number of actors that can be used in the first scene. The text is intriguing open-ended, like a choose-your-own-adventure book.[9]

In the first scene, the lines of dialogue are unattributed, with no pre-determined characters. Churchill provides shards of sentences – words, short phrases – letting the reader or audience member fill in the blanks (assuming there are blanks). An impression of conversation is generated, alongside an impression of the main subject of the conversation: the man whose funeral has just taken place. We get a sense of who this man was, what he had done in his life, and how people felt about him, based on what is said. As is to be expected, there does not seem to be uniformity of opinion concerning his character:

> so wonderful
> never complained
> well he did
> terrible temper
> I never saw
> swore at the nurses
>
> (*ibid.*: 14–15)

The collective (re-)constitution of the personal identity of the deceased by those who knew him accords with Brown's articulation, previously discussed, of partially shared selves: the way in which 'various components of ourselves, spiritual, genetic, or cultural', may continue to survive in non-individual form by being socially distributed (Brown, 2008: 11). This is akin to the idea of keeping people 'alive' by remembering them, but it also points to the collective construction of personal identity (i.e., the way in which our identities are shaped by those who have influenced us, but also the proposition that we may not be the sole, or even the primary, author of our identities). The self is thereby understood as a wave that alters as it moves through time and space (e.g., getting older, having contact with different people).[10] Churchill's non-designated characters are hazy textual entities (on the page, at least); they suggest ontological porosity. Having them evoke, through dialogue, the character of a recently deceased person emphasises this porosity and highlights the way in which the *self-as-wave* can live on, after a fashion, even after one has died.

Predictably, the occasion of the funeral prompts those in attendance to turn their thoughts to the matter of death itself. The way in which death can occur suddenly (especially if one is learning about another's death, with little or no warning) is mentioned. A character uses an apt simile: 'it comes at you suddenly doesn't it / like stepping on a rake' (Churchill, 2015: 19). Churchill cleverly integrates the suddenness of death into the scene's dramatic composition. She instructs that the actors should individually make a statement at some point in the scene regarding how and when their character dies (spoken as their character). Ten first-person death-accounts are provided, allowing those staging the text to select and assign the statements, modify the time-frame of the character's death, if appropriate, and determine when the statements are made in the scene. The statements are supposed to be inserted randomly into the dialogue in any order and the number of statements made in performance is dependent upon the number of actors used in the scene. Here are some examples:

> I die eleven years later. I have a heart attack swimming in the North Sea in January. I'd done it before all right. ...
> I die forty years later in my sleep, which is a relief. I was expecting to live to see the baby. ...
> I die sixty-two years later. More and more things aren't working. They put pneumonia on the death certificate.
> I die twenty-three years later after nine years of Alzheimer's. I don't know anyone who's there. (*ibid.*: 21–2)

As well as highlighting the general precariousness and fragility of human life (which we can all too easily forget or disregard), these statements foreground the philosophical proposition and reality of death-in-life (which we can also forget about or disregard). Funerals are reminders about death, of course, but these 'impossible' utterances go one step further and flash-forward to the circumstances of each person's individual death, as though by chronesthesia (mental time-travel). This is science-fiction territory, but Churchill uses the posthumous statements as a dramatic conceit. They connect the characters in the scene to that of the deceased man, punctuate the conversation, and remind us of our own inevitable expiry dates – just like the 'Tikker' watch, an electronic gizmo one can wear on one's wrist that (helpfully?) provides a countdown of one's estimated life expectancy. (Best paired with a Fitbit for maximum bodily/existential apprehension!)

In the 2015 NT production, the actors delivered the first-person death-statements to the audience in an off-the-cuff, detached manner, in keeping with the 'cool' visual aesthetic of the set design (by Vicki Mortimer), which resembled the interior of an Apple store. The actors did not vocally distinguish these statements from their lines of dialogue, as one might expect, nor were any scenographic adjustments made (e.g., with lighting) to make these reports from the future stand out. They were simply spoken, and then the conversation continued. This did not render the statements less odd, or troubling. These lines generated some (nervous?) laughter in the audience, although there is nothing intrinsically funny about the lines themselves – quite the opposite. The matter-of-fact death-divination by characters who are still alive is an ontological incongruity. It is therefore unsettling, and may prompt laughter or unease. How are the characters speaking these lines? If they can report on their own deaths, then logically they must continue to exist in some form, and not just as 'components of self' that have figuratively been dispersed among those who are still living, whose lives they have touched. The contradictory positionality implicit in the title of this scene and the play itself ('here we go') has bearing here. 'Here' indicates fixity; 'we go' indicates movement (but go where?). In this play, Churchill proposes paradoxical states of being, making temporality and spatiality seem fluid.

The second scene, 'After', extends the dramatic device of posthumous vocalisation – or at least it appears to do so. An unnamed person (henceforth referred to as 'the person') gives a free-flowing, stream-of-consciousness-style monologue about being dead. Churchill provides little in the way of explanatory or prescriptive stage directions ('*One person. Very fast.*') (23). This is either a monologue given by a deceased character or an imaginary, future-projection of self into a posthumous existence by a still-living character (who may be dying, or near death).

Trying to imagine oneself 'being' dead is difficult – at least from an 'interior' perspective (see Kagan, 2012: 186–204). Also challenging is the prospect of imagining nothingness, or projecting oneself into nothingness. Warraich notes: 'As beings capable of an imagination that can span the universe, we to date remain incapable of imagining nothingness. Thinking about nothing is to watch a cat catch its tail' (2017: 142). (A brain-twister: thinking about nothing is not the same as not thinking about anything!)[11] Zygmunt Bauman elaborates on this epistemological conundrum vis-à-vis death:

> Death is an absolute *nothing* and 'absolute nothing' makes no sense – we know that 'there is nothing' only when *we can perceive* the absence of perception; every 'nothing' is a faced, perceived, contemplated nothing, and so no 'nothing' can be absolute – an unqualified nothing. But death is the cessation of the very 'acting subject', and with it, *the end* of all perception. Such an end of perception is one state of affairs the perceiving subject cannot conjure up: it cannot 'blot oneself out' of the perception and still wish the perception to be. ... Faced with such impossibility, the perceiving subject may only delude itself with a play of metaphors, which conceals rather than reveals what is to be perceived, and in the end belies the state of non-perception which death would be. (1992: 2)

If we are unwilling or unable to accept the 'absolute *nothing*' of death, which can fill us with horror (though, as Bauman observes, if we cannot and will not experience it, then logically it should not be a cause of concern), we may project on to it and imagine it into being, and thus imagine *being in it*, in some form of afterlife, furnishing it with the 'stuff' of life (e.g., ideas, tropes, fears, fantasies) (*ibid.*: 3). Religion may provide assurance about an afterlife, but in a multi-faith, yet also rapidly secularising, society, such as twenty-first-century Britain, these assurances are not universally held. Religious ideas about an afterlife may seem outmoded, may be selectively believed, and/or may be mixed with ideas from other traditions, as is evident in *Here We Go*.

The 'dead' person in Scene 2 of Churchill's play describes herself or himself (sex is not specified) in an apparent null-space where the person's thoughts ostensibly shape that which appears and is perceived (see Figure 5.2).[12] (Although, it should be noted that it is not always entirely clear in this scene whether the *idea* of a thing precedes apperception of it or vice versa.) The person 'encounters' a jumble of death-related figures and images from multiple mythologies and religions. These include St Peter and the pearly gates; the great golden scale of the Egyptian god

5.2 Patrick Godfrey in the afterlife scene from the National Theatre's 2015 production of Caryl Churchill's *Here We Go*

Osiris; Valhalla; the old Norse giantess or goddess Hel (custodian of the underworld); Charon in his boat in Hades; and Odysseus (who travels to the underworld in Book 11 of Homer's *The Odyssey*). The person does not reflect on the significance of 'discovering' an afterlife replete with cultural mishmash, or acknowledge this to be at all remarkable. The person unquestioningly accepts that this is a multicultural, 'anything-goes' afterlife (or else has preconceived it as such).

This version of the afterlife is apparently whatever one imagines or wishes it to be. Here, there is no divine judgement, though the person states: 'I always was afraid despite everything there'd be a judgement', and wonders if God exists and is 'here somewhere' (Churchill, 2015: 24). Like Duffy's Everyman, the person questions how much good they did in their life. The person speculates that, even though 'they don't emphasise hell these days ... maybe there is a hell of arms chopped off and piles of bodies with bags on their heads and hanging upside down', given that 'we know people do just that sort of thing quite a lot' in the world (*ibid.*: 24). Personal belief appears to be a governing factor, as indicated in the person's passing consideration of purgatory:

> or is it purgatory do they have that still where it's burned out of you not for ever yes I can feel it getting hotter the blast of it on my ridiculous I don't believe it of course never did that's not happening ... (25)

Likewise, the person considers becoming a ghost but dashes the idea, saying: 'I'm not a ghost story' (26). The person also contemplates 'going back and having another life my own life over again like that movie and do it better of course', before acknowledging that reincarnation as someone or some*thing* else is more typically posited (*ibid.*). The person's lack of belief in reincarnation quashes this notion. Moreover, as the person wants to be the self-same entity after death, reincarnation as someone or something else is unappealing and insufficient. 'I wouldn't be me this one I've been doesn't remember others it's extinction of me even if I'm part of some cosmic whatsit drop gone back to the ocean no' (28).

The *carte blanche* afterlife depicted in this scene has a certain appeal, if one discounts the ultimate dissatisfaction that eternity would inevitably bring, as philosopher Shelly Kagan has proposed (2012: 238). As an apparently reconfigurable, non-prescriptive, person-specific afterlife, it is in keeping with the culture of individualism in the early twenty-first century. If one can personalise one's own death (e.g., by making idiosyncratic funeral arrangements) and die in one's own way (a contentious issue, as I will discuss in relation to *Cosy*), then it stands to reason that one might have the afterlife one wishes as well! This is fanciful, and there is arguably a slight air of silliness or whimsy about this scene, which might lead one to consider it a run-through of the 'play of metaphors' (Bauman's phrase) humans have used to ideate life-after-death, and its myriad possibilities (see Eagleman, 2009). As the person in this scene reflects on the afterlife he or she wants based on prior actions and personal beliefs, the reader or audience member is encouraged to do the same. One may, of course, decide that one would not like an afterlife at all, irrespective of the possibilities presented here. In the final scene of the play, Churchill takes a step backward and challenges us to consider how we would like to get 'there', wherever or whatever 'there' may be (or not be).

The last scene is the shortest of the three, on the page, comprising about sixty-seven words. There is no speech, only stage directions. There are two featured characters: '*a very old or ill person and a carer*'

(Churchill, 2015: 29). The carer helps the old or ill person to remove her or his nightclothes and to get dressed. This is done *'slowly and with difficulty because of pain and restricted movement'* (ibid.). Once the old or ill person is dressed, the carer helps her or him to get back into nightclothes, before dressing the person again, then undressing the person again, and so on *'for as long as the scene lasts'* (ibid.). This is a curious textual construction – undramatic (in a conventional sense) and cryptic. Juxtaposing the scene's title, 'Getting there', with the title of the previous scene, 'After', suggests that the 'Getting there' scene is about approaching death, but, if this is so, the old or ill person appears to be making an elliptical approach. To use an aviation analogy, he or she is stuck in a holding pattern, circling the runway. The direction that the cycle of dressing and undressing should continue *'for as long as the scene lasts'* means that action is notionally unending, or can be so, in a reader's 'mental theatre'. This is a rather unhappy prospect. As infinite time-loops go, this one is not very appealing.

Churchill does not say that the *'very old or ill'* person in this scene is dying, but this is a reasonable interpretation. The liminality of the old or ill person's mode of being – ostensibly suspended between living and dying, possibly exemplifying death-in-life – is illustrative of the way in which the process of dying is frequently protracted, and not always clearly marked *as* 'dying', in the twenty-first century. (This topic was previously touched upon in relation to Everyman's parents in Duffy's play.) People in 'advanced' societies are living longer, but often with chronic illnesses, degenerative diseases, and disabilities.

This has, unsurprisingly, generated much commentary. Warraich remarks: 'Death, in most cases, is no longer a sudden conflagration, but a long, drawn-out slow burn. In fact, doctors grappling with this change named the time of debility before death "pre-death"' (2017: 32–3). Similarly, Brown notes the shift from 'acute to chronic death', invoking Tithonus from Greek mythology, who was granted the wish of immortality, but not eternal youth, and so became increasingly debilitated and demented, but could never die. 'Tithonus's fate now threatens us all', Brown writes: 'ever-increasing enfeeblement, ill health and dementia' (2008: 8, 10). The 'Tithonus scenario' means that, oftentimes, 'dying is becoming indistinguishable from daily living'; it is deferred for as long as possible (Kellehear, 2007: 219). This can mean that 'dying in modernity is something to be managed and controlled away from the day-to-day business of life' – in a hospice or care home, for instance (Heaphy, 2007: 149). This has become common. 'For those who are able to avail themselves of palliative care, the managed death of the urban age where there is such a reliance on professionals to guide and support people through dying, is the one most likely to be experienced' (Howarth, 2011: 17). Walter probes this issue, noting that 'the dying person needs to be able both to assert control and to accept dependency, and it is the unpredictability of this mixture of control and dependency that makes each death unique' (1994: 139). Elsewhere, he queries a possible consequence of professional management of the dying, asking: 'is hospice and palliative care empowering families and communities to care for their dying members, or giving the message that you need training to deal with the dying?' (2008a: 12).

Churchill's scene of a carer attending to an old or ill person evokes the professional management of dying in the twenty-first century, the elongation of this process, and the existential grey area, or limbo, it opens for the living or dying person, who may figuratively be neither 'here' nor 'there'. It is tempting to interpret the scene as an implicit critique of this situation. The purely functional series of actions and the lack of verbal interaction between the two figures in the scene suggest clinical detachment and routine, and aside from the reference in the stage directions to the old or ill person's pain there is no other indication of feeling. This little sphere is seemingly cut off from society; the old or ill person may be experiencing a form of 'social death' (discussed in the Introduction). The scene is open to interpretation, however, and it is easy to read meaning into it, depending on one's outlook.

The NT production endeavoured to keep multiple interpretative possibilities open and allow audience members to make it meaningful (or not) for themselves. Obviously, staging decisions and performance choices had to be made that concretised and framed the scene in a certain way. Patrick Godfrey performed the role of the very old or ill person; Hazel Holder performed the role of the carer. Godfrey also performed the role of the speaker in the previous scene, lending an impression of overall unity to the play, making it seem that all three scenes related to his character at different points of his life and death. The third scene was the longest in the production, clocking in at about twenty-two minutes (compared with eight minutes for the first scene and twelve minutes for the second).[13] The actors completed two cycles of dressing and undressing. The dressing took about six minutes to complete; the undressing took about five minutes. The last few minutes were conducted in a slow fade-out, finishing in darkness.

The actors did not embellish the text, and yet, of course, their execution of the actions was unique, intricate, and full of 'minor' details. Significantly, though, they did not highlight the cyclical aspect of their actions. There was a seamless transition between the dressing and undressing sequences. Once Godfrey had made it to an armchair and was dressed, he and Holder immediately began the undressing routine, which led back to him sitting on a bed in his pyjamas, and so forth. The two actors did not make eye contact; their interaction was limited to the task at hand. Their relationship looked professional, impersonal. Holder, as the carer, treated Godfrey respectfully – for example, ensuring that his shirt was on and hanging loose before removing his underwear, thus keeping his genitals covered. Yet, they both seemed to be going through the motions, however carefully, and to be only perfunctorily present. Godfrey periodically stared out into space, blankly. And we stared back.

This scene, which resembled performance or installation art and experimental dance (e.g., Yvonne Rainer's work with the Judson Dance Theatre in the 1960s, which highlighted everyday movements and tasklike actions), got mixed responses from audiences and critics. Unsurprisingly, some people were put off and even angered by it. At the performance I attended, the audience became restless. There was a fair bit of coughing, then stray chuckles as the first clothing reversal occurred, followed by a whispered 'is this it?' Later in the scene, I heard one woman say 'this has gone far enough!' Someone applauded at the end of one of the sequences. I wondered if the applause was intended to curtail or end the performance, making this decision for the production team. The actors continued anyway.

The audience's frustration was understandable. From my perspective, the twenty-two minutes passed slowly. Once the absurdist illogic of the repetitions became clear, it was hard not to die a little inside, so to speak. Each sequence of dressing and undressing and moving from one location to another took so much effort, and was such an involved procedure, that the ostensible purposelessness was rather galling. Dressing and then undressing this person did not facilitate him to do anything other than to begin the reverse process. Reading it on the page is one thing, witnessing it in performance is another. In performance, it is not an intellectual proposition, an abstract scenario, but rather a shared reality taking place in the seemingly interminable present. Like durational performance art, the scene made it possible, if one were open to it, to apprehend what Alice Rayner calls an 'adverbial' sense of time: time as 'a modality that dismantles fixed subjects and objects and turns past, present and future into ways of manners of attention' (2014: 32). Time, thus conceived, 'becomes a mode or a way of my knowing through which I recognize the way of living presently through my body; in the past through my memory, and towards a future, which is (ultimately) death' (2014: 35). Trying to get into sync with the modes-of-being of Godfrey as the old or ill person and Holder as the carer in this scene was challenging – uniquely so for each audience member. (I remember that my father, who had died two months previously, and who had been similarly debilitated near the end of his life, continually came to mind as I watched this scene in the Lyttelton Theatre. I saw him in the character, which made for uncomfortable viewing.)

Attending to the performers in this scene non-critically – just getting into the groove of their skipping record, so to speak, and accepting it – was difficult, and potentially disorientating, but in a good way. As Jon Sherman remarks in his study of stage presence and the ethics of attention: 'The simultaneously mutual and different experiences of disorientation embody the "strange proximity" of a relation to others who cannot be known and yet *whose unknowability fosters a shared experience of the perceptible world*' (2016: 117, emphasis in original). Sherman articulates the phenomenological experience of losing oneself as the centre of orientation by experiencing a relationship of shared uncertainty with a stage performer, and imaginatively intertwining with her or him: 'My habits of perception and relation briefly dissolve and I am forced to confront the lengths to which I will go to (re-)assert what I find familiar or recognizable. I am left with a choice to orient myself into a strange world centered between others and myself or in myself' (*ibid.*). This production similarly challenged audiences to forgo the feeling of being entertained and self-content in lieu of apprehending a distinctive form of existence in which one is physically constrained, locked into a restrictive pattern of action, and where time is experienced differently from normal 'clock-time'. Notably, the production did not actively seek to maintain the audience's interest in repetitions of the sequences. The repetitions did not markedly differ or acquire layered meaning as they proceeded; the action was not aesthetically compelling. At one level, it 'was what is was', although, as analysis of theatre semiotics has taught us, this is not strictly true. Despite the apparent meaninglessness, there was still meaning to be made and responses to be reflected on.

Dan Rebellato, in a blog post about the production, hailed this scene as a 'remarkable piece of naturalism' (despite the non-naturalistic repetitions, an incongruity he acknowledges) (2015). For Rebellato, its naturalism derived from the 'minimum amount of editorialising' on the part of the production team (including the actors), and the invitation to 'observe things themselves' (*ibid.*). Rebellato's commentary is insightful, and worth quoting at length:

> One of things we were watching was the body: the actor's body as much as the character's. We were watching an old body being dressed and undressed. We saw the hair on his chest, the old veins in his legs, his rotund body, his pale skin ... At one moment the old man on stage coughed bron-

chially; the actor I think, not the character. The way you do when someone stumbles on stage, I became intensely aware of his old bodily presence. And then two people in the audience coughed too and it seemed like we were all a bit more conscious of our bodies. Maybe even our mortality but that may be putting it a bit grandly. I felt throughout that I was intensely focused on what was actually happening on stage, which may sound weird because what else am I doing? But what was happening was intensely what was happening ...

And this is what I think that last scene is inviting us to do: to watch. Steadily, unusually, without panic or the protection of some attitude or belief, to watch someone near the end of their life ... It felt to me afterwards that there was an unsettling affinity between the intolerable prolongation of a piece of theatre and an impatient attitude towards the old to which I'm sure we are all sometimes momentarily prone (*why are you so slow? why are you still here? why don't you just go?*). (*ibid.*)

Here we (do not) go.[14] This could be the motto of the elderly, whose number is increasing, even as life expectancy increases as well. Churchill, notably, was seventy-seven at the time of the production. Dominic Cooke, the director, has spoken about the political aspect of staging old age in this scene, and making audiences confront this reality:

I think one of the provocations of it is asking us to look, physically, at something we don't want to look at. Our culture is so obsessed with beauty, immortality, never getting old. We don't like looking at frailty. We don't *really* like looking at old age. Older people are pushed aside in the culture. So ... it's not just that [the scene is] repetitive and in some ways not dramatic, in a traditional sense. It's also that the content is *uncomfortable* for us. Because people are living longer ... we tend to avert our gaze from what that means, what it feels like. (Mountford and Cooke, 2016)

Another easily overlooked aspect of this scene is the carer, and her labour in attending to the old or ill person. What does it mean for her to be doing this job? What is the cost of this, in all senses of the word? Is it sustainable? What degrees of agency do both these characters have? To what extent are they co-dependent? Should we attach significance to the fact that in this production it was a young black woman who was caring for an old white man? Churchill's oblique text raises many questions about end-of-life, prompting us to grapple with this often-painful reality and to try to make sense of it. Watching the repetitious routine in the final scene, a routine that appears to offer an unrewarding existence, one might think of oneself, or a loved one, in that situation, and consider whether an alternative arrangement could, and perhaps should, be made – an exit strategy before the final curtain.

Rehearsing dying: *Cosy*

The final example in this chapter, Kaite O'Reilly's play *Cosy*, which premiered at the Wales Millennium Centre in Cardiff in 2016 in a production directed by Phillip Zarrilli, is thematically connected to the scenario presented at the end of Churchill's *Here We Go*. Churchill presents a seemingly unrewarding, and possibly maddening, existence for a very old or ill person in a scene comprising a cyclical series of movements and actions. O'Reilly dramatises the related issues of the right to die and assisted suicide, offering multiple, conflicting perspectives on these topics, and plots the development an 'exit strategy' from life. Her play, which is not set in a specified country but is linguistically and socially indicative of both Britain and Ireland, is a dark, realistic comedy (or possibly a tragicomedy) with some overtly stylised elements.[15] It is 'cosy' in form and genre, especially in comparison with *Here We Go*. O'Reilly's play is a family drama containing finely drawn, identifiable characters with rich and complicated backstories, a linear narrative, and a five-part structure. It is not, however, especially 'cosy' in content, which gives it a subversive edge. On this point, O'Reilly stated in an interview with me in 2016: 'I find the way to get an audience away from their fear and superstition is to make them laugh. It's like foreplay. Get them all relaxed. Give them a nice little massage before the main event. And then kick them in the fucking stomach. Not because I want to hurt or punish the audience, but because it's live. It's the most extraordinary art form'.[16]

In *Cosy*, the 'kicker' is that the family matriarch, Rose, who is seventy-six, has announced that she wishes to end her own life, to her family's shock and general consternation. The play is centred on this contentious desire, which is gradually revealed before being articulated in pithy verbal exchanges, hashed out in vigorous debates, physically rehearsed with the aid of an unwitting dupe, and privately contemplated in a final monologue. The cast of characters for this 'ominous comedy', as one reviewer called it, includes two generations of Rose's family – her daughters Ed, Camille, and Gloria; and her granddaughter, Isabella (Camille's daughter) – along with Rose's companion, Maureen, a woman of 'atypical' health and physicality who has recently come to live in the family home with Rose and Ed (Raymond, 2016).[17] Rose and Ed have a strained, long-term, co-dependent relationship. The situational set-up and character relationships in this play are complicated, and O'Reilly does not grant the reader or audience member much in the way of privileged information at the outset. Instead, she presents us with a curious, 'messy' situation with many ambiguous elements. This makes the play true to life. We are left to figure things out along with Camille, Gloria, and Isabella, who have been prompted to visit because of Rose's declared death wish.

Rose's desire to end her own life is hinted at in the first and second scenes and then spelled out in the third. We learn that Rose has a medical condition that is progressive and degenerative, but we are not given more specific information. Rose is not, apparently, dying from this condition, nor is she in marked physical pain or discomfort. Indeed, she seems quite hale and hearty and *compos mentis* (unlike the disaffected aesthete, Dartigny, in Rachilde's *Madame La Mort*, discussed in Chapter 1). This differentiates *Cosy* from what is probably the best-known 'euthanasia drama', Brian Clark's *Whose Life Is It Anyway?* (1978), which features an accident victim who has been made a quadriplegic. *Cosy* makes a different case for self-termination.

Rose's justification for wishing to end her own life is not based on current physical suffering or on a terminal diagnosis, but on fears for the future. Rose does not want to advance into decrepitude. She scorns the idea of living to be ninety, saying: 'I don't want to be one of those breathing fossils from an earlier epoch lingering on, joints creaking, uterus sagging, everything giving out' (O'Reilly, 2016: 233). She does not wish to have to cede to ever-diminishing physical capabilities, to be trapped in an eventually 'useless' body, or to 'give up my life in order to live' (*ibid.*: 290). This last part is linked to the prospect of selling her home so that she can move into a nursing home, where she imagines being 'patronised and dressed in communal clothing, not even my own knickers, kept in the world when I'd really rather leave it' (283). She wishes to remain the 'author' of her own story, and rejects Gloria's suggestion that she is simply 'caving in' and 'giving up' because she is tired or unhappy:

> What about being in pain? Or grief? In terror? The fear of losing control? How about for that future little plastic tube protruding from my back to drain the poison from my kidneys? Or avoiding incontinence and the hallucinations, where I could be screaming COCKROACHES! COCKROACHES! convinced they're crawling all over me and there's nothing you or anyone else can do? How about to avoid a living death? (290)

Rose wishes to have 'dignity' in her dying (in line with the UK-based, assisted-dying campaigning organisation, Dignity in Dying), and says she does not forgive herself for the way her husband died. 'He wouldn't have wanted every Tom, Dick, or Harry poking and prodding and doing procedures to prolong his life when we all knew he was done for. ... It was a horrible end of life. No dignity, no peace' (264–5). To this end, Rose has had the words 'DO NOT RESUSCITATE' printed in felt tip across her sternum (264).

Rose's rationale for wanting to end her life is reasonable, even though she is apparently still in relatively good health and retains her dynamic personality. Her argument is that she is justified in ending her life at this point *because* she still has agency, mental wherewithal, and physical capability. She is still 'p-functioning' (person-functioning), to use philosophy lingo, and wants to keep her personhood intact and script her own dying rather than yield to a natural process that will inevitably take over, and that may end up being managed by others (Kagan, 2012: 20). Rose, like characters from other plays discussed in this chapter (e.g., Duffy's Everyman, Carr's Woman, the 'dead' person in Churchill's 'After' scene), is not religious; she does not believe in a 'higher power' or an afterlife. She is blunt about this. 'It's only a hole in the ground and compost. That's it' (291). Rose is hoping to achieve a 'good death' for herself, given her life philosophy and what she sees as the probability of her situation from this point forward. Her desire to end her own life soon so that she can have a 'good death', as she sees it, is somewhat unusual, given that she is still seemingly able to enjoy life (as indicated in her lively verbal exchanges with her family members and her companion, Maureen). What is *not* unusual are her fears for the future and her baulking at the prospect of living-for-the-sake-of-it, no matter what this takes or what it might constitute. (Flashback to the final scene of *Here We Go*. Flash-forward to the speculative, future erasure of death, discussed in the book's conclusion.)

Medicalised death treated as a spectre has haunted the cultural imaginary for decades (as in Buzzati's 1953 play *A Clinical Case*, discussed in Chapter 3), and still retains its grip in people's minds, often with just cause, yet medicalised death can obviously be advantageous and preferable (e.g., the provision of morphine to the dying), and 'easier dying' should not be swapped out for 'better living' as a matter of course. Warraich, in his book on modern death, provides this summation: 'The more medicalized death gets, the longer people are debilitated before the end, the more cloistered those who die become, the more terrifying death gets. ... The only way to make any real change is to tear away the vines of terror that creep up our legs whenever we talk about death and dying' (2017: 9).

Cosy, like the death café initiative, combats continued fear about death and dying by openly verbalising this sentiment, bringing 'unsafe' subject matter into the 'safe' environment of a domestic space (Rose's home), and, by extension, the theatre, which can also function as a 'safe space' (though it does not *have* to do so, as in the case of Howard Barker's theatre, discussed in the previous chapter). Indeed, theatre's capacity to provide an ostensibly 'safe' – yet simultaneously or alternately 'unsafe' – space is arguably a vital part of its power and a reason for its endurance. It is also why theatre provides such a valuable site for apprehending mortality and rehearsing death and dying, both individually and collectively. *Cosy* mobilises this delicate operation by conducting a darkly comic, deadly serious debate, one that exposes privately held, yet mutually shared, mortal dread. This sharing is beneficial, but the play does not pretend to offer a magic salve for existential angst; O'Reilly allows that death can still be considered frightful, even when faced head-on.

The boisterous debate about Rose's death-wish in *Cosy*, held over multiple scenes by different combinations of characters, signals the complexity of the issue of the right to die and the difficulty of determining 'absolute' truths, or 'one-size-fits-all'-type solutions, even in this social microcosm (i.e., Rose's home), which is visited by people with diverse viewpoints and life experiences. Maureen, who is Rose's ally in her plan to end her own life, nevertheless wishes to keep on living herself, even though her health is uncertain (she is attached to a catheter and passes blood for much of the play). A provider of gallows humour, she professes to be dedicated to 'the adventure of seeing what part of me fails next' (O'Reilly, 2016: 298). Maureen's physical condition and health status are not specified, but she presents herself as being atypical (a 'walking miracle … A legend in my own diagnosis'), and appears to advance a 'crip' perspective (*ibid.*: 223):[18]

> When you're not the usual meat and two veg, shelf life can be a real problem. There's always some chancer waiting to be compassionate and help you out of your misery. If it were up to others, I'd've been put out of my misery years ago … The trick is to keep moving. (264)

And so she does, dragging her sometimes blood-filled catheter-on-wheels along with her as she goes, periodically exiting to feed the roses with her 'bucket of blood' (223). This seems like an aberrant, unnatural thing to do, but Maureen claims that roses thrive on human blood.

Questions about what is natural or unnatural, morally right or wrong, are raised throughout the play. Gloria, who works in a community home, criticises the 'care industry' for the way in which it has been interposed – deleteriously, in her opinion – into human affairs:

> There was a time when people used to care. Now, it's a profession. We're so industrialised in our looking after one another, so processed and medicalised, we've lost the simplicity, the connection of just being. We're

so far from life and death and the natural and the real. Our comings and goings are managed, sanitised, delayed, prolonged, speeded-up, made inhuman. (257)

The Sisyphean loop of professional care presented in *Here We Go* comes to mind here. Gloria expresses a widely-held sentiment – also articulated by Ariès in his historical study of death in the West (1981) – that death has acquired an increasingly unnatural character in modernity, and that the traditional practice of dying at home, without having had sustained medical intervention in the run-up period, is preferable.[19] Gloria rails against the medicalisation of death and the practice of working to extend life by making repeated, *unnatural* interventions:

> [Our] doctors are taught to solve and mend as though we're immortal and can always get better. We can't. We're *supposed* to have a 'best before' date; we've been designed to expire. We're organic matter, not Teflon. And so that natural pause, the final full stop has been ostracised ... moved from the centre of the family to being outsourced, just another unpleasant job someone else can deal with without inconveniencing us too much. (O'Reilly, 2016: 258)

Gloria, befitting her name, believes in God and fated, personal destiny, and so for her the prospect of authoring one's own death is unnatural, and a sin to boot. Further underlying her opposition to Rose's declared intention to kill herself, and making her outbursts seem retrospectively ironic, is the (presumably true) circumstance that Gloria herself is dying, which she dramatically reveals to her family near the end of the play, but gives few details about.

At the beginning of Scene 5, Rose and Maureen, in cahoots, rehearse the act of killing someone – in this case, Ed – by putting a plastic bag filled with ice over her head and mock-suffocating her, to Ed's real distress. They do this without Ed's knowledge or consent, leading to this comical exchange:

> ED: She almost killed me with a plastic bag.
> GLORIA: What?!
> MAUREEN: It was just a dry run. Rehearsing.
> ED: You might have warned me. Asked my permission?
> ROSE: Don't be silly, darling, that would ruin the element of surprise and we needed an authentic reaction, to see if we can handle it, or need more help.
> ED: The way I feel at the moment, Mother, I could quite happily help kill you – in fact, I'd do it all by myself, with the greatest of pleasure.
> ROSE: That's the spirit. (295)

Although this is not a serious attempt (they have poked holes in the ironically named 'Tesco Bag for Life' they have used), it is still an outrageous thing to do, and an indicator of the dysfunctional relationship between elderly mother and co-dependent daughter. In performance, the scene provoked uncomfortable laughter in the dark, a signature element of the play.

Cosy further subverts expectations by evading narrative resolution. One might expect the play to end with Rose either killing herself or changing her mind about wanting to die; the play seems to be setting up a narrative 'pay off'. But O'Reilly opts to do something different – something less immediately satisfying, but ultimately more rewarding: she ostensibly suspends the matter of Rose's dying. The play finishes with a monologue given by Rose in which she articulates her night terrors – her fear of dying, and death – and highlights the difficulty of facing one's own extinction:

> You think it's fine and a fearless thing, a natural progression, life to death, cradle to grave. You think it's natural and easy. There is nothing natural about death. There is nowhere to take your ease, just the scrabbling, the terrible scrabbling of fingers in the earth, the clawing, the fear and all the time thinking: who'll be there to hold my hand when the time comes? (301)

At this point, the stage directions state that the other characters are revealed at the back of the stage, watching Rose. It seems an aesthetic shift has occurred, though this is not mentioned in the stage directions. Are we no longer in the shared reality that has been presented hitherto in the play? Or have we perhaps jumped to a point in the future? Rose's monologue ends poetically, ambiguously, making it seem that she is speaking herself out of existence:

> Let me not fall into darkness
> Ssssh …
> No no no no not into the dark, not into the dark, please –
> Ssssh
> Cosy, cosy. It comes, it comes
> Not into the dark!
> Stars. Stars.
>
> *Blackout.* (302)

In performance, Sharon Morgan as Rose delivered this monologue delicately and devastatingly (see Figure 5.3). Spot-lit in a plush, red armchair, with the shadowy presences of the other characters standing behind her, she spoke into the darkness of the auditorium, her eyes

5.3 Sharon Morgan as Rose (seated) at the end of the 2016 (captioned) production of Kaite O'Reilly's *Cosy* at the Wales Millennium Centre, Cardiff

glistening, her delivery capturing the alternating notes of hope and fear – elemental counterpoint of being human – inscribed in O'Reilly's text. As Rose cosies up to death, she perceives pinpricks of light, suggesting solace. Cold comfort, perhaps, though stars burn brightly before they are extinguished.

Conclusion

The four plays discussed in this chapter each grapple with realities of death and dying in the early twenty-first century, experienced on an individual level. These realities are inevitably plural, given the 'mixed picture' (as Walter describes it) of death and dying in this period. The 'mixed picture' is in line with the 'contradictory and uncertain' space (Noys's phrasing) in which death operates in modern Western societies. Pressing social issues, such as assisted suicide, remain contested, and, in many places, unresolved. Death conceived in 'big-picture' fashion may well be 'contradictory and uncertain', but the four plays discussed in this chapter have highlighted points of contact and connection – shared concerns among dramatists about the prospect of dying at this period of human history, in relatively privileged socioeconomic circumstances, and with the benefit (or mixed blessing?) of modern medicine.

These plays dramatise the 'contradictory and uncertain' space of death in the early twenty-first century, and, in doing so, make us better acquainted with this uncertainty, and perhaps better able to (en)counter it. As O'Reilly remarked to me in an interview in 2016: '[theatre] gives us a space to breathe with the piece, and it gives us the courage to … sit, and dare, and then, once you dare look, and think about it, it's never as bad as our imagination thinks it will be'. (Rose may be thought to be doing something similar at the end of *Cosy*.) Elaine Storkey, discussing the NT's production of Duffy's *Everyman* on BBC Radio 3's *Free Thinking* programme, mentioned that an audience's coming-together for the duration of the performance, and the consequent likelihood of them individually reflecting on their own mortality, might work to challenge social fragmentation, 'the way in which we have all gone in different directions' (quoted in Dodd, 2015). She wondered if recognition of our shared mortality through theatrical performance might bring us back together again. This is, most likely, a 'utopian performative', but it is a noble pursuit, nonetheless (Dolan, 2005: 7).

Each of the plays discussed in this chapter dramatises unease and uncertainty at the end of life. Uncertainty about what, if anything, 'happens next' (i.e., after we die) is age-old, but this question is being examined anew in the context of modern resuscitation science, which is challenging the ostensible fixity and irreversibility of death. 'One of the things that makes existence bearable is the certainty it's finite', observes Rose in *Cosy* (O'Reilly, 2016: 244). Amazingly, this certainty is being eroded, and the future of death as an absolute end is being rewritten and reimagined. However, it is not clear that this is necessarily a good thing (as in the looped sequence in the 'Getting there' scene in Churchill's *Here We Go*). Rose's existential suspension at the close of *Cosy* likewise points to the deferral of an ending – an unending, so to speak. This book's concluding chapter will negotiate an ending, and unending, by looking to the future of death while reflecting on the past and reconsidering the accounts of death in modern theatre presented thus far.

Notes

1 This is not to say that individuals cannot use representations of death and dying in popular culture, and accounts of death in the media, to structure their own understanding of mortality, both individually and in dialogue

with others. See Coombs (2014). Additionally, there are video games that explore mortality meaningfully, such as *That Dragon, Cancer*, published by Numinous Games in 2016.
2. Tony Walter makes this observation in a video contribution to the digital programme of the National Theatre production of *Everyman*, available as a digital download via the National Theatre's mobile app.
3. According to Funeralcare's website, the 2016 study was based on responses from over thirty thousand funeral homes: www.co-operativefuneralcare.co.uk/arranging-a-funeral/organising-the-day/funeral-music/2016/ (accessed 28 August 2017).
4. Photos of people posing under the giant finger are viewable on Twitter (search using '#IamEveryman').
5. The last line echoes Matthew 3:17, concerning the transfiguration of Christ on the mountain: 'And lo a voice from heaven, saying This is my beloved Son, in whom I am well pleased'.
6. This is not new, but it still has contemporary relevance. Fiona Macintosh writes of characters in Ancient Greek tragedy 'dying into death', tussling with 'the arduous process of dying' and endeavouring to gain 'eloquence and insight' (1994: 58).
7. The most famous precedent of this type of character splitting in Irish drama is probably Brian Friel's 1964 play *Philadelphia, Here I Come!*, which features the bifurcated characters of Gar O'Donnell (Public) and Gar O'Donnell (Private). Relatedly, Edward Albee's play *Three Tall Women* (1991) splits a dying woman into three differently aged selves.
8. This also relates to the practice of 'natural burial', a topic explored in Laura Wade's 2005 play *Colder Than Here*.
9. Churchill's 2012 play *Love and Information* similarly features anonymous lines of text, many of which are fragmentary.
10. For a philosophical discussion of personal identity in relation to death, and an elaboration of the concept of a person as a 'space-time worm', see Kagan, 2012: 98–131.
11. 'Thinking of nothing in the negative sense of simply not thinking is very different from the positive sense of actually thinking in real time about nothing or about the concept of nothingness' (Jacquette, 2015: 8). See Chapter 1 for Maeterlinck's comments on nothingness.
12. Compare with Robert Johnson's imagined afterlife in J.B. Priestley's *Johnson Over Jordan*. Johnson is accompanied on his afterlife journey by a nameless and ultimately benign Death figure; the person in Churchill's scene has no guide.
13. Timings are based on the production recording held at the National Theatre Archive.
14. Compare with the famous ending of *Waiting for Godot*, in which Vladimir and Estragon agree that they should go, and the stage directions state: '*They do not move*' (Beckett, 2006: 87). One also thinks of Clov's exit and unannounced return at the end of *Endgame*.

15 The 2016 production of *Cosy* featured a company of Welsh actors, implicitly situating the play in Wales.
16 Interview with Kaite O'Reilly on 20 November 2016 in Exeter.
17 'Atypical' is the term O'Reilly uses for her 2016 collection of plays (including *Cosy*) that, in her words, '"answer back" to the moral and medical models of disability and attempt to subvert (often invisible) cultural norms and negative representations of disabled people' (O'Reilly, 2016: xi).
18 O'Reilly uses the term 'crip' when discussing disability culture. There is a section on her website (kaiteoreilly.com) concerning 'crip culture'.
19 Relatedly, the 'natural death movement', which has taken off in the early twenty-first century, seeks to restore individual agency over death and dying. See Wienrich and Speyer (2003), Doughty (2015), and the website www.naturaldeath.org.uk.

Conclusion: Unending

I was once slightly bemused by a student – a young man in his early twenties – who blithely stated, during a class discussion, that he had not given much thought to what would happen to him when he reached old age, and was not too bothered about this future stage of his existence. The reason for his nonchalance? He assumed that by the time he was in advanced years, scientists would have found cures for the major illnesses that are currently the main causes of death in the elderly, thus allowing him to stay in relatively good health, perhaps in perpetuum. Dying as an old man did not seem very 'real' to him. Oho! I thought. A classic case of death denial, wrapped up in youthful naivety and blind faith in scientific progress. I'll sort him out. Give him a dose of existential angst. He'll thank me later.

Subsequently, though, I wondered if *I* was the one who was out of touch. As it happens, there *are* people who take seriously the idea that their future death is not necessarily set in stone, or that lifespans might be greatly extended in comparison to what is considered normal today. I don't think my young optimist knew anything specific about this. He merely articulated a fuzzy belief in the curative potential of medical science – discoveries and breakthroughs that will hopefully happen in the not-too-distant future. But perhaps such thinking is not totally specious or wishful. In the early twenty-first century, there is a raft of scientific initiatives that aim to keep death perpetually at bay, render it impermanent, or eliminate it altogether. Instead of accepting death as inevitable, unavoidable biological destiny, proponents of these initiatives regard death as something that can be scientifically vanquished, or 'cured'. In this way of thinking, death will be denied by being reclassified as 'a *disease*, a *treatable condition*. Death is perhaps a serious disease – no need to minimize it – but no different in principle, to the scientifically ambitious thinker, from any other severe derangement of organ function' (Keith, 2009: 104).

Here is a small selection of current medical schemes that might result in circumventing death. Enthusiasts of cryogenics advocate freezing people immediately after their death so that they may be revived, and their ailments cured, when medical science has evolved. (This does not preclude dying again in the future, though.) Transhumanists think we should seek to enhance humans artificially with technology (e.g., artificial intelligence, nanobots) so we are no longer simply human; this might include having longer lives, and possibly living for ever (Brown, 2008: 203). Other proponents of radical life extension, such as Aubrey de Grey, aim to stave off death by eliminating the damaging effects of ageing. De Grey, a biomedical gerontologist, is the founder of the SENS Research Foundation, based in California. The acronym SENS stands for 'Strategies for Engineered Negligible Senescence'. This refers to a detailed plan that would bring about 'a state in which medical treatments and biotechnology have reduced age-related disease to the point at which there is no statistically detectable change in a population's death rate with the increasing age of the population' (Keith, 2009: 105). In other words, old age will not make death more likely, no matter how old one gets. One will be able to live on, even into advanced years, without having a reduced quality of life (unlike the scenario presented in the 'Getting there' section of Churchill's *Here We Go*, discussed in the previous chapter). One would not get frailer or have diminished faculties as one gets older. De Grey states: 'the defeat of aging will entail the elimination [of the customary period of debilitation and disease near the end of life], by postponing it to indefinitely greater stages so that people never reach it' (2007: 8). Ageing is 'no more or less than the collective early stages of the various age-related diseases', de Grey maintains; it need not result in death if one course-corrects for it (*ibid*.: 18). 'There is no ticking time bomb', he states, 'just the accumulation of damage. Aging of the body, just like the aging of a car or a house, is merely a maintenance problem. ... [Aging] can be postponed indefinitely by sufficiently thorough and frequent maintenance' (*ibid*.: 21). De Grey envisions using gene therapy and other techniques to engineer periodic rejuvenation of the human body, lowering the cumulative amount of damage caused by ageing to a healthier, sustainable level – one that does not trigger age-related diseases. This would give new meaning to the famous closing remarks of Beckett's 1953 novel *The Unnameable*: 'you must go on, I can't go on, I'll go on' (2010: 134). If de Grey is proved right, those of us who are still young enough to take advantage of molecular and cellular damage-reduction therapy *may* – if we have the means, the opportunity, and the motivation – 'go on' much longer than we would if we let biology take its natural course and get medical treatment only when we become ill. How much longer might we ultimately 'go on', barring accidents and other misadventures, and when might this start happening? This is unclear.[1] De Grey has speculated that the first thousand-year-old human might already be alive, and that, in the future, the average age of death 'will be in the region of a few thousand years' (2004).

Visions of radically longer-living humans who have achieved mastery over ageing, and thus greater control over life and death, who have altered themselves using bio-technology, or have otherwise merged with artificial intelligence to become more-than-human (or less than human?) are the stuff of science fiction; it remains to be seen how much of this will become science fact. The prospect of 'curing' ageing and extending human life by centuries is disputed; some researchers believe it to be impossible (see, for example, Nelson and Masel, 2017). Likewise, 'cryonauts' – people whose bodies are preserved by cryonics – will not necessarily be 'themselves' even if technologies are developed that will reverse the damage inflicted by the long-term freezing of cells; memories, which are key to continuity of identity, may not survive this process (Brown, 2008: 243). Additionally, the transhumanist desire to expand human capacities by becoming more entangled with technology – even more than we are currently are – is not a universally shared dream, and may remain a niche, avant-garde pursuit. To wit: the performance artist Stelarc who has grown a third ear on his arm and proposed using it to broadcast sound to the internet, does not appear to have started a trend for this type of 'body hacking'. But the day is young.

There is, of course, nothing new about the desire to extend human life. Dreams of prolonging the human lifespan – potentially beyond all limits – are age-old and appear in diverse mythologies and world literatures (Guthke, 2017: 1). Twentieth-century dramatists also took up this theme. George Bernard Shaw's five-part drama *Back to Methuselah* (1921) is premised on the idea that humans can extend their lives greatly (up to three thousand years, he suggests) through 'creative evolution'. Shaw explains this unusual notion: 'the will to do anything can and does, at a certain pitch of intensity set up by the conviction of its necessity, create and organize new tissue to do it with. ... Among other matters apparently changeable at will is the duration of individual life' (1930: xviii). Shaw's eccentric extravaganza dramatises the invention of birth and death in the Garden of Eden, the revelation of the first super-long-lived humans in the late twenty-second century, and finally ventures to the year 31,920, when great longevity of human life is the norm and ancient humans are anticipating eternal existence in non-corporeal form, as pure thought. These ancient humans seem markedly different to the more recently *hatched* youngsters (for this is how the humans of this far-distant future come into the world). Alas, the ancient ones are apparently not very happy with their lot, as Acis, a younger human, observes.

> They manage to change themselves in a wonderful way. You meet them sometimes with a lot of extra heads and arms and legs: they make you split laughing at them. Most of them have forgotten how to speak: the ones that attend to us have to brush up on their knowledge of the language once a year or so. Nothing makes a difference to them as far as I can see. They never enjoy themselves. I don't know how they can stand it. (*ibid*.: 219)

The younger generation cannot grasp the appeal of the projected future existence of the ancient ones as eternal thought. One of the younger humans, an artist, hopes to die an accidental death before morphing into a non-corporeal form of existence where there are '[no] limbs, no contours, no exquisite lines and elegant shapes, no worship of beautiful bodies, no poetic embraces ...' (253). Shaw thus sounds a note of disquiet about the prospect of radical human transmogrification and the dubious benefit of living forever.[2]

Karel Čapek makes the case for the undesirability of immortality more overtly in his 1922 play *Věc Makropulos* (*The Makropulos Case*), published one year after Shaw's *Back to Methuselah*.[3] Čapek's play features a long-lived character, initially referred to in the play as Emilia Marty, who was born in 1585, given an elixir of life when she was sixteen, and has now lived for over three hundred years, though she has the appearance and physical capabilities of someone in their thirties. Her centuries of existence have proved harmful to her psychological wellbeing. Life, for her, has been voided of meaning and potency; she has lost a sense of reality and finds her existence purposeless. 'Everything's so stupid', she says, addressing the mortals in her midst. 'Empty, pointless. Do you really exist? Perhaps you're not real, perhaps you're objects, or shadows. What am I supposed to do with you? (1999: 254). She has become thoroughly disenchanted with life and feels detached from those around her. She thinks her soul has died:

> You find you don't believe in anything. Nothing. Just this emptiness. ... Singing's the same as silence. Everything's the same. There's no difference. ... People never get better. Nothing changes, nothing. Nothing matters, nothing happens. Shootings, earthquakes, the end of the world – nothing! You're here, and I'm somewhere far, far away, three hundred years away. If you only knew how easy your lives are! (*ibid.*: 254–5)

Emilia envies those who are mortal, for whom '[everything] means something' and 'has value' and is enjoyed to the full 'because of the stupid accident that you'll soon be dead' (256). Despite her profound ennui, Emilia still clings to life – she wants the formula for the elixir – but only because she '[dreads] death' (*ibid.*). She is caught between the proverbial rock and a hard place. At the end of the play, the formula is destroyed, releasing Emilia from her impossible existence.

Čapek's play has a parable-like quality, reminding us that death helps to give meaning to life and that we become deathless at our peril – something the current crop of extreme life-extension and immortality enthusiasts might heed. Čapek suggests exceptionally long life might come to be regarded more as a curse than a blessing, and drain life of its meaning. If death were removed from life's equation, would living still be (as) potentially meaningful or (as) potentially enjoyable at a certain point? Emilia's situation of existing but (to her mind) not 'truly' living does not seem enviable. Advanced care directives are put in place for this reason, forbidding 'heroic measures' on the part of medical providers, for example, if quality of life looks to be greatly diminished and will not likely be restored or much improved.

Dead or alive

> The dead are not always as dead as we think nor the living as living as they think. (Cixous, 2004: 29)

Medical science cannot grant us lifespans of multiple centuries (yet), but it can, sometimes, bring us back from the dead, like the biblical Lazarus. This means that, setting aside the possibility of an afterlife, one's death may not be the final episode of one's life. We can live again to die another day![4] It is now possible, with the aid of resuscitation techniques and technologies, to restore someone to life three or four hours after cardiac arrest, if conditions are suitable, often with no long-term consequences. The length of time one can be a viable candidate for resuscitation might be increased in the future, as resuscitation science and technology evolve.[5] Sam Parnia, a cardiopulmonary resuscitation expert, remarks: '"death" is not the end we once thought it to be. Death is no longer a specific moment in time, such as when the heart stops beating, respiration ceases, and the brain no longer functions. That is, contrary to common understanding, death is not a moment. It's a process – a process that can be interrupted well after it has begun' (Parnia and Young, 2014: 20). Death, therefore, can be temporary and reversible; one can alternate between being dead and being alive, like a stage actor rising to their feet after their character has bit the dust. As such, there is now a weird, liminal zone, a grey area, between life and (permanent) death that one may occupy for a while.[6] In this state, one may be considered technically dead – a corpse – but potentially restorable to life. The significance of conceiving death as a reversible process, a temporary state of (non-)being, should not be overlooked; it affects our understanding of our mortality, and reveals anew the interchange between life and death (glimpsed in different forms, for different reasons, throughout this book).

A piece of devised theatre by the British company Unlimited entitled *Am I Dead Yet?*, which premiered in 2014, explored the 'grey zone' of human mortality in the early twenty-first century, given the latest advancements in resuscitation science, and also looked ahead to a possible future of death, inspired by initiatives to extend the human lifespan radically.[7] The piece featured two performers, Jon Spooner and Chris Thorpe, who narrated a trio of interlaced, death-related stories, interposed with scripted dialogue with the audience and cabaret-style musical offerings. In one section, a CPR demonstration was given by a trained professional from the area in which the show was performed. (The piece has been performed around the UK and elsewhere since its premiere.)[8] The creators have described *Am I Dead Yet?* as a 'show about developments in resuscitation science, resurrection, death, why we as a society are so bad at talking about death and how might our lives be improved if we were able to talk about death more frequently, honestly and openly' (Spooner and Thorpe, 2014: 1).[9] The show aimed to inform and enlighten audience members about subjects they might not know much about, and provide an experience that allowed them to contemplate their mortality, and that of others, in a 'safe' space and an entertaining manner. Relatedly, the performers hosted death cafés in conjunction with the show.

One of the tales related in this piece was inspired by true stories of people who have been dead for several hours and later resuscitated. This story involves a young girl who is walking alone on an icy pond; the ice breaks, causing her to plunge into the water and drown. When her mother finds her, and breaks through the ice, the girl has turned blue. The performers tell how paramedics helicopter the girl and her mother to the hospital, all the while performing chest compressions on the girl. The mother knows her child is dead, but slowly appreciates that this might not be a permanent condition. There is hope yet.

> JON: For the first time since the pond she allows her daughter's name to come out of her mouth.
> Amy. Come on.
> Amy. Come on.
> Amy. Come on.
> Amy. Come on.
> Amy. Come on.
> Amy. Come on.
> Amy. Come on.
> Come back.
> CHRIS: And science takes the blood out of her daughter, and reunites her with it. And repeats. And on a monitor her small heart lies impossibly still and cold. Inert. And her daughter's spark is inactive, gone out, but, she begins to understand, that spark is possibly still somewhere within her. Waiting in that mechanical matrix to loop round through time and reappear at the same point it left the Earth. (Spooner and Thorpe, 2014: 26–7)

The 'science' in question refers to an extra-corporeal membrane oxygenation (ECMO) machine, which allows medical staff to 'reroute a patient's blood out of the body, feed it oxygen, and return it to the circulatory system', gradually warming it in the process (Parnia and Young, 2014: 11). In the story told by the performers, the medical procedures are successful and the girl's heart begins to beat again.

In another story, the performers tell of two policemen in the 1970s or early 1980s, who, one summer evening, are searching railway lines for the body of a man hit by a train – a possible suicide. They find various body parts, including a severed head. Later that night, off-duty at the police station, the officers sit together drinking tea and try to process the awful thing they have just had to do: find and bag body parts. They reflect on the nature of corporeal existence and that mysterious thing – the 'spark' of life. 'You … look at the ambulatory … tubes of meat around you and wonder what it is that goes out of us at the moment we're turned from what we are into something that resembles cheap steak', one of them says (*ibid*.: 21). The younger policeman predicts that, in the future, people who want to 'really stay dead' will kill themselves in such a way as to make it impossible to be restored to life by medical means. In the future, the copper imagines, 'they'll be able to fix death, whether you want that or not. So the only alternative will be to make sure you're in so many bits it's impossible to give you another go' (23).

The third main story told in *Am I Dead Yet?* is set at an unspecified future date. In this scenario, reminiscent of the science fiction of Philip K. Dick, the performers, Jon and Chris, are much older versions of themselves. In this reality, '[there] is no such thing as death' – or rather, permanent death – at least for people who can avail of death-defeating technology (28). The future versions of Jon and Chris have reached a point in their lives when their doctors have advised them to undergo a procedure in which they die, temporarily. And so, they enter a white room in a medical facility where they consent to die and have their genes re-capped ('[painted] over like teeth') and their organs and support structures (monitoring software, nanopumps) modified (36). They are then brought back to life, newly rejuvenated, and end up looking younger than Jon's youngest son, who is ninety-two years old (echoes of de Grey's SENS project here). This process can be repeated at a later stage, apparently indefinitely. In this way, they can keep 'one step ahead of permanent death' (37). The story concludes thusly:

> JON: And we no longer worry.
> CHRIS: We no longer worry.
> JON: There are no major problems to solve.
> CHRIS: We don't even wake up any more
> JON: In the morning
> CHRIS: And worry about anything.
> JON: We know this can go on for as long as we want it to.
> CHRIS: Now.
> JON: These days.
> CHRIS: And all the days.
> JON: Why would we worry?
> CHRIS: Why would we worry?
> JON: What would be the reason to worry? (*ibid*.)

The question is, should *we*, in the present day, be worried about the future outlined in this story?

The scenario presented here is vaguely unsettling, and may be thought to better resemble dystopia than utopia. These future-humans, who apparently no longer have any cause for concern, are not altogether recognisable *as* human, but are strangely placid creatures, wrapped up in their own technologically mediated reality. (This is not so far from the present day.) They are existential drifters. (Flashback to the decadent aesthete, Dartigny, in Rachilde's *Madame La Mort*, and Max Nordau's polemic *Degeneration*, discussed in Chapter 1.) This impression was heightened in performance by Pete Malkin's sound design, which here consisted of a trancelike, ambient drone, evoking a waiting-room in limbo. Other details about this future world do not inspire confidence in it. We are told there are 'many, many' more suicides and that people 'edit themselves out of the world' by literally turning a blind eye to things (a device installed in the optic nerve allows them to 'only see the thing we want or need to') (33). One of the unseen things are the 'invisible majority' – the 'people for whom implants are not an option', who have not been 'granted access', and who thus live shorter lives and have become '[almost] a different species' (34–5). An implication of this story is that deathlessness will have a financial and spiritual cost that may not be worth paying, even if one has the means. Ironically, deathlessness might lead to a peculiar form of lifelessness.

Am I Dead Yet? ended with the performers singing a wistful, piano-accompanied song, the chorus of which is 'Oh, I think I'll die. / Oh, I know I'll die.' The verses were comprised of responses written by audience members before the show to the prompt 'I think I'll die …'. Responses ranged from the glib (e.g., 'I think I'll die stylish') to the grimly sober ('I think I'll die of cancer – I've had it twice already and I reckon it'll get me in the end'). Despite the preceding narratives about death's impermanence and indefinite deferment, the performers restated audience members' declarations about their own mortality, singing their words back to them in a kind of musical echo-chamber. The show therefore sent a mixed message: on the one hand, death may not be as permanent or inevitable as you think, but, on the other, we will all die and you should reconcile yourself to that reality. *Am I Dead Yet?* did not resolve this conundrum or tie up this open-ended situation, but let audience members ponder it for themselves. This is fair. After all, the future of death is unknowable, but, as has been shown throughout this book, theatre allows us to (re-)stage our ever-shifting, always imperfect, understanding of our mortality, and to face this existential challenge 'alone together'.

Flashes before your eyes

It's Fool's Day. I'm attending a performance. I hear the recorded voice of an older woman with a Northumbrian accent. This, I presume, is Helen.

'Y'see, I can't see now. Oh, well. It doesn't matter. You can put the eyes in my eyes'.

Who's Helen and why should I be feeling sad about her?

Lines from a poem I learned at school ...
  Every old man I see
  In October-coloured weather
  Seems to say to me:
  'I was once your father.'

From a newspaper article:

> Your life really does flash before your eyes when you die, a study suggests – with the parts of the brain that store memories last to be affected as other functions fail. Research on those who have had 'near death' experiences suggests that the phenomenon rarely involves flashbacks in chronological order, as happens in Hollywood films. Participants said that there was rarely any order to their life memories and that they seemed to come at random, and sometimes simultaneously. ... Those involved in the study said they lost all sense of time, with memories flying back at them from all periods of their life. One wrote: 'There is not a linear progression, there is lack of time limits ... It was like being there for centuries. I was not in time/space so this question also feels impossible to answer'. (Donnelly, 2017)

The unnamed person in Churchill's play – apparently dead, and in a null-space where one's thoughts shape that which appears ...

An early idea for this project was to investigate the ways in which theatre artists associated with a particular aesthetic (e.g., expressionism) explored death and dying in their work. It soon became apparent that this would not provide an optimal framework for the book. The fact that artists create work in a particular style does not mean they will necessarily explore a shared set of concerns. There is no guarantee their work will cohere around themes relating to mortality in a discernible or insightful manner. Chapter 1 reveals the differences of approach to the topic of death taken by dramatists associated with, or influenced by, the symbolist movement. Symbolists writing in the *fin de siècle* were inspired by the 'deathly tenor of the age' and the vogue for spiritualism, so their work has conceptual coherence in this regard; nevertheless, it makes use of these influences uniquely.

I have generally opted to focus on an identifiable, historical sensibility in relation to mortality, and locate examples of drama and theatre that manifest this sensibility and explore it thematically. This has allowed for a varied mix of case studies, as plays written in different styles and forms but engaging with similar attitudes toward mortality have been juxtaposed and interrelated. This has admittedly given rise to strange bedfellows in some of the chapters (e.g., Ernst Toller and Vernon Lee in Chapter 2; Dino Buzzati and the Open Theater in Chapter 3; Józef Szajna and Howard Barker in Chapter 4). Happily, these combinations have highlighted previously unrecognised connections between dramatists and theatre-makers working in different cultural contexts. I have shown how these artists endeavoured to make sense, as best they could, of specific aspects of mortality in the modern world. Form is found, or (re-)made, to suit content, but there is more than one way to explore these sensibilities – hence, the mixing-and-matching arrangements in this book. From a scholarly perspective, thinking across aesthetic lines and national borders reveals a trove of conceptual correspondences and thematic parallels in the (cob)webs of modern theatre.

Static theatre –
all is silent … all is still …
A noise. Death steals in.

The examination of symbolist theatre in Chapter 1 sets the scene for the rest of the book. Symbolism occupies a slightly nebulous territory in theatre history. Its relationship to theatrical modernism is contested, with some scholars (e.g., Berghaus, 2005) regarding it as a precursor to the historical avant-garde rather than an avant-garde proper. It has a 'foot' in more than one world, to be sure, but its use of mythic subject matter and esoteric ideas should be understood in the context of late nineteenth-century *modernity*. As I have stated elsewhere, '[while] symbolist art … seems pointedly divorced from the everyday world, it was nonetheless informed by it' (2014: 35). Moreover, sometimes symbolist authors called attention to the modernity of their work, as Maeterlinck does in *The Intruder*, which is *'set in modern times'*, per the stage directions (1985: 52).

Symbolist drama is inflected by the Zeitgeist of the *fin de siècle*, which was marked by a morbid sensibility (much to the chagrin of cultural commentators such as Nordau). Rather than simply replicate this sensibility uncritically, however, or casually exploit its frisson (like the Cabaret du Néant), symbolist theatre artists presented death onstage in such a way as to undermine audience members' ontological security about that which lies 'beyond the veil'. Symbolist theatre offered dramas of doubt and uncertainty about the presence of death in life and the prospect of life after death, suggesting possibilities of being (and non-being), but eschewing firm beliefs. This tallies with Marshall Berman's previously cited conception of what it means to 'be modern': 'to be modern is to experience personal and social life as a maelstrom, to find one's world and oneself in perpetual disintegration and renewal, trouble and anguish, ambiguity and contradiction: to be part of a universe in which all that is solid melts into air' (1988: 345). This is highly suggestive of the world of symbolist drama, which is full of nervy, frightened, insecure characters gaping into the void and shivering – spooked by things they cannot comprehend. I have argued that death was presented atmospherically in symbolist theatre to make this into a potentially shared experience for characters and audience members alike. The ontological and epistemological flux found in symbolist drama aptly sets the stage for the later theatrical explorations of mortality in this study. These later stages of mortality, which are prompted by historical events and changing social dynamics, hark back to the symbolists; they are equally unsettled and unsettling.

Requiem for Andreyev:
'Oh, how desolate the night is. Never since the world began has there been such a desolate night as this, its gloom is frightful, its silence fathomless, and I am utterly alone'.

Rose in her armchair at the end of O'Reilly's Cosy:
'Let me not fall into darkness
Ssssh ...
No no no no not into the dark, not into the dark, please –
Ssssh
Cosy, cosy. It comes, it comes
Not into the dark!
Stars. Stars'.

As discussed in the Introduction, the 'stages of mortality' explored in each of the chapters are not completely divided; there is crossover and overlap between them. Each new 'stage' is ghosted by previous 'stages'. Just as symbolist dramatists writing in the late nineteenth century picked up on pre-existing attitudes to, and representations of, death and dying, so too did twentieth- and twenty-first-century dramatists and theatre-makers; in some cases, this may have involved conscious or unconscious borrowing.

One may locate echoes of the symbolists' ambiguous, death-themed scenarios in which characters and audience members are suspended in states of uncertainty and confusion in the broken-down world of Beckett's *Endgame*; the oblique, elliptical dramaturgy of Duras's *Yes, Maybe*; the surrealistic nightmare-world of Barker's *Found in the Ground*; and in the scene depicting the afterlife in Churchill's *Here We Go*, in which a character has to make sense of her or his experience in an existential void. Furthermore, one might recall the symbolists' atmospheric evocation of death when considering Buzzati's depiction of the hospital as a sinister environment (or instrument) of death in *A Clinical Case*; Ionesco's presentation of a domestic space infiltrated by the presence of a fantastical corpse in *Amédée*; Szajna's scenographic depiction of ruined civilisation and traumatised humanity in *Replica*; and the final scene of Churchill's *Here We Go*, which presents a looped sequence of what might be considered a form of death-in-life. The situational circumstances are different in each of these cases, but the means of evocation are similar – death hangs 'in the air'.

Two parts of this book that are obviously linked are Chapters 2 and 4, both of which concern mass death. In these chapters I examined how dramatists and theatre-makers attempted to represent historical and/or future catastrophes, considering how major 'death events' (or just the threat of same) affect conceptions of mortality and lived experience. A significant point of connection between these chapters is the use of fantasy and abstraction to conjure the extent of the devastation and its breach of formerly held perceptions of reality. Toller scripts a face-off between duelling, ideologically opposed personifications of death in *The Transfiguration*. Lee reimagines the First World War as a grotesque ballet masterminded by Satan and orchestrated by Death in *Satan the Waster*. Kraus blends real events from the First World War with expressionist phantasmagoria in *The Last Days of Mankind*. Likewise, in Chapter 4, the selected 'theatres of catastrophe after Auschwitz and Hiroshima' use fantasy and abstraction, vis-à-vis dramaturgy and/or staging, to explore atrocities of the Second World War and what they might foreshadow. Global conflicts have their own complex histories, of course, but these examples all share a commitment to grapple with the enormity of modern, industrialised, techno-bureaucratically organised mass death and to indicate its profound, lasting psychological effects. In doing so, they eschew – or otherwise disrupt – realism, and confront readers or audience members with difficult-to-fathom death events.

A naked, headless woman, symbolising the victims of the Holocaust, perambulates. (If you're without your head, you're probably dead, or possibly dreaming.) Barking.

Carr in conversation: 'I love the idea of the tragedy of man and woman. It is the only significant thing about us – that we are going to die, and that we all get it so wrong'.

Mitford on the rhetoric of American funeral directors: 'The deceased is beautified, not with makeup, but with "cosmetics". Anyway, he didn't die, he "expired"'.

A young man blithely remarks that he has not given much thought to what will happen to him when he reaches old age, and is not too bothered about this future stage of his existence. Dying does not seem very 'real' to him.

Death denial is not wholly specific to the cultural milieux and period (1950s to 1970s) explored in Chapter 3. Maeterlinck writes about death denial in one of his philosophical treatises written in the early twentieth century: 'The more our thoughts struggle to turn away from it, the closer do they press around it. The more we dread it, the more dreadful it becomes, for it battens but on our fears' (1912: 5). Spiritualism, with its promise of the posthumous survival of the spirit (and continuity of self) can be considered a form of death denial, in that it rejects the prospect of nothingness after death. Spiritualism has not died out, either, even if its heyday has long passed. Examples of death denial continue to appear in later chapters of this book – think of Winnie ignoring the reality of her gravelike situation in Beckett's *Happy Days*; the character of Fourth Woman in Bond's *The Tin Can People*, who, at one point in the play, paradoxically tries to avoid death by pretending to be dead while upright and walking; Everyman's materialistic, wasteful, self-centred ways in Duffy's update of the medieval morality play; Woman's bugaboo about death, which takes form as the avian 'Thing in the Wardrobe' in Carr's *Woman and Scarecrow*; and Gloria's refusal to accept Rose's desire to end her own life in O'Reilly's *Cosy*. The contemporary scientific initiatives that aim to deny death by classing it as a treatable condition, related as a science fiction story in *Am I Dead Yet?*, provide further evidence of death denial's longevity and likely persistence. Death denial is not a totalising sensibility, however, nor has it ever been. In the early twenty-first century, death denial and the 'death awareness' movement vie with one another, contributing to the 'contradictory and uncertain space of death in modern culture' (Noys, 2005: 3).

The cabaret of 'nothingness' – a chamber dimly lit by wax tapers and a chandelier made of human skulls attached to bones clutching candles. Wooden coffins, resting on biers, are ranged about the room.

Death as a ballet-master – his bones have worked his evening suit into rags, his wig has fallen off, and through the rents of his once smart waistcoat and shirt there is a glimpse of something far worse than a mere skeleton ...

The 'Thing' is mostly heard but not seen, though he does extend a wing and a clawed foot out of the wardrobe at the end of the first act – an intimation of his inevitable approach.

Thousands of crosses in a snowfield. (The apparition vanishes.)

The ways in which death is represented in the examples discussed in this book are manifold. Personification of death persists in modern drama, though is often conducted in an ironic or self-reflexive manner. The Veiled Woman in Rachilde's *Madame La Mort* is a cipher, and may be regarded as a fanciful projection of a dying man – a clichéd union of *eros* and *thanatos*. In Toller's *The Transfiguration*, Death-by-Peace tells Death-by-War that the latter is 'a modern Death, / A product of the times' by virtue of the fact that he has been co-opted by the human-engineered war machine and its implementation of the 'Fordism' (i.e., industrialisation) of death (1986 [1919]: 163). This is not meant as a compliment. In contrast, Lee presents Death as an old-fashioned ballet-master in *Satan the Waster*, depicting him as an antiquity who is getting increasingly ragged and out of touch. In Carr's *Woman and Scarecrow*, the Thing in the Wardrobe, an embodiment of death, merges with Scarecrow, Woman's alter ego, at the end of the play to take Woman's life. Is this all happening in her head in her dying moments? This is how Duffy arranges the mental drama of *Everyman*, in which Death is presented as a wise-cracker, a 'heavy' – a charactersation seemingly drawn from Everyman's imagination. Duffy thus points to the familiarity of this stock figure, who has not yet been permanently retired.

Allied to recurrent personification of death is repeated dramatisation of the idea that supernatural forces can be instrumental in bringing about one's death. This does not seem to be a very modern – or at least a rational – point of view, but, confusingly, 'premodern' ideas and sensibilities can still be part of modernity and modernism. Hence, the series of offstage voices who act as harbingers of death in van Lerberghe's *The Night-Comers*; the spectral force that stalks the family in Maeterlinck's *The Intruder*; the phantom death personae who operate undetected in society in Toller's *The Transfiguration*; Satan's supernatural machinations in Lee's *Satan the Waster*; the mysterious, deathly siren in Buzzati's *A Clinical Case*; and the folkloric, demonic figures of Carr's *Woman and Scarecrow*. However, in some cases (e.g., Maeterlinck, Buzzati, Carr) the reality of these supernatural elements is questionable; they may be *imagined* by characters rather than 'really' existing in the worlds of these plays. Again, this speaks to the lingering importance of folkloric elements and supernatural beliefs, even in scientifically oriented, supposedly rationalist, modern societies. Relatedly, this book has featured examples of spirits haunting the living (or seeming to haunt the living), as in Yeats's *Purgatory* and Barker's *Found in the Ground*, or otherwise being invoked by the living (e.g., the 'calling up' of spirits followed by spirit possession in the Open Theater's *Terminal*).

Conceptions of death as absolute termination (rather than as 'expiration' of the soul into some other realm) are, nonetheless, presented in the plays discussed in this book.[10] Andreyev's *Requiem* is an early example, with the character of The Manager sitting in an empty theatre, bewailing the void in which he finds himself – symbolically dead. The play offers a nihilistic vision of human mortality. Characters in plays written in the early twenty-first century similarly espouse a lack of belief in life-after-death (e.g., Woman in *Woman and Scarecrow*; Rose in *Cosy*). Their belief in the finality of death is qualified, or contested, though. Rose's frank view of death ('It's only a hole in the ground and compost') is juxtaposed with Gloria's religious beliefs; O'Reilly cultivates a clash of viewpoints and does not fully resolve them (2016: 291). Woman, in Carr's play, hopes her children will keep her alive in their memories, thus allowing her to endure after her death via genetics and memetics (cultural transmission), even if she has little faith in the posthumous existence of her soul. Duras's *Yes, Maybe*, written during the Cold War, sketches the reverse situation: a world in which human history has been erased and memory curtailed, thus severing the connection between the living and the dead and effecting the 'death of death' (making death meaningless).

Death in modern theatre is thus presented in diverse, sometimes opposed, ways, in line with the generally 'mixed picture' of death in Western societies in the period under survey.[11] One can discern recurrent strokes and familiar patterns, as well as a multitude of minor details, but the overall composition is messily arranged; it is an abstract collage, the work of many hands.

St Peter and the pearly gates. The great golden scale of the Egyptian god Osiris. Valhalla. The old Norse giantess/goddess Hel (custodian of the underworld). Charon in his boat in Hades. Odysseus.

Churchill's character does not reflect on the significance of discovering an afterlife replete with cultural mishmash, or acknowledge this to be at all remarkable.

The plays and productions discussed in this book are all informed by the cultural circumstances of their creation, of course, but some are more obviously connected to a specific culture than others. Anglo-Irish, Protestant-Catholic dynamics infuse Yeats's *Purgatory*, though this play is also inspired by Japanese Noh. Carr's *Woman and Scarecrow* likewise mines Irish folklore and cultural practices about death and dying. Toller's *The Transfiguration* is shaped by the author's Jewish-German identity. The Open Theater's *Terminal* explicitly addresses the 'American way of death', as Jessica Mitford puts it. Nevertheless, there are several examples in this study that bypass cultural specificity and strive for wider valence: for example, Szajna's largely wordless piece *Replica* and Duras's *Yes, Maybe*, which jumbles national signifiers. This book has also examined productions of plays in translation in a different cultural context, and has shown how these plays have been made newly resonant: for example, Zarrilli's American production of Buzzati's *A Clinical Case*, and the English Stage Company's 1963 production of Ionesco's *Exit the King*. It stands to reason that plays and performance pieces that engage with the theme of mortality may travel well, so to speak, as they have the potential to reach a wide audience: death is a common denominator, after all, which helps to account for its perennial treatment by dramatists and theatre-makers, its 'eternal return', as it were. One might productively consider how the theme of mortality is addressed in the theatre of a single national tradition, but then mutually shared concerns about death and dying in an international context might recede from view.

There is a nexus between theatre and death: an interchange of absence and presence, 'ghosting' from the past in the present, conjuring of the

Conclusion: Unending

inanimate through the animate, and reminder of our mortality in moments of experiencing live performance with people who are with us – and sometimes remembering people who have 'passed' – as time slips by.

I find all this quite moving.

O'Reilly on theatre audiences: 'Get them all relaxed. Give them a nice little massage before the main event. And then kick them in the fucking stomach'.

I notice my breathing has become shallow and more rapid.

This is what theatre can do, and this is why you wrote this book.

While it is widely known that there is a plethora of plays from the late nineteenth century onward that treats some aspect of death or dying, and that certain dramatists and theatre-makers have been especially taken with the theme of mortality, this study is unique in providing a synoptic account of this phenomenon, covering a time-span of over a hundred years and engaging multiple cultural contexts. This has revealed some of the richness and diversity of modern theatre's engagement with death and dying, whilst also identifying shared interest in certain topics via a series of interrelated, mostly chronological, micronarratives. This book has thus re-examined what has hitherto been regarded as a largely unrelated and idiosyncratic set of activities. The 'stages of mortality' outlined herein show that modern dramatists and theatre-makers have been, and continue to be, attuned to the ever-evolving ways in which death and dying are understood. They are, in fact, a vital part of this enterprise. Modern theatre artists regularly invite audience members to contemplate mortality (both their own and that of others), highlighting the sometimes hidden or unacknowledged presence of death in everyday life. They use theatre's quintessential element – play – to evoke 'the real', often drawing on registers of the symbolic and the fantastical to present painful truths that can be difficult to accept or even to comprehend. When all is said and done, theatre can help us to better understand what it means to be mortal, what it means to be human.

The figure on the stage remains visible for a short time before fading into a kind of mist ...

Notes

1 Life-extension programmes cannot guarantee immortality. As Kevin T. Keith notes, 'death by violence or accident would always be a danger, and even death by untreated disease or unique genetic defect would remain possible. Thus everyone would face some possibility of death even if no "natural" source of death were to be feared' (2009: 109).
2 In the first part of the play, Adam, in the Garden of Eden, declares his frustration about being immortal: 'I am tired of myself. And yet I must endure myself, not for a day or for many days, but for ever. That is a dreadful thought. That is what makes me sit brooding and silent and hateful' (Shaw, 1930: 5).
3 Leoš Janáček adapted Čapek's play as an opera with the same name; it premiered in 1926.
4 Friedrich Dürrenmatt dramatises the strange scenario of a person repeatedly dying and coming back to life – not due to medical intervention but for unexplained reasons – in his comedy *Der Meteor* (*The Meteor*, 1966).
5 '[If] someone asked me the question "Exactly when after death does irreversible death become an absolute reality, and when exactly does death become completely permanent?" I would answer, "We don't really know, and whatever point we choose will still likely be arbitrary and most likely will need redefining again in the future as science and technology improve and our ability to resuscitate people progresses"' (Parnia and Young, 2014: 274–5).
6 This relates to a type of Tibetan meditation practice called '*thukdam*', in which practitioners who have died while meditating show no noticeable signs of death for a week or more.
7 *Am I Dead Yet?* was written by Chris Thorpe and Jon Spooner in consultation with Dr Andy Lockey. The piece was directed by Amy Hodge.
8 A recording of a full-length version of the show, performed at the Bush Theatre in London in 2014, is available on the company's website, as of the time of this writing: www.unlimited.org.uk/aidy/. I attended a performance at the Lincoln Performing Arts Centre on 11 November 2016, from which my observations derive.
9 I am grateful to Chris Thorpe for providing me with a copy of the unpublished script for *Am I Dead Yet?* and allowing me to quote from it.
10 This is Sandra M. Gilbert's distinction – discussed in Chapter 4.
11 As discussed in Chapter 5, Tony Walter characterises death in Britain in the twenty-first century as a 'mixed picture'; I extend the range of reference here.

REFERENCES

Ackerman, A.L. (2012) *Reading Modern Drama*. Toronto: University of Toronto Press.
Adorno, T.W. (2003) *Can One Live After Auschwitz?: A Philosophical Reader*. Translated by R. Livingstone. Stanford: Stanford University Press.
Altman, P. (1975) '"A Clinical Case" Slashes Hospital Open with Satire'. *Minneapolis Star*, 29 May.
Anderson, B. (2009) 'Affective Atmospheres', *Emotion, Space and Society* 2 (2): 77–81.
Andreyev, L. (1985) 'Requiem', in *Doubles, Demons, and Dreamers: An International Collection of Symbolist Drama*, edited by D. Gerould, 209–24. New York: Performing Arts Journal Publications.
Anon. (1963a) 'Civilisation Decays – in 100 Minutes'. *Newcastle Journal*, 28 August.
—. (1963b) '"Exit the King": Enter Ionesco'. *Sunday Times*, 1 September, 22.
—. (1963c) 'Slow Exit'. *Eastern Press*, 16 September.
Arendt, H. (1963) *Eichmann in Jerusalem: A Report on the Banality of Evil*. London: Faber and Faber.
Ariès, P. (1976) *Western Attitudes Toward Death: From the Middle Ages to the Present*. London: Marion Boyars.
—. (1981) *The Hour of Our Death*. New York: Vintage Books.
Barfield, S., P. Tew and M. Feldman, eds. (2009) *Beckett and Death*. London: Continuum.
Barker, H. (1987) *The Possibilities*. London: John Calder.
—. (1997) *Arguments for a Theatre*. 3rd ed. Manchester: Manchester University Press.
—. (2001) *Collected Plays: Volume Five*. London: Calder.
—. (2005) *Death, the One and the Art of Theatre*. London: Routledge.
—. (2007) *A Style and Its Origins*. London: Oberon Books.
—. (2012) *Plays Seven*. London: Oberon.
—. (2014) *These Sad Places, Why Must You Enter Them?* London: Impress.
Barnett, D. (2017) 'Corporeal Disintegration as Last-Gasp Vocal Act: The Final Works of Murobushi, Artaud, and Chéreau', *New Theatre Quarterly* 33 (2): 169–78.
Baudelaire, C. (1909) *The Flowers of Evil*. Translated by C. Scott. London: Elkin Matthews.

Bauman, Z. (1989) *Modernity and the Holocaust*. Cambridge: Polity Press.
—. (1992) *Mortality, Immortality and Other Life Strategies*. Cambridge: Polity.
Bayes, H. (2009) 'Found in the Ground – Riverside Studios, London'. *Public Reviews*, accessed 23 August 2017. http://thepublicreviews.blogspot.co.uk/2009/10/found-in-ground-riverside-studios.html.
Becker, E. (1973) *The Denial of Death*. New York: Free Press.
Beckett, S. (1957) *Krapp's Last Tape and Other Dramatic Pieces*. New York: Grove Press.
—. (1958) *Endgame*. New York: Grove.
—. (1963) *Happy Days*. London: Faber and Faber.
—. (2006 [1956]) *Waiting for Godot*. London: Faber and Faber.
—. (2010) *The Unnameable*. London: Faber & Faber.
Bendle, M.F. (2001) 'The Contemporary Episteme of Death', *Cultural Values* 5 (3): 349–67.
Benson, D.J. (2007) *Music: A Mathematical Offering*. Cambridge: Cambridge University Press.
Berghaus, G. (2005) *Theatre, Performance, and the Historical Avant-Garde*. New York: Palgrave Macmillan.
Berman, M. (1988) *All That Is Solid Melts into Air: The Experience of Modernity*. London: Verso.
Bettelheim, B. (1979) *Surviving, and Other Essays*. New York: Knopf.
Blake, W. (1992 [1794]) *Songs of Innocence and Songs of Experience*. New York: Dover Thrift Editions.
Blau, H. (1982) *Take Up the Bodies: Theater at the Vanishing Point*. Urbana: University of Illinois Press.
—. (1990a) *The Audience*. Baltimore: Johns Hopkins University Press.
—. (1990b) 'Universals of Performance; or Amortizing Play', in *By Means of Performance: Intercultural Studies of Theatre and Ritual*, edited by R. Schechner and W. Appel, 250–72. Cambridge: Cambridge University Press.
—. (2011) *Reality Principles: From the Absurd to the Virtual*. Ann Arbor: University of Michigan Press.
Bleyen, J. (2009) 'Ariès's Social History of Death', in *Encyclopedia of Death and the Human Experience*, edited by C.D. Bryant and D.L. Peck, 65–8. Los Angeles: Sage.
Böhme, G. (1993) 'Atmosphere as the Fundamental Concept of a New Aesthetics', *Thesis Eleven* 36 (1): 113–26.
—. (2013) 'The Art of the Stage Set as a Paradigm for an Aesthetics of Atmospheres', *Ambiances*, last modified 10 February, accessed 28 July 2018. https://journals.openedition.org/ambiances/315.
Bond, E. (1998) *Plays 6*. London: Methuen.
Bond, E., and I. Stuart. (1995) *Edward Bond: Letters*. Vol. 2. Amsterdam: Harwood Academic Publishers.
Booth, A. (1996) *Postcards from the Trenches: Negotiating the Space between Modernism and the First World War*. Oxford: Oxford University Press.
Borgstrom, E., and J. Ellis. (2017) 'Introduction: Researching Death, Dying and Bereavement', *Mortality* 22 (2): 83–104.
Bosanquet, T., and J. Caird. (2009) 'Brief Encounter with … Howard Barker'. whatsonstage.com, Accessed 7 February 2012. www.whatsonstage.com/interviews/theatre/london/E8831254919348/Brief+Encounter+With+…+Howard+Barker.html.
Bosworth, R.J.B. (1993) *Explaining Auschwitz and Hiroshima: History Writing and the Second World War 1945–1990*. London: Routledge.
Boyer, P.E. (1998) *Artists and the Avant-Garde Theater in Paris, 1887–1900*. Washington, DC: National Gallery of Art.
Brennan, M., ed. (2014) *The A–Z of Death and Dying: Social, Medical, and Cultural Aspects*. Santa Barbara: Greenwood.
Brockington, G. (2006) 'Performing Pacifism: The Battle between Artist and Author in *The Ballet of the Nations*', in *Vernon Lee: Decadence, Ethics, Aesthetics*, edited by C. Maxwell and P. Pulham, 143–73. Basingstoke: Palgrave.

Bronfen, E., and S.W. Goodwin, eds. (1993) *Death and Representation*. Baltimore: Johns Hopkins University Press.
Brooke, R. (2014) *The Complete Poems of Rupert Brooke*. Keighley: Pomona Press.
Brown, G.C. (2008) *The Living End: The Future of Death, Aging and Immortality*. London: Macmillan.
Brown, M., ed. (2011) *Howard Barker Interviews 1980–2010: Conversations in Catastrophe*. Bristol: Intellect.
Bryant, C.D., and D.L. Peck. (2009) *Encyclopedia of Death and the Human Experience*. Vol. 2. Los Angeles: Sage.
Budgen, F. (1960) *James Joyce and the Making of 'Ulysses'*. Bloomington: Indiana University Press.
Buzzati, D. (1975) *A Clinical Case*. Unpublished script.
Cannadine, D. (1981) 'War and Death, Grief and Mourning in Modern Britain', in *Mirrors of Mortality: Studies in the Social History of Death*, edited by J. Whaley, 187–242. London: Europe.
Canning, J., H. Lehmann and J.M. Winter. (2004) *Power, Violence and Mass Death in Pre-Modern and Modern Times*. Aldershot: Ashgate.
Čapek, K. (1999) *Čapek: Four Plays*. Translated by C. Porter and P. Majer. London: Bloomsbury.
Carlson, M. (1984) *Theories of the Theatre: A Historical and Critical Survey, from the Greeks to the Present*. Ithaca: Cornell University Press.
—. (2001) *The Haunted Stage: The Theatre as Memory Machine*. Ann Arbor: University of Michigan Press.
Carpenter, C.A. (1999) *Dramatists and the Bomb: American and British Playwrights Confront the Nuclear Age, 1945–1964*. Westport, CT: Greenwood Press.
Carr, M. (2006) *Woman and Scarecrow*. Loughcrew: Gallery Press.
Celan, P. (1996) *Selected Poems*. Translated by M. Hamburger. London: Penguin.
Chamberlain, F. (1997) 'Presenting the Unrepresentable: Maeterlinck's *L'Intruse* and the Symbolist Drama', *Contemporary Theatre Review* 6 (4): 25–36.
Chambers, J. (2010) '"Or I'll Die": Death and Dying on Page and Stage', in *Theater Historiography: Critical Interventions*, edited by H. Bial and S. Magelssen, 162–74. Ann Arbor: University of Michigan Press.
Chambers, L. (2001) *Theatre Talk: Voices of Irish Theatre Practitioners*. Dublin: Carysfort Press.
Chapple, H.S., B. Bouton, A. Chow et al. (2017) 'The Body of Knowledge in Thanatology: An Outline', *Death Studies* 41 (2): 118–25.
Chéroux, C., A. Fischer, P. Apracine et al. (2005) *The Perfect Medium: Photography and the Occult*. New Haven: Yale University Press.
Chew, S. (2009) 'Found in the Ground'. whatsonstage.com, accessed 7 February 2012. www.whatsonstage.com/reviews/theatre/off-west+end/E8831254728361/Found+in+the+Ground.html.
Churchill, C. (2015) *Here We Go*. London: Nick Hern Books.
Cioffi, K.M. (1996) *Alternative Theatre in Poland, 1954–1989*. Amsterdam: Harwood Academic.
Cixous, H. (2004) *Selected Plays of Hélène Cixous*. London: Routledge.
Clapp, S. (2015) 'Everyman Review – A Rousing Display'. *Guardian*, 3 May. Aaccessed 4 April 2017. www.theguardian.com/stage/2015/may/03/everyman-olivier-national-theatre-review-chiwetel-ejiofor-carol-ann-duffy.
Clodfelter, M. (2017) *Warfare and Armed Conflicts: A Statistical Encyclopedia of Casualty and Other Figures, 1492–2015*. 4th ed. Jefferson, NC: McFarland.
Cody, G.H. (2000) *Impossible Performances: Duras as Dramatist*. New York: Peter Lang.
Connor, S. (2006) 'Haze: On Nebular Modernism'. Accessed 5 September 2017. http://stevenconnor.com/haze.html.
Coombs, S. (2014) 'Death Wears a T-shirt: Listening to Young People Talk about Death', *Mortality* 19 (3): 284–302.

Corrieri, A. (2016) *In Place of a Show: What Happens Inside Theatres When Nothing Is Happening*. London: Bloomsbury.
Craig, E.G. (1911) *On the Art of the Theatre*. London: William Heinemann.
Croyden, M. (1970) 'To Joe Chaikin, Burning Bridges Is Natural'. *New York Times*, 29 March, 77.
Cruz, D.T. (2014) *Postmodern Metanarratives: Blade Runner and Literature in the Age of Image*. Basingstoke: Palgrave Macmillan.
Curtin, A. (2013) 'Vibration, Percussion and Primitivism in Avant-Garde Performance', in *Vibratory Modernism*, edited by A. Enns and S. Trower, 227–47. Basingstoke: Palgrave.
—. (2014) *Avant-Garde Theatre Sound: Staging Sonic Modernity*. New York: Palgrave Macmillan.
de Grey, A. (2004) "We Will Be Able to Live to 1,000'. *BBC News*, accessed 9 November 2017. http://news.bbc.co.uk/1/hi/uk/4003063.stm.
—. (2007) *Ending Aging: The Rejuvenation Breakthroughs that Could Reverse Human Aging in Our Lifetime*. New York: St Martin's Griffin.
Deák, F. (1993) *Symbolist Theater: The Formation of an Avant-Garde*. Baltimore: Johns Hopkins University Press.
Dennis, D. (2014) 'Definitions of Death', in *The A-Z of Death and Dying: Social, Medical, and Cultural Aspects*, edited by M. Brennan, 156–9. Santa Barbara: Greenwood.
Dent, M. (2001) 'The [Fallen] Body: The Crisis of Meaning in Sankai Juku's "Jomon Sho"', in *Ordinary Reactions to Extraordinary Events*, edited by R.B. Browne and A.G. Neal, 122–36. Bowling Green: Bowling Green State University Popular Press.
Dodd, P. (2015) *Free Thinking*. BBC Radio 3. 29 April. Accessed 28 April, 2017. www.bbc.co.uk/programmes/b05s3rrp.
Dolan, J. (2005) *Utopia in Performance: Finding Hope at the Theater*. Ann Arbor: University of Michigan Press.
Dollimore, J. (2001) *Death, Desire and Loss in Western Culture*. New York: Routledge.
Donnelly, L. (2017) 'Your Life Really Does Flash Before Your Eyes Before You Die, Study Suggests'. *The Telegraph*, 29 January. Accessed 9 April 2018. www.telegraph.co.uk/news/2017/01/29/life-really-does-flash-eyes-die-study-suggests/.
Doughty, C. (2015) *Smoke Gets in Your Eyes: And Other Lessons from the Crematorium*. Edinburgh: Canongate.
Downes, S. (1994) 'Letter: Ionesco: Zen and the Art of Absurdity'. *The Independent*, 30 March. Accessed 20 May 2016. www.independent.co.uk/voices/letter-ionesco-zen-and-the-art-of-absurdity-1432812.html.
Doyle, A.C. (1930) *The Land of Mist*. New York: Doubleday.
Dryden, J. (1971) *The Works of John Dryden: Prose 1668–1691: An Essay of Dramatick Poesie and Shorter Works*. Berkeley: University of California Press.
Duffy, C.A. (2015) *Everyman: A New Adaptation*. London: Faber & Faber.
Duras, M. (1968) *Théâtre II*. Paris: Gallimard.
Eagleman, D. (2009) *Sum: Forty Tales from the Afterlives*. Edinburgh: Canongate.
Eksteins, M. (1989) *Rites of Spring: The Great War and the Birth of the Modern Age*. New York: Doubleday.
Ellmann, M. (2013) 'More Kicks than Pricks: Modernist Body-Parts', in *A Handbook of Modernism Studies*, edited by J.M. Rabaté, 255–80. Chichester: Wiley-Blackwell.
Enders, J. (1999) *The Medieval Theatre of Cruelty*. Ithaca: Cornell University Press.
Esslin, M. (1965) 'Introduction', in *Absurdist Drama*, edited by M. Esslin, 7–24. West Drayton: Penguin.
—. (2001) *The Theatre of the Absurd*. 3rd ed. London: Methuen.
Etchells, T. (1999) *Certain Fragments: Contemporary Performance and Forced Entertainment*. London: Routledge.
Eynat-Confino, I. (2008) *On the Uses of the Fantastic in Modern Theatre: Cocteau, Oedipus, and the Monster*. New York: Palgrave Macmillan.

Fasching, D.J. (2004) 'Ethics after Auschwitz and Hiroshima', in *The Genocidal Temptation: Auschwitz, Hiroshima, Rwanda, and Beyond*, edited by R.S. Frey, 1–24. Dallas: University Press of America.
Fischer-Lichte, E. (2008) *The Transformative Power of Performance: A New Aesthetics*. London: Routledge.
Fitzgerald, M., ed. (2002) *The Words upon the Window Pane: Manuscript Materials by W.B. Yeats*. Ithaca: Cornell University Press.
Fleischer, M. (2007) 'Incense & Decadence: Symbolist Theatre's Use of Scent', in *The Senses in Performance*, edited by S. Banes and A. Lepecki, 105–14. London: Routledge.
Freud, S. (1985 [1915]) 'Thoughts for the Times on War and Death', in *Civilization, Society and Religion: Group Psychology, Civilzation and Its Discontents, and Other Works*, edited by A. Dickson, 57–89. London: Penguin.
Frey, R.S., ed. (2004) *The Genocidal Temptation: Auschwitz, Hiroshima, Rwanda, and Beyond*. Dallas: University Press of America.
Friedman, A.W. (1995) *Fictional Death and the Modernist Enterprise*. Cambridge: Cambridge University Press.
Friedman, S.S. (2015) *Planetary Modernisms: Provocations on Modernity Across Time*. New York: Columbia University Press.
Fuchs, E., ed. (1987) *Plays of the Holocaust: An International Anthology*. New York: Theatre Communications Group.
—. (1999) 'The Apocalyptic Century', *Theater* 29 (3): 7–40.
Fulton, R., and G. Owen. (1988) 'Death and Society in Twentieth Century America', *Omega: Journal of Death and Dying* 18 (4): 379–95.
Fussell, P. (1975) *The Great War and Modern Memory*. New York: Oxford University Press.
Gaëll, R. (1916) *Priests in the Firing Line*. Translated by H. Hamilton Gibbs and M. Berton. London: Longmans, Green and Co.
Gardner, L. (2009) 'Found in the Ground'. *The Guardian*, 7 October. Accessed 15 August 2017. www.theguardian.com/stage/2009/oct/07/found-in-the-ground.
Gerould, D., and J. Kosicka. (1980) 'The Drama of the Unseen: Turn-of-the-Century Paradigms for Occult Drama', in *The Occult in Language and Literature*, edited by H. Riffaterre, 3–42. New York: New York Literary Forum.
Giddens, A. (1991) *Modernity and Self-Identity: Self and Society in the Late Modern Age*. Stanford: Stanford University Press.
Gilbert, S.M. (2006) *Death's Door: Modern Dying and the Ways We Grieve*. New York: W.W. Norton.
Goldingay, S. (2012) 'Contra Mortem, Petimus Scientiam: Pain, Tragedy, Death and Medicine in *Blok/Eko*', *Studies in Theatre and Performance* 32 (3): 347–58.
Gontarski, S.E. (1977) *Beckett's Happy Days: A Manuscript Study*. Columbus: Publications Committee, Ohio State University Libraries.
Goodman, D.G. (1994) *After Apocalypse: Four Japanese Plays of Hiroshima and Nagasaki*. Ithaca: East Asia Program.
Gorer, G. (1955) 'The Pornography of Death', *Encounter* 5 (4): 49–52.
Gorky, M. (1934) *Reminiscences of Tolstoy, Chekhov, and Andreev*. Translated by K. Mansfield, S.S. Koteliansky and L. Woolf. London: Hogarth Press.
Green, M. (1964) *The Art of Coarse Acting*. London: Hutchinson & Co.
Griffero, T. (2014) *Atmospheres: Aesthetics of Emotional Spaces*. Farnham: Ashgate.
Gritzner, K. (2010) *Eroticism and Death in Theatre and Performance*. Hatfield: University of Hertfordshire Press.
—. (2012) 'Poetry and Intensification in Howard Barker's Theatre of Plethora', *Studies in Theatre and Performance* 32 (3): 337–45.
—. (2015) *Adorno and Modern Theatre: The Drama of the Damaged Self in Bond, Rudkin, Barker and Kane*. Basingstoke: Palgrave Macmillan.
Grotowski, J. (1969) *Towards a Poor Theatre*. London: Methuen.

Guthke, K. S. (1999) *The Gender of Death: A Cultural History in Art and Literature*. Cambridge: Cambridge University Press.

—. (2017) *Life Without End: A Thought Experiment in Literature from Swift to Houellebecq*. Rochester, NY: Camden House.

Hachiya, M. (1955) *Hiroshima Diary: The Journal of a Japanese Physician, August 6–September 30, 1945*. London: Victor Gollancz.

Hand, R.J. (2010) 'Labyrinths of the Taboo: Theatrical Journeys of Eroticism and Death in Parisian Culture', in *Eroticism and Death in Theatre and Performance*, edited by K. Gritzner, 64–79. Hatfield: University of Hertfordshire Press.

Harper, M.M. (2006) 'Yeats and the Occult', in *The Cambridge Companion to W.B. Yeats*, edited by M. Howes and J. Kelly, 144–66. Cambridge: Cambridge University Press.

Haughton, M. (2013) 'Woman's Final Confession: Too Much Hoovering and Not Enough Sex. Marina Carr's *Woman and Scarecrow*', *Mortality* 18 (1): 72–93.

Heaphy, B. (2007) *Late Modernity and Social Change: Reconstructing Social and Personal Life*. London: Routledge.

Hendrickson, R. (2000) *The Facts on File Dictionary of American Regionalisms*. New York: Facts on File.

Hogan, M.J. (1996) *Hiroshima in History and Memory*. Cambridge: Cambridge University Press.

Howard, T., and T. Łubiensk. (1989) 'The Theatres of Józef Szajna', *New Theatre Quarterly* 5 (19): 240–63.

Howarth, G. (2011) 'The Emergence of New Forms of Dying in Contemporary Societies', in *Death, Dying, and Social Differences*, edited by D. Oliviere, B. Monroe, and S. Payne, 8–18. Oxford: Oxford University Press.

Hulton, D. (2010) 'Joseph Chaikin: The Presence of the Actor', *Studies in Theatre and Performance* 30 (2): 219–24.

Hurd, A. (1914) 'The Clink of Glasses and the Roar of Guns', *Great Deeds of the Great War* 1 (1): 15.

Hutcheon, L., and M. Hutcheon. (2004) *Opera: The Art of Dying*. Cambridge, MA: Harvard University Press.

Ibsen, H. (1936 [1867]) *Peer Gynt: A Dramatic Poem*. Translated by R. Farquharson Sharp. Philadelphia: J.B. Lippincott.

Innes, C. (1981) *Holy Theatre: Ritual and the Avant Garde*. Cambridge: Cambridge University Press.

Ionesco, E. (1965 [1956]) 'Amédée or How to Get Rid of It', in *Absurdist Drama*, edited by M. Esslin, 25–116. West Drayton: Penguin.

—. (1994) *Exit the King, The Killers, Macbeth*. Translated by C. Marowitz and D. Watson. New York: Grove Press.

Jacobs, R.A. (2010) *Filling the Hole in the Nuclear Future: Art and Popular Culture Respond to the Bomb*. Plymouth: Rowman & Littlefield.

Jacobs, W.D. (1972) 'Ionesco's Amédée', *The Explicator* 31 (3): 33–7.

Jacquette, D. (2015) *Alexius Meinong, the Shepherd of Non-Being*. Cham: Springer.

Jalland, P. (2010) *Death in War and Peace: Loss and Grief in England, 1914–1970*. Oxford: Oxford University Press.

James, P. (2013) *The New Death: American Modernism and World War I*. Charlottesville: University of Virginia Press.

Jelewska-Michas, A. (2006) 'Inspiration from Edward Gordon Craig in Tadeusz Kantor and Józef Szajna's Artistic Theories', *Meno Istorija ir Kritika* 2: 80–7.

Joyce, J. (1986 [1922]) *Ulysses*. New York: Vintage.

Kaes, A. (2009) *Shell Shock Cinema: Weimar Culture and the Wounds of War*. Princeton: Princeton University Press.

Kagan, S. (2012) *Death*. New Haven: Yale University Press.

Kalb, J. (1989) *Beckett in Performance*. Cambridge: Cambridge University Press.

Kaye, N. (2012) 'Photographic Presence: Time and the Image', in *Archaeologies of Presence: Art, Performance and the Persistence of Being*, edited by G. Giannachi, N. Kaye and M. Shanks, 235–56. London: Routledge.
Keith, K.T. (2009) 'Life Extension: Proponents, Opponents, and the Social Impact of the Defeat of Death', in *Speaking of Death: America's New Sense of Mortality*, edited by M.K. Bartalos, 102–51. Westport, CT: Praeger.
Kellehear, A. (2007) *A Social History of Dying*. Cambridge: Cambridge University Press.
Keshavjee, S. (2006) 'The Enactment of the Supernatural in French Symbolist Culture', in *Technologies of Intuition*, edited by J. Fisher, 31–43. Toronto: YYZ Books.
Khapaeva, D. (2017) *The Celebration of Death in Contemporary Culture*. Ann Arbor: University of Michigan Press.
Kipp, L. (2017) 'Between Excess and Subtraction: Scenographic Violence in Howard Barker's *Found in the Ground*', *Sillages Critiques* 22, accessed 24 August 2017. http://sillagescritiques.revues.org/4830.
Kirkland, W. (1918) *The New Death*. Boston, MA: Houghton Mifflin.
Knight, G.W. (1946) *Hiroshima: On Prophecy and the Sun-Bomb*. London: Andrew Dakers Limited.
Kobialka, M. (2009) *Further On, Nothing: Tadeusz Kantor's Theatre*. Minneapolis: University of Minnesota Press.
Kosmos, V. (2014) 'Hell Époque: Death-themed Cabarets & Other Macabre Entertainments of Nineteenth-Century Paris', in *The Morbid Anatomy Anthology*, edited by J. Ebenstein. Brooklyn: Morbid Anatomy Press.
Kosok, H. (2007) *The Theatre of War: The First World War in British and Irish Drama*. Basingstoke: Palgrave Macmillan.
Krasner, D. (2016) *A History of Modern Drama*. Vol. 2. Chichester: Wiley-Blackwell.
Kraus, K. (1922) *Die letzen Tage der Menschheit: Tragödie in Fünf Akten mit Vorspiel und Epilog*. Vienna: Die Fackel.
—. (2015) *The Last Days of Mankind*. Translated by F. Bridgham and E. Timms. New Haven: Yale University Press.
Kselman, T. (1987) 'Death in Historical Perspective', *Sociological Forum* 2 (3): 591–7.
Kübler-Ross, E. (1970) *On Death and Dying*. London: Tavistock.
Kyle, L.D. (1976) 'The Grotesque in *Amédée* or How to Get Rid of It', *Modern Drama* 19 (3): 281–90.
Lachapelle, S. (2011) *Investigating the Supernatural: From Spiritism and Occultism to Psychical Research and Metapsychics in France, 1853–1931*. Baltimore: Johns Hopkins University Press.
Lahr, J. (1970) 'On-stage'. *Village Voice*, 23 April, 43.
Lamont, R.C. (1993) *Ionesco's Imperatives: The Politics of Culture*. Ann Arbor: University of Michigan Press.
Lapisardi, F.S. (1992) 'A Task Most Difficult: Staging Yeats's Mystical Dramas at the Abbey', in *Staging the Impossible: The Fantastic Mode in Modern Drama*, edited by P.D. Murphy, 30–43. Westport, CT: Greenwood Press.
Lee, R.L.M. (2008) 'Modernity, Mortality and Re-Enchantment: The Death Taboo Revisited', *Sociology* 42 (4): 745–59.
Lee, V. (1920) *Satan the Waster: A Philosophic War Trilogy with Notes & Introduction*. New York: The Bodley Head.
Leeney, C., and A. McMullan. (2003) *The Theatre of Marina Carr: 'before Rules was Made'*. Dublin: Carysfort Press.
Lensing, L.A. (1982) '"Kinodramatisch": Cinema in Karl Kraus' *Die Fackel* and *Die Letzten Tage der Menschheit*', *The German Quarterly* 55 (4): 480–98.
Levy, R.S. (2005) *Antisemitism: A Historical Encyclopedia of Prejudice and Persecution*. Santa Barbara: ABC-CLIO.
Ley, G. (2014) *Ancient Greek and Contemporary Performance*. Exeter: University of Exeter Press.

Lifton, R.J. (1968) *Death in Life: The Survivors of Hiroshima*. London: Weidenfeld & Nicolson.
Lively, F. (1998) 'Introduction', in *Madame La Mort and Other Plays*, edited by K. Gounaridou and F. Lively, 3–53. Baltimore: Johns Hopkins University Press.
Luckhurst, M., and E. Morin. (2014) *Theatre and Ghosts: Materiality, Performance and Modernity*. Basingstoke: Palgrave.
Macintosh, F. (1994) *Dying Acts: Death in Ancient Greek and Modern Irish Tragic Drama*. Cork: Cork University Press.
Maeterlinck, M. (1904) *The Double Garden*. Translated by A.T. de Mattos. New York: Dodd, Mead and Company.
—. (1912) *Death*. Translated by A.T. de Mattos. New York: Dodd, Mead & Company.
—. (1913) *Our Eternity*. Translated by A.T. de Mattos. New York: Dodd, Mead and Company.
—. (1914) *The Unknown Guest*. Translated by A.T. de Mattos. New York: Dodd.
—. (1985) 'The Intruder', in *Doubles, Demons, and Dreamers: An International Collection of Symbolist Drama*, edited by D. Gerould, 51–66. New York: Performing Arts Journal Publications.
—. (1994 [1890]) 'Small Talk – The Theatre', in *Symbolist Art Theories: A Critical Anthology*, edited by H. Dorra, 143–52. Berkeley: University of California Press.
Mailer, N. (1961) *Advertisements for Myself*. London: Deutsch.
Malachy, T. (1982) *La mort en situation dans le théatre contemporain*. Paris: Editions A.G. Nizet.
Malkowski, J.C. (2011) '"Dying in Full Detail": Mortality and Duration in Digital Documentary', PhD Dissertation, University of California, Berkeley.
Malpede, K. (1974) *Three Works by the Open Theater*. New York: Drama Book Specialists/Publishers.
Markusen, E. (2004) 'Reflections on the Holocaust and Hiroshima', in *The Genocidal Temptation: Auschwitz, Hiroshima, Rwanda, and Beyond*, edited by R.S. Frey, 25–40. Dallas: University Press of America.
Martin, A. (1969) *Soundings*. Dublin: Gill & Macmillan.
Martin, K. (2013) *Modernism and the Rhythms of Sympathy: Vernon Lee, Virginia Woolf, D.H. Lawrence*. Oxford: Oxford University Press.
Maunder, A., ed. (2015) *British Theatre and the Great War, 1914–1919: New Perspectives*. London: Palgrave.
Mayor, R. (1963) 'Little to Carp at in the Festival Drama'. *Scotsman*, 17 August.
Mellor, P.A., and C. Shilling. (1993) 'Modernity, Self-Identity and the Sequestration of Death', *Sociology* 27 (3): 411–31.
Milchman, A., and A. Rosenberg. (2004) 'Auschwitz and Hiroshima', in *The Genocidal Temptation: Auschwitz, Hiroshima, Rwanda, and Beyond*, edited by R.S. Frey, 187–92. Dallas: University Press of America.
Miles, L., and C.A. Corr. (2015) 'Death Cafe: What Is It and What We Can Learn From It', *Omega: Journal of Death and Dying* 75 (2): 1–15.
Miscellaneous. (1985) 'The War Plays by Edward Bond (Reviews)', *London Theatre Record* 5 (15): 717–23.
Mitford, J. (1980 [1963]) *The American Way of Death*. London: Quartet Books.
Monk, R. (2012) *Inside the Centre: The Life of J. Robert Oppenheimer*. London: Jonathan Cape.
Morrow, W.C., and E. Cucuel. (1899) *Bohemian Paris of To-Day*. London: Chatto & Windus.
Mountford, F., and D. Cooke. (2016) 'Directors in Conversation: Dominic Cooke on Here We Go'. National Theatre Podcasts, Accessed 24 April 2017. https://audioboom.com/posts/3915471-dominic-cooke-on-here-we-go.
Mueller, J. (1991) 'Changing Attitudes Towards War: The Impact of the First World War', *British Journal of Political Science* 21 (3): 1–28.
Muse, J. (2010) 'The Dimensions of the Moment: Modernist Shorts', *Modern Drama* 53 (1): 76–102.

References

Neill, M. (1997) *Issues of Death: Mortality and Identity in English Renaissance Tragedy*. Oxford: Clarendon.
Nelson, P., and J. Masel. (2017) 'Intercellular Competition and the Inevitability of Multicellular Aging', *Proceedings of the National Academy of Sciences*. doi: 10.1073/pnas.1618854114.
Neocleous, M. (2005) 'Long Live Death! Fascism, Resurrection, Immortality', *Journal of Political Ideologies* 10 (1): 31–49.
Niewyk, D.L., ed. (2003) *The Holocaust: Problems and Perspectives of Interpretation*. Boston, MA: Houghton Mifflin Company.
Niewyk, D.L., and F.R. Nicosia. (2000) *The Columbia Guide to the Holocaust*. New York: Columbia University Press.
Nordau, M. (1993) *Degeneration*. Lincoln: University of Nebraska Press.
Noys, B. (2005) *The Culture of Death*. Oxford: Berg.
O'Gorman, R. (2007) 'Woman and Scarecrow: Review', *Theatre Journal* 59 (1): 102–3.
O'Reilly, K. (2016) *Atypical Plays for Atypical Actors*. London: Oberon.
Oe, K. (1995) *Hiroshima Notes*. New York: Marion Boyars.
Parnia, S., and J. Young. (2014) *Erasing Death: The Science that Is Rewriting the Boundaries between Life and Death*. New York: HarperOne.
Pavis, P. (2003) *Analyzing Performance: Theater, Dance, and Film*. Ann Arbor: University of Michigan Press.
Perdigao, L.K., and M. Pizzato. (2010) *Death in Twentieth-Century American Texts and Performances: Corpses, Ghosts, and the Reanimated Dead*. Farnham: Ashgate.
Perloff, M. (2014) 'Avant-Garde in a Different Key: Karl Kraus's *The Last Days of Mankind*', *Critical Inquiry* 40 (2): 311–38.
Phelan, P. (1992) *Unmarked: The Politics of Performance*. London: Routledge.
Porter, R. (1999) 'The Hour of Philippe Ariès', *Mortality* 4 (1): 83–90.
Presner, T.S. (2006) '"The Fabrication of Corpses": Heidegger, Arendt, and the Modernity of Mass Death', *Telos* 2006 (135): 84–108.
Puchner, M. (2002) *Stage Fright: Modernism, Anti-Theatricality, and Drama*. Baltimore: Johns Hopkins University Press.
Rabaté, J.-M. (2013) *A Handbook of Modernism Studies*. Chichester: John Wiley & Sons.
Rachilde, K. Goundariou and F. Lively. (1998) *Madame La Mort and Other Plays*. Baltimore: Johns Hopkins University Press.
Ragon, M. (1983) *Space of Death: A Study of Funerary Architecture, Decoration and Urbanism*. Charlottesville: Virginia University Press.
Ray, G. (2005) *Terror and the Sublime in Art and Critical Theory: From Auschwitz to Hiroshima to September 11*. Basingstoke: Palgrave Macmillan.
Raymond, G. (2016) 'Review: Cosy'. Accessed 25 April. www.theartsdesk.com/theatre/cosy-wales-millennium-centre.
Rayner, A. (2006) *Ghosts: Death's Double and the Phenomena of Theatre*. Minneapolis: University of Minnesota Press.
—. (2014) 'Keeping Time', *Performance Research* 19 (3): 32–6.
Rebellato, D. 2015. 'Here We Go'. *Dan Rebellato*, last modified 2 December, accessed 21 April 2017. www.danrebellato.co.uk/spilledink/2015/12/2/here-we-go.
Roach, J.R. (1996) *Cities of the Dead: Circum-Atlantic Performance*. New York: Columbia University Press.
Rodenbach, G. (2007) *Bruges-la-Morte*. Translated by M. Mitchell and W. Stone. Sawtry: Dedalus.
Romanska, M. (2012) *The Post-Traumatic Theatre of Grotowski and Kantor: History and Holocaust in 'Akropolis' and 'Dead Class'*. London: Anthem Press.
Ryder Ryan, P., and R. Sklar. (1971) 'Terminal: An Interview with Roberta Sklar', *TDR/The Drama Review* 51 (3): 148–57.
Sang-Hun, C. (2016) 'South Koreans, Seeking New Zest for Life, Experience Their Own Funerals'. *New York Times*, 26 October, A4.
Schechner, R. (2002) *Performance Studies: An Introduction*. London: Routledge.

Schell, J. (1982) *The Fate of the Earth*. New York: Avon.
Schleunes, K.A. (1970) *The Twisted Road to Auschwitz: Nazi Policy toward German Jews 1933-1939*. Urbana: University of Illinois Press.
Schneider, R. (2014) *Theatre & History*. Basingstoke: Palgrave.
Sebald, W.G. (2003) *The Emigrants*. Translated by M. Hulse. London: Vintage.
Shaw, G.B. (1930) *Back to Methuselah*. London: Constable & Co.
Shepherd-Barr, K. (2016) *Modern Drama: A Very Short Introduction*. Oxford: Oxford University Press.
Sherman, D. (2014) *In a Strange Room: Modernism's Corpses and Mortal Obligation*. Oxford: Oxford University Press.
Sherman, J.F. (2016) *A Strange Proximity: Stage Presence, Failure, and the Ethics of Attention*. London: Routledge.
Shucksmith, J., S. Carlebach, and V. Whittaker. (2013) *Dying: Discussing and Planning for End of Life: British Social Attitudes (30)*. London: NatCen Social Research.
Siegel, S.F., ed. (1986) *Purgatory: Manuscript Materials Including the Author's Final Text*. Ithaca: Cornell University Press.
Sihra, M. (2008) 'The Unbearable Darkness of Being: Marina Carr's *Woman and Scarecrow*', *Irish Theatre International* 1 (1): 22-37.
Small, C. (1963) 'Taking Ionesco in One Gulp'. *Glasgow Herald*, 3 September.
Sofer, A. (2013) *Dark Matter: Invisibility in Drama, Theater, and Performance*. Ann Arbor: University of Michigan Press.
Soloski, A. (2011) 'What Makes a Good Stage Death?'. *Guardian*, 2 November. Accessed 17 October 2017. www.theguardian.com/stage/theatreblog/2011/nov/02/what-makes-good-stage-death.
Spooner, J., and C. Thorpe. (2014) *Am I Dead Yet?* Unpublished theatre script.
Stoppard, T. (1967) *Rosencrantz and Guildenstern Are Dead*. London: Faber & Faber.
Sword, H. (2002) *Ghostwriting Modernism*. Ithaca: Cornell University Press.
Szajna, J. (1987) 'Replika: A Performance Scenario', in *Plays of the Holocaust: An International Anthology*, edited by E. Fuchs, 148-52. New York: Theatre Communications Group.
Thomas, D. (2003) *Collected Poems: Dylan Thomas*. London: Phoenix.
Thompson, E. (2014) *Waking, Dreaming, Being: Self and Consciousness in Neuroscience, Meditation, and Philosophy*. New York: Columbia University Press.
Toller, E. (1986 [1919]) 'The Transfiguration', in *Expressionist Texts*, edited by M. Gordon, 155-208. New York: PAJ Publications.
—. (1991 [1934]) *I Was a German: The Autobiography of a Revolutionary*. Translated by E. Crankshaw. New York: Paragon House.
Twitchin, M. (2016) *The Theatre of Death – The Uncanny in Mimesis: Tadeusz Kantor, Aby Warburg, and an Iconology of the Actor*. London: Palgrave.
Unterecker, J. (1965) 'An Interview with Anne Yeats', *Shenandoah* 16 (4): 7-9.
Van Lerberghe, C. (1895) 'The Night-Comers', in *The Evergreen: A Northern Seasonal*, 61-71. Edinburgh: Fisher Unwin.
Walker, J.A., and G. Odom. (2016) 'Comparative Modernist Performance Studies: A Not So Modest Proposal', *Journal of Dramatic Theory and Criticism* 31 (1): 129-53.
Waller, J. (2007) *Becoming Evil: How Ordinary People Commit Genocide and Mass Killing*. 2nd ed. Oxford: Oxford University Press.
Walter, T. (1994) *The Revival of Death*. London: Routledge.
—. (2003) 'Historical and Cultural Variants on the Good Death', *British Medical Journal* 327 (7408): 218.
—. (2008a) 'Death in Britain Today', *Self & Society* 36 (2): 9-16.
—. (2008b) 'The Sociology of Death', *Sociology Compass* 2 (1): 317-36.
—. (2016) 'The Dead who Become Angels: Bereavement and Vernacular Religion', *Omega: Journal of Death and Dying* 73 (1): 3-28.
Walter, T., R. Hourizi, W. Moncur and S. Pitsillides. (2011) 'Does the Internet Change How We Die and Mourn?', *Omega: Journal of Death and Dying* 64 (4): 275-302.

Ward, N. (2010) 'The Death of the Actor', *Performance Research* 15 (1): 140-8.
Warraich, H. (2017) *Modern Death: How Medicine Changed the End of Life*. New York: St Martin's Press.
Watson, A. (2006) 'Self-Deception and Survival: Mental Coping Strategies on the Western Front, 1914-1918', *Journal of Contemporary History* 41 (2): 247-68.
Watts, F.W. (1930) 'A Night Counter-Attack', in *Everyman at War: Sixty Personal Narratives of the War*, edited by C.B. Purdom, 66-72. London: J.M. Dent and Sons.
Weafer, J.A. (2014) *Irish Attitudes to Death, Dying and Bereavement 2004-2014*. Dublin: Irish Hospice Foundation.
Wertheim, D. (2009) 'Remediation as a Moral Obligation: Authenticity, Memory, and Morality in Representations of Anne Frank', in *Mediation, Remediation, and the Dynamics of Cultural Memory*, edited by A. Erll and A. Rigney, 157-72. Berlin: Walter de Gruyter.
Whaley, J. (1981) *Mirrors of Mortality: Studies in the Social History of Death*. London: Europe.
White, K. (2009) *Beckett and Decay*. London: Continuum.
Whittall, A. (2011) 'Tritone'. *The Oxford Companion to Music*, accessed 15 May 2015. www.oxfordreference.com/view/10.1093/acref/9780199579037.001.0001/acref-9780199579037-e-6939.
Wienrich, S., and J. Speyer. (2003) *The Natural Death Handbook*. 4th ed. London: Rider.
Wilder, T. (1957) *Our Town: A Play in Three Acts*. New York: Harper & Row.
Wilson, B.A., and M.M. Wilson. (2004) *First Year, Worst Year: Coping with the Unexpected Death of Our Grown-Up Daughter*. Chichester: Wiley.
Wright, N.T. (2011) *Surprised by Hope*. London: SPCK Publishing.
Yankowitz, S. (1974) 'Terminal', in *Three Works by the Open Theater*, edited by K. Malpede, 38-65. New York: Drama Book Specialists/Publishers.
Yeats, W.B. (1922) *The Trembling of the Veil*. London: T. Werner Laurie.
Yeats, W.B., and R. J. Finneran. (2002) *The Yeats Reader: A Portable Compendium of Poetry, Drama, and Prose*. Basingstoke: Palgrave Macmillan.
Zerubavel, E. (2006) *The Elephant in the Room: Silence and Denial in Everyday Life*. Oxford: Oxford University Press.
Zilboorg, G. (1943) 'Fear of Death', *The Psychoanalytic Quarterly* (12): 465-75.

INDEX

Note: titles of plays, productions, and literary works can be found under authors' or theatre companies' names.

afterlife 53–4, 71, 141, 182, 200–1, 203, 205–8, 222n.12
  see also heaven; hell; purgatory
ageing 128, 201, 225–6
Andreyev, Leonid
  Requiem 47–50, 239
anti-theatricality 83
apocalypse 67, 94, 142, 144, 160–1, 177
Ariès, Philippe 15–18, 22, 27n.17, 101–3, 106, 121, 127, 130–1, 181, 218
Ars moriendi 16, 197
  see also good death
Artaud, Antonin 85, 175
atmosphere in theatre 31, 39–43, 45–7, 49, 62, 118

Barker, Howard 12, 136, 178, 217
  Found in the Ground 166–77, 236, 239
  The Possibilities 137
  Und 172

Baudelaire, Charles
  The Flowers of Evil 38–9
Bauman, Zygmunt 107, 141, 206, 208
Becker, Ernest 99–100, 108
Beckett, Samuel
  Breath 160
  Endgame 143–5, 222n.14, 236
  Happy Days 2, 145–6, 237
  Krapp's Last Tape 4
being dead 57, 64n.11, 134n.13, 155, 206–8, 228–30
bereavement 3–4, 17, 66, 70, 99, 102, 113, 127, 136, 141, 153, 183–4, 187, 203
  see also stages of grief
Berman, Marshall 23
Blau, Herbert 8, 10–12, 27n.13
Bond, Edward
  The Tin Can People 149–57, 172, 176, 237
Bronfen, Elisabeth 18, 26n.2, 26n.7, 66
Brown, Guy 63n.5, 193, 201, 204, 209

Index

burial practices 16, 56, 63n.1, 77, 101, 112–15, 117, 184, 222n.8
Buzzati, Dino
   A Clinical Case 20, 98, 103–12, 216, 236, 239–40
Brown, Guy 63n.5, 193, 201, 204, 209

Cabaret du Néant 31–5, 41, 56
Čapek, Karel
   The Makropulos Case 227–8
Carlson, Marvin 11–12
Carr, Marina
   Woman and Scarecrow 196–202, 238–40
Chaikin, Joseph 111–12, 119
Churchill, Caryl
   Here We Go 202–13, 221, 225, 236
closet drama 79, 86, 95
   see also mental theatre
Cold War, the 110, 136, 142, 239
conscious dying 123–4
corpses 8, 14, 26n.9, 33–4, 37–8, 44, 48, 72, 74–5, 90–3, 96n.8, 107, 110, 114, 126–32, 140, 144, 154, 161, 170, 172, 173, 229, 236
corpsing 5
   see also dying onstage
Craig, Edward Gordon 29, 160, 164

dance of death 36, 72–3, 79–83, 85, 95
dark matter 11, 46, 52
death awareness movement 98–9, 108, 112, 133, 181, 238
death café 183, 188, 216
death denial 20, 97–134 *passim*, 140, 186–7, 224, 237–8
death drive (Freud) 200
   see also eros and *thanatos*
death in film 6, 26n.6, 75, 169–70
death-in-life 75, 117, 127, 136, 143, 148, 164–5, 201–2, 205, 209, 236
death studies 18–19, 24–5, 181
definitions of death 13–15, 27n.16, 184, 229
De Grey, Aubrey 225–6, 231
Dryden, John 7
Duffy, Carol Ann
   Everyman 156, 186, 189–96, 197–9, 207, 209, 216, 221, 237–8

Duras, Marguerite
   Yes, Maybe 146–9, 152–3, 176, 236, 239, 240
Dürrenmatt, Friedrich
   The Meteor 242n.4
dying onstage 7–8, 10–11, 26n.10, 27n.12
   see also corpsing

ecological destruction 90–2, 142, 193–4
end of life 33, 184, 216, 221, 225, 228
   see also old age
eros and *thanatos* 37, 59, 129, 167, 238
   see also death drive (Freud)
Esslin, Martin 98, 103, 126
Etchells, Tim 26n.9, 49
expressionism 73–4, 78, 88, 90–1, 94, 118
extinction 77, 143, 153, 157, 194
   see also mass death

Fort, Paul 29, 47, 49, 52
Frank, Anne 168, 170
Freud, Sigmund 97–8, 100, 197, 200, 202
funerals 63n.1, 112–14, 131–2, 133n.7, 187–8, 200, 203–5, 208

genocide 108, 135–6, 178n.1
   see also killing; mass death
ghosts 11–12, 55–9 *passim*
   see also spiritualism; the supernatural
Gilbert, Sandra 15, 107, 141, 163, 242n.10
God 19, 44, 141, 185, 190–3, 195–6, 200–1, 218
good death 182, 185, 216
   see also ars moriendi
Goodwin, Sarah Webster 18, 26n.2, 26n.7, 66
Gorer, Geoffrey 100–1
Grand-Guignol 34, 41, 84, 156
Grotowski, Jerzy 4, 158

heaven 31, 141, 222n.5
   see also hell; purgatory
Heidegger, Martin 107–8

hell 31, 68-9, 77, 79, 86, 150, 189, 208
  see also heaven; purgatory
Hibakusha 135, 148, 150, 153, 161
historiography of death 15-17, 68-71, 101-2
Holocaust (Nazi) 77, 107-8, 135-43 *passim*, 158-78
hospice 181, 184, 209-10

Ibsen, Henrik
  Peer Gynt 63n.9
immortality 69, 80, 97, 99, 201-2, 213, 218, 227-8, 242n.1
industrialisation of death 77-8, 93, 135, 138, 140-1, 152, 161-3, 217, 236-8
  see also genocide; mass death
Ionesco, Eugène
  Amédée 126-32, 236
  Exit the King 120-5, 127, 131, 185, 190, 240
  Killing Game 8

Jooss, Kurt 96
Joyce, James 92, 179n.14

Kane, Sarah 22
Kantor, Tadeusz 18, 158, 160, 164-5
killing 57, 68, 78, 87, 88-9, 92, 108, 135, 139, 169, 183, 218-19
  see also genocide; mass death
Kirkland, Winifred 69-71, 95, 96n.4, 141
Kraus, Karl
  The Last Days of Mankind 87-95
Kübler-Ross, Elisabeth 22, 108, 120-1

Lee, Vernon
  Satan the Waster 78-87, 95
limbo 62, 210, 232
  see also purgatory
liminality 4, 42, 55, 61-2, 209, 229

Macintosh, Fiona 18
Maeterlinck, Maurice 35, 43, 52-4, 63n.6
  The Intruder 44-7
Mailer, Norman 139-40, 145, 165
Malachy, Thérèse 18-19, 136

mass death 66, 93, 98, 108, 140-2, 145, 153, 157, 163
  see also extinction
medicalised death and dying 17, 21, 68, 74, 103-11 *passim*, 182, 216-18, 225-6, 228
  see also resuscitation
mental theatre 67, 190, 198, 209, 238
Miller, Arthur
  Death of a Salesman 112
Mitford, Jessica 112-15

natural death movement 222n.8, 223n.19
nihilism 50, 54, 103, 143, 148-9, 153, 166, 178, 239
  see also nothingness, the void
Nordau, Max 34-6, 51, 55
nothingness 31, 206, 222n.11, 237
  see also nihilism; the void
Noys, Benjamin 140, 165, 186, 220, 238
nuclear destruction 110, 135-8, 142-53, 155-7, 160-1, 178, 186

old age 192, 213, 219, 224-5
  see also end of life
Open Theater
  Terminal 101, 111-20, 127, 130, 133n.9, 239, 240
O'Reilly, Kaite 133n.10
  Cosy 188, 197, 208, 214-21, 223n.15

personification of death 6-7, 31-3, 36, 38, 40, 67, 72-8 *passim*, 80-1
Phelan, Peggy 11
Priestley, J.B.
  Johnson Over Jordan 64n.11, 222n.12
purgatory 195, 208
  see also limbo; Yeats, W.B., *Purgatory*

Rachilde
  Madame La Mort, 36-9, 52
Rayner, Alice 12, 55, 211
resuscitation 216, 221, 228-30, 242n.5
  see also medicalised death and dying
Roach, Joseph 3, 56

Rodenbach, Georges
  Bruges-la-morte 39–40
Schechner, Richard 4, 46
Schell, Jonathan 143–4, 148, 153, 179n.6
secularity 182, 186, 195–6
self, the 63n.9, 75, 100, 119, 121, 123–4, 139, 153, 188, 196–7, 201, 204–6, 212, 222n.10
Shaw, G.B.
  Back to Methuselah 63n.10, 226–7, 242n.2
Sherman, David 28n.19, 93
Sklar, Roberta 111–12, 115, 119
social death 15, 188, 201
Sofer, Andrew 46
soul 13, 32, 37, 51, 56–8, 69, 185, 195, 198, 228, 239
spiritualism 30, 51–5, 66, 117, 134n.13, 141, 237
  see also ghosts; the supernatural
stages of grief 22, 120
  see also bereavement
Stoppard, Tom
  Rosencrantz and Guildenstern are Dead 8, 12
suicide 37, 214, 220, 230, 232
supernatural, the 44, 46, 51–3, 55, 89, 105, 190, 198, 239
  see also ghosts; spiritualism
Szajna, Józef
  Replica 158–66, 168, 172, 176, 179n.8, 236, 240

Toller, Ernst
  The Transfiguration 71–8, 81, 85, 95, 152
trauma 75, 138, 146, 148, 149–51, 153, 161, 173, 176, 187, 236

Unlimited Theatre
  Am I Dead Yet? 229–32

Van Lerberghe, Charles
  The Night-Comers 43–4
Vietnam War, the 109–10, 116, 140, 148
void, the 48–9, 50, 235–6, 239
  see also nothingness; nihilism

Wade, Laura
  Colder Than Here 222n.8
Walter, Tony 14, 18, 68, 79, 185–7, 189, 197, 210, 220, 242n.11
Wilder, Thornton
  Our Town 64n.11

Yeats, W.B. 30
  The Dreaming of the Bones 57–8
  Purgatory 55–62
  The Words upon the Windowpane 55

Zarrilli, Phillip 103, 108–11, 133n.2, 214
Zilboorg, Gregory 99–100, 108
zombies 75, 154

EU authorised representative for GPSR:
Easy Access System Europe, Mustamäe tee 50,
10621 Tallinn, Estonia
gpsr.requests@easproject.com